Still Amazed

A collection

Miles Beauchamp

Pacific Indigo

Still Amazed

ISBN: 978-1-7348857-3-6

Library of Congress Control Number: 2020907825

Pacific Indigo
Books & Media
San Diego, CA
United States

pacific@mpb.me

Edited by Paisley Prophet

A note of gratitude for permission to use photos and graphics:

Pexels: https://www.pexels.com/photo-license

Unsplash: https://splash.com/license

Many of these works have been published in milespb.com, Asian Journal, @milespb1, and others.

Pacific Indigo
books & media

To Michelle

"It is not like I have gone crazy; I just don't want to take any chances. You never know what could happen."

Ruth Bader Ginsburg

CONTENTS

Foreword

I have been part of the San Diego literary community for well over thirty years, and I found a kindred spirit in Miles Beauchamp, who has been holding court as a constant in San Diego for as long as I have known him, steady as the heartbeat of San Diego, the place we call home. Miles really came into his own when his publisher turned him loose and told him to just have fun, giving him permission to share his unique perspective of the human condition through a weird kaleidoscope of disbelief, paranoia, and humor, with the occasional rant.

I invite you to sit back and enjoy these unique journalistic snapshots of the human condition through a rare and very special lens.

Matthew J. Pallamary
Author, Editor, Shamanic Explorer

Preface

Recently, I've heard authors dreamily discussing their love affairs with books. Not me. My love is not for books, but rather what the books communicate. And for that, it can be paper, electrons, smoke signal, semaphore—any old way to send a thought across time and space. When I first saw Amazon's Kindle, I just kept staring. A library in your hand.

Of course, it's not so simple. A book of paper and cardboard is more than information. It's an artifact that both transmits and preserves the ideas and emotions that words represent. And it never needs to be charged. That said, books stored and transmitted by computers have helped make publishing those words infinitely more democratic.

Most of my words are shared in newspaper columns, essays, blogs, tweets, and the occasional book. Over time, I've become comfortable with the short form. Give me the space of an essay and I'll make the keyboard sing—unless I'm pounding on it because I can't come up with the right word. I've learned to do less and less pounding over time because keyboards, while not overly expensive, are still valuable tools that deserve to be treated a bit better. Or so I'm told.

A while back, I decided to put together a collection of my favorite columns and essays. Most of them appeared in the *Asian Journal*, a San Diego newspaper where I'm allowed to play on keyboards to my heart's content. As long as I have the piece in on time, the publisher, Simeon Silverio, puts up with me. We've tolerated each other for years, and I'm in awe of his professionalism. His act of turning me loose helped create this book.

You'll meet various family members in the book, as well as thoughts on the things we all go through in life, the people we meet, and the loves we encounter and hang onto.

Now, if you'll excuse me, I'll go remind my daughter of her flute lesson. Enjoy the read.

CHAPTER ONE

Families and Other Bizarre Oddities

A h, yes. Families. We all have them in one form or another. The term "families" certainly does not simply mean a person or group of people you were born or adopted into. It can also mean, by extended definition, your work, school, sports, close friends, etc. In trying to sort it all out and keep it straight, we've come up with terms like "birth family," "adopted family," "extended family," "nuclear family," "work family," and more.

The pieces in this section look at families in one form or another and, just for the heck of it, *other bizarre oddities*. I mean, let's face it: in all the forms that families can take—and some of them can be pretty strange—there are other bizarre oddities living next door or down the street. Your street, not mine. Everyone in my neighborhood is perfectly sane and friendly. *Wink, wink.*

A strong beverage may help with this section. Just sayin'.

Kids and Dogs and Other Fun Things

As I sit here trying to work, my son and his dog are running circles around my chair. Is it raining outside? No. Is either one of them too ill to be playing outside? No.

The question is, then, why are they here in my office with me, running circles around my chair while my son makes siren sounds, and the dog keeps looking back to make sure he does not get too far ahead?

What do I do while all of this is going on? I start getting annoyed, of course, which leads me to begin saying things like:

* Knock it off!
* Knock it off!
* Knock it off!
* Knock it off!
* I'm not kidding, knock it off!
* I'm not kidding, knock it off!
* I'm not kidding, knock it off!
* I'm not kidding, knock it off!
* I mean it!
* I mean it!
* I mean it!
* I mean it!

Now, don't think that I just keep saying these things without thinking about it. No, I pay attention to what is going on and definitely to who is not paying attention to me. It's pretty much always kids and dogs who are not paying attention.

It's not always that I expect them to pay attention, it's just that I would like them to when I want it, not when it suits them. That rarely happens.

So, where were we? Oh, yeah. Well, by now, my vocabulary has more or less sunk to the following level:

* I told you two to go play outside! Daddy has to work.
* I mean it, go play outside or in your room.

* I told you two to go play outside! Daddy has to work.

* I mean it, go play outside or in your room.

Have they left yet? No. So, what do I do? I slowly start to get out of my chair. I think that this will get their attention, make them think that they are really in trouble, and they will leave (have you noticed that, by now, I have started thinking that the dog is just another kid out to bug me? Sometimes, I almost do think that, and yes, it is a bit weird).

"Daddy sit down! You are getting in the way!"

"Getting in the way? This is my office!"

"Daddy!"

"Daddy, nothing! You two, scram."

"But, Daddy, can't you see we're playing?"

"Yes, I can see that, but can't you two see that I am trying to work?" (Yes, I'm still talking as if the dog understands every word. Give me a break, I'm a bit frustrated.)

"We're just playing."

"Well, play somewhere else."

"We like playing here." (Notice that Ryan also talks as if the dog is human.)

"Yeah, well, why do you like playing here so much?"

"Because you're here."

Do you know what I did after Ryan said that? I turned off the computer, took off my shoes, and crawled down onto the floor with the two of them. As soon as I did that, it wasn't hard to concentrate at all. I had simply been concentrating on the wrong thing.

The important things…

3

A Dog Named Poppy

Let me bring you up to speed on Poppy. He is the Lhasa Apso breed of dog that we have running around our house because, well, I guess because we need torture in our lives. Basically, he's dumb as a rock, ugly, and has the personality of a rattlesnake with morning sickness.

His name used to be Popcorn but now is Poppy because I refused to wander around the neighborhood calling out, "Popcorn!" when he ran away, as he so often did. Now, he no longer runs away. And I desperately wish he would.

Personally, I want to get an aquarium and start raising interesting, colorful, tropical fish. I have just the place in my house for the tank, except that where I want to place it has dimensions that do not match the dimensions of any tank I have been able to find. I'm told that I must have a tank made.

As soon as I heard what a custom-made tank cost, my eyes glazed over and I started hyperventilating.

A custom-made tank would be pretty cool, though. Unique size, interesting tropical plants, multi-colored rocks and lava for the bottom. In it would swim fish of fantastic colors and shapes, just begging to be looked at. My son would probably want to pet them, but I should be able to persuade him not to. Petting fish is not the best of ideas, particularly if you take them out of the water to do it.

The dog would undoubtedly want to try to get them out of the water and play with them…or eat them. You know how dogs are, especially dumb ones.

The soft glow of an aquarium

A lit aquarium is a beautiful object. The plants undulate in the water, swirling colors everywhere. It can be an always-changing panorama of nature at its most remarkable. Or it can be something that needs cleaning. Like everything else in life, it's all how you look at it.

One thing I have discovered while aquarium shopping is how expensive some fish are. It seems that most tropical fish are not cheap. Some are fairly expensive, and some are downright outrageous. I'm not buying any of those.

I have had aquariums before, although not for many years now. I discovered a few things about fish and aquariums and the various and sundry things that go with them; I thought I might pass on some of those things to you, should you decide to go off the deep end (aquarium joke) and get one of the things too.

1. The tank needs to be cleaned.
2. The fish do not need to be cleaned—in fact, they dislike it a lot.
3. Fish eat fish food. They do not like leftover BBQ ribs.
4. The life span of any fish I've ever cared for is not long.
5. As the fish go to that grand aquarium in the sky, you will need to get more of them, and the prices will have increased.
6. When cleaning your tank (see number one, above), realize that you are cleaning fish urine, feces, leftover food that is rotting away on the bottom, and all sorts of other not-particularly-pleasant things. Well, that's gross and time-consuming, so you may decide to obtain the services of an aquarium-cleaning service. Well, there goes the Jeep…or Porsche…

In re-reading the above list, it is becoming clear that perhaps an aquarium is not a good idea. Hell, those make a litter box look downright beautiful.

*I'd love to have an aquarium, but like
most beautiful things, it's all about maintenance.*

A Sick Child Makes a Night Last Forever

This past Sunday evening was nothing out of the ordinary. Dinner, a last bit of homework for the kids, showers, reading, then a smidgen of wind-down time with TV, and finally bedtime. Like I said, nothing out of the ordinary.

Then midnight rolls around. As I pick up the remote to find something—there must be something—to watch, I hear that first plaintive, "Daddy!"

Warning: graphic language ahead that may make you sick if you have a weak stomach. In other words, if you gag when hearing someone else gag, well, go watch Cartoon Network for a few minutes.

Okay, it wasn't all that plaintive. Maybe plaintive mixed with panic as dinner made its way back up the throat. Aw, gee, I'm not going to like this at all.

Earlier in the evening, everything seemed fairly normal. No one was sick, the kids were both doing fine. And it lasted that way until the first wail from my daughter. After that first wail, things turned downright ugly. That is to say, the barf started flowing. As I watched her poor little head bent over the bowl, I couldn't help wondering just where on earth it was coming from.

But let's back up just a bit—back to that first cry, followed by the unmistakable sound of liquids and solids being forcefully expelled from a stomach. It's amazing how quickly that sound can get a parent up from their chair.

I looked around and there she stood, looking stricken, with rather vile fluids coming out of places they shouldn't. And she was crying. I, being the calming father that I am, quietly said (okay, not so quietly), "Get in the bathroom!"

She nodded and took off, hurling across the carpet, the entryway rugs, the hall carpet, the bathroom floor, the bathroom walls, and finally the toilet, where some of it managed to actually get in the bowl. The rest? Around the bowl, the seat, the TP dispenser, the towels, the bathtub—well, I could go on, but why?

What? I warned you, didn't I?

Of course, before we even got to the point of her calling me, she had thrown up all over her pillow, the sheets, the blankets, the bedspread, and assorted stuffed animals.

And now, there she was, head bent, heaving away. After a while, it quit, and she began to feel better. I got her all cleaned up (not an easy task with her hair), changed the bed, and tucked her back in. All was quiet in the house once again.

Well, yeah, sure it was quiet—everyone was sleeping but me. I was busy cleaning walls, floors, doors, and bathtubs. Add to that the starting of loads of laundry, mopping, scraping, and trying to convince the dog that puke isn't food. After a while, I looked up and it was two a.m. and I was tired. Very tired.

Unfortunately, while I was tired, I was also wide awake. Luckily, for those of us conscious at that time, the web presents an enormous number of choices of things to watch or do. Regrettably, not very many of them were worth spending much time with.

I thought about watching a film, but then I realized that sometimes when you're tired, you really don't need that. You just want peace and quiet. You want the opportunity to reset yourself with something to drink and just sit in your chair and stare at the lights of the city.

And I managed to do that. For ten minutes. And then it started up again. I went in again, saw that she had thrown up all over the bed and her clothes again, and I started the cleaning process all over again.

Finally

Eventually, all the fun had to come to an end, and the vomiting stopped. She cuddled into her bed, in the almost darkened room, a bit of music in the background, and finally drifted off to sleep.

As for me, I was glad that it seemed finally over. I was so tired I could barely keep my head up, but too awake to be able to sleep. I was in that state of sleep despair and unable to do anything about it except whimper. I just had one thought that kept running through my head, namely, *Where did all that stuff come from?* I knew how much she had eaten that day and it just didn't seem to be as much as I cleaned off the walls, toilet, carpets, blankets, towels, my clothes, her clothes, and the floor. Make that floors.

It takes a lot out of you when a lot comes out of you (possibly my favorite line of the entire book)

I kept checking on her, making sure she was okay, still asleep, still dry. Definitely still dry. She just kept snoozing away. I was not quite so lucky and spent most of the rest of the night awake. The next morning, of course, we kept her home from school. I stayed home with her and we had a marathon cartoon day. She was very tired after that "Night of the Heaves."

Luckily, being a generally healthy kid, she bounced back quickly. After a day of lying around the house with me, she was once again ready to take on the world. As for me, I needed a vacation—I don't recover as quickly from missing a night of sleep as I used to.

But the loads of laundry managed to get finished, the carpets got cleaned, the floors mopped, and the house aired out. Life is back to our version of normal.

A Hit, a Win, and a Birthday

Last Saturday was a day essentially built around my daughter. She had a softball game in the morning and then a birthday sleepover party that afternoon/night/next morning.

A sleepover birthday party? With ten little girls? Sigh, yes. But more on that later.

First, the softball game. My daughter has been a soccer player from the moment she started playing sports. She liked soccer, her brother played soccer before he moved on to lacrosse, and it seemed ordained. And, for a few years, it was. But then her brother got a new girlfriend (interesting how girlfriends change the dynamics of so many things, isn't it?) and the GF plays softball. GF plays on a team in Orange County, likes it, and is good at it. And so now, Daughter wants to try it.

Trying out new sports is a good thing; kids can find a favorite, see what they're best at, and at that age, why not? The only downside is the new equipment. Lots of new equipment, and as you know, sports equipment is not cheap. But you're the parent, so you look in your little child's eyes, grit your teeth, smile, and hand over the credit card.

And that's how it was with us. GF donated a few old things to Daughter to get her started, to see if she really wanted to go forward. Daughter did. And that meant a trip to the sporting goods store. Ah, the sporting goods store. A place of dreams, vigor or the wish for vigor, dynamic youth, and a cash register that sucks every wallet dry the minute you enter the store.

Practice

And then there was practice. Her team holds practice twice weekly, which means girls and coaches practicing and parents watching (texting), taking photos (looking at YouTube videos), yelling encouragement (talking on the phone), and generally being supportive (collecting money for uniforms, deciding on where to hold parties, and figuring out who is bringing snacks to the game).

Practices are interesting. You get to see how good the coaches are and how bad some of the parents are. Not bad in a criminal sense (well, a few are iffy), just bad in a sense that they won't quit giving instructions to their kid while the coach is trying to do what coaches do. Knock it off, Mom and Dad (and you know who you are).

During the practices, I noticed that the girls were slowly coalescing into a team. Oh, not a good one yet, but one that had potential. You have to love that word. Potential gives you so much hope while still allowing for a less-than-stellar present. Yep, our girls had potential—lots of potential. And we parents were going to do everything we could to help that along, including deciding on snack rotation. We're nothing if not involved.

Finally, a game

The "Big Day" arrived. Game day was bright and sunny, and the girls had confidence. The game started fairly evenly, but soon, one of our girls scored a run and we never looked back. Yeah, yeah, yeah—the other team had a score or two, but honestly, who cares? The main thing is, we won. Sorry, that's not the main thing. The main, *main* thing is dear Daughter stepped up to the plate, took her stance, and nailed a ball straight down the field. Two girls scored from her hit, and after a few more girls had hits, my daughter ran to home and scored. She had a smile on her that lasted for days.

And now, a birthday party

If a hit and a win at softball weren't enough, there was also her birthday party. Excuse me, birthday party/sleepover. What is a birthday party/sleepover? The short answer is, it's just one long birthday party that ends up with ten very tired girls on a sugar high. The full answer is one (very) long birthday party that ends up with ten very (very, very) tired girls on a sugar high with a frazzled dog, a big brother who has had enough of helping (he did a great job but one can only ask so much of someone), and parents who want to run away from home.

We probably would have run away, except we've seen enough CSI and other shows to know that, sooner or later, we'd be found and they would drag us, kicking and screaming, to be given back to kids plotting revenge. Who needs that?

It was a great birthday party with all the important things, such as pizza, an ice cream birthday cake, presents, candy, movies-on-demand, and all the usual stuff. The girls slept in one large pile in the family room. At midnight, with the giggles, the dog, the sugar in the tummies, and everything else, they would not go to sleep. Well, duh. Finally, we did the only thing we could do. Mom went downstairs, sat on a coffee table in the middle of them, and played guard dog. That woman is a high school teacher—she could stop a train with her glare. It worked, and slowly, they fell asleep.

The aftermath

The next morning, everyone looked rough, to say the least. The girls were dragging, the parents were pale and shaky, the dog refused to get up, and big brother would have slept for three days solid except he had a training exercise.

But the idea of chocolate chip pancakes soon had the girls scrambling in the kitchen. Quick, what do you get with girls and pancake batter? Enough smoke to set off the fire alarm. Which it did, twice. When I told the person who called to check on the alarm that it was just girls and pancakes, she burst out laughing. The smell of it had me gagging, and the dog ran outside. He's the smart one, apparently.

But they had fun, and that was one weekend my daughter will re-member forever. Score one for the positive side of parenting.

Boys and Noise

Have you ever listened to boys? I mean, really listened to them for an extended period (not that it always takes much time at all)? Boys (some, most, all—take your pick) truly have an ability to make the weirdest sounds.

Well, some are weird, and others are simply their approximation of sounds they have already heard. You know, sounds like sirens, birds, trucks, tractors, and hundreds of others. I've been listening to Son, our energetic, athletic, bright, and very vocal son lately, and he has been making some very bizarre sounds. And by bizarre, I simply mean sounds that humans don't always make—but bulldozers, jets, and tanks often do.

Here are just a few of the sounds that have escaped his vocal cords lately, a sampling, if you will.

Sounds from ten-year-old vocal cords

- Sirens—one of his favorites
- Any truck, but especially:
- Dump trucks
- Garbage trucks
- Fire trucks
- Diesel semis
- Earth movers
- Earth graders
- Tractors
- Furniture moving trucks
- Tank trucks
- Flatbed trucks
- Delivery (if they're big)
- Multi-stop
- Platform
- Bottler

- Cement mixer
- Refrigerator
- Isotherm
- Tank
- Log carrier
- Bowser
- Box
- Electric platform
- Food
- Ice cream
- Tow truck

There are more of them, I'm sure, but that gets the main ones listed. And let me ask you this—did you have any idea there were that many types of trucks? Me either. But there are, and Son can mimic almost all of them. But, wait! It gets even better.

Truck companies

I'm listing companies only because he's sure that each company has its own sound, depending on the type of truck. I'm not sure, myself, but hey, he's the expert.

- GMC
- Iveco
- Kenworth
- Peterbilt
- Ford
- Freightliner
- Mack
- Mitsubishi Fuso
- Navistar
- Volvo Trucks

He also enjoys pointing out assorted models and brands of trucks to his sister and me. She doesn't much care, but then again, she is starting to see trucks almost as fast as he does.

Beyond trucks

Huge, gargantuan trucks are not the only causes of Son's vocalizations. Oh, no. There are many other things, including:

- Jets
- Bells
- Whistles
- Horns
- Anything heard on television or in a film
- Walk through the San Diego Zoo and pick out pretty much any animal and he can mimic it. Yes, it gets a bit spooky at times, but there you go.
- Ships
- Explosions
- Bike horns
- Toys
- Heavy machinery
- His sister, mom, or me
- Flying saucers
- Fighter planes
- Bombers
- Military tanks
- Jackhammers
- Entire construction sites
- Entire airports
- Entire amusement parks
- Entire freeways
- Entire aircraft carriers
- Entire Army
- Entire Navy
- Entire Air Force
- Entire Marine Corps
- Every single sound my car makes

- Every single sound his mom's car makes
- Every single sound his toy cars make
- Every weapon sound from World War II
- Pretty much anything else on television
- Ships' bells
- Ships' whistles
- Ships' anchors being raised or lowered
- Trains
- Pumps—pick a pump, any pump
- Farm animals (when he gets tired of mimicking zoo animals)

I could go on, and on, and on, and on, and on, and on, and on, and on, and on, and on, and on, and on, and on, and on, but we'd both get bored, and besides, by now, I'm sure that you get the idea. This kid is a whiz at mimicking sounds.

The other thing about his mimicking sounds is that he likes to do it. Now, I'm not sure just how many kids like to mimic sounds, although I'm sure that it's quite a few.

I'm also not sure just when kids finally stop making bizarre sounds—although, to judge by some of them in the stands at sporting events, a few of us will never outgrow the need to sound off.

First Birthday

In just a few short days, my daughter will turn one year old. It's hard to believe that an entire year has gone by so quickly, but it has, whether I choose to believe it or not.

It seems like it was just yesterday that I saw her being delivered, saw her face for the first time, saw her take her first breath, saw her eyes open.

When those eyes opened, I was the very first thing she saw. She was delivered, she took a breath, opened her eyes and there I was. I had a huge smile, but she did not—she was still getting used to the whole thing. She didn't actually "see" me, of course, but it felt good, nonetheless.

I will never forget looking into those eyes for the first time, the first time they were ever open. I was in awe then, and I am still. I probably always will be.

And now that tiny baby is turning one year old. She is tiny no longer, and her eyes have seen a great deal, but somehow I am still in awe.

The past year

Over the last year, Daughter has learned to eat solid foods, to talk (some in English, most in a language all her own), to crawl, and to walk (more or less).

It's been an interesting year, one full of surprises for both of us (okay, for Mom and Brother too). I must keep reminding myself that every day there are things she is seeing that she has never seen before. Every day she is now tasting things she has never tasted (some she is supposed to taste—like new foods—and some she is not supposed to taste—like bugs, rocks, and leaves). She, like most babies, has started learning by tasting, and it's a constant struggle to keep things out of her mouth that shouldn't be there.

Over the past month, I have fished out of her mouth a hundred different things that are on the ground that we adults don't see. But she sees everything down there because that's where she is.

Yes, I am constantly worried that I'll never be able to get her "grown up."

It's fascinating to watch her look at the world around her and see more and more. Sometimes, I'll be watching her and see her notice something for the first time. At first, she glances at it, then looks away. Then she'll stop, get a puzzled look on her face, and look back. Then she stares—hard. You can see the wheels in that little head spinning as she struggles to understand it.

For instance, the other day, I had her outside with me while I was attempting to bring order to the garage. She was sitting in her stroller, happily drinking from a cup (okay, sipping some and pouring some on the ground) while I was putting things away and talking to her as I worked. Then I noticed her staring at something. I went over to where she sat and stood behind her to see what she was looking at.

I soon discovered that she was looking at a four-foot-long model of a sailing boat my late uncle had made decades ago. She had never seen it before and was trying hard to figure out exactly what it was. The model looked a bit familiar because of the boats she has in the tub, but this was big! I took her over to it so she could get a better picture of it and touch it.

So many things are like that—she sees it, then has to see it much closer, touch it, and then file the knowledge in that growing brain of hers.

And, ah, that brain. Aren't you amazed at how a child's brain grows, how it functions, how it stores away memories, becoming knowledge? I certainly am. Living with that brain of hers, watching it become "her" more and more, has to be one of the most incredible things I've ever witnessed.

Uh-oh

This morning, when she and I were taking her brother to school, she did something, and he said, "Uh-oh." She then promptly repeated it exactly, tone and everything. Brother asked, "Dad, did you hear that? She said, 'Uh-oh.'"

Of course I did, and then Brother said it again, and she repeated it again. This went on all the way to school. Hearing that "uh-oh" from her little voice had us both laughing and me, again, amazed. Not amazed that it would happen because, intellectually, I knew someday it would, but amazed that it did right then, and I heard it. I love the sound of that "uh-oh" like few things on earth.

In a way, I am a bit jealous of her. She is starting new on the road of life, and while I'm not yet at the end of that road, I have traveled a rather long way on it. She is going to get to see so much, do so much, and be so much. The planet keeps doing more with technology, with science, with medicine, and every day, new vistas open for people. Additionally, never has there been a better time to be a woman. She is not as restricted by her gender—she can go anywhere, study anything, be anything she wants to be.

Of course, I hope she ultimately is happy, but I also hope she does great things for this world. I hope she uses her life to further the human race, to aid humanity, to leave the world better than it was when she came in. And I think she can. She has a terrific brother to help her, a brilliant, successful mother to guide her, and…well, me. I'm there to help her as well, in whatever way I can, to see that she can be what she wants to be. It's going to be one heck of a ride, little girl, and I'll always be there—in one way or another—to help.

Can There Ever Be Peace?

In this world of ours, it has been decreed that there shall be both morning and non-morning people. It has also been decreed that, too often, the same type will never marry each other. And this is a very unfortunate thing.

My wife and I are not the same kind of person when it comes to the morning. She is not a morning person, and I am. I love mornings, the sound of birds, the quiet of dawn, the feel of a city just waking up. She loves those things too, but just at a later hour.

Another interesting thing is that our kids are polar opposites as well. My daughter wakes up by 6:30–7 a.m., calls out "Daddy!" and is ready to get out of bed. And when she wants to get out of bed, she wants it then. So I go into her room, softly get her out of bed, we go into the kitchen where I get tea and she gets milk, and then she's happy—give her a book to read, a dog to annoy, or a lap to sit on and life's good.

My wonderful son, on the other hand, would love to get up a little after that—a few hours after that, actually. He would prefer sleeping until nine or ten…or noon. That never happens, but that's his preference. And when he finally does get out of bed, with me or his mother threatening to pour ice water all over his bed, he is one grumpy-looking individual.

Picture it: he staggers out of bed, staggers to the bathroom, staggers to the family room, and then collapses. Sometimes, there is a bit of whining going on, but most of the time, there is just silence; the family knows to stay out of his way until he's pried his eyes open. In all of that, he's just like his mom, only she wants coffee—strong coffee—instead of milk or juice as she attempts to get her eyes to focus.

Now, all this might lead one to think that the two sides in our house are constantly at war—morning-hating mother and son against morning-loving (or at least tolerating) father and daughter. That might be true, except for the fact that father/daughter insist that mother/son be at least somewhat nice in the morning, or we'll talk and sing to each other very loudly.

So, we have a semblance of an uneasy truce. This truce doesn't always hold, and there can be exceptions to it, but by and large, we all manage to get along in the mornings.

In an effort to assist all of you unfortunate souls trying to deal with a spouse of the opposite type, I have assembled a list of attributes that both can use to try and understand the other.

The morning person

* Loves the look of the sun rising over the horizon
* Enjoys the chirping of birds as they go about looking for food or mates
* Relishes an early cup of steaming-hot coffee
* Likes the early news programs
* Likes being first to read the paper
* Wants to be on the road before the traffic hits
* Enjoys the friendship of other morning people standing in line for coffee and a doughnut
* Likes the quiet of the neighborhood
* Uses the time available to work, read the paper, putter around the house, or do any of a myriad of other things, in peace
* Adores cracking jokes at 6 a.m.

The non-morning person

• Loves to see the sun at the crack of noon
• Hates the sound of birds or any other thing before 10 a.m.
• Loves a steaming cup of coffee after 9 a.m.
• Reads the paper last
• Hates traffic, but not enough to get up any earlier
• Enjoys the friendship of other people in line at Starbucks after 10 a.m.
• Likes a quiet neighborhood too, but not at the expense of actually noticing it
• Ignores the jokes of those obnoxious morning people
• Loves the comfort of a warm bed long after it should have been made
• Eats brunch instead of breakfast
• Can shoot death rays out of their eyes at jovial individuals if that person chooses to be jovial before noon

- Figures it's better to be married to a morning person than live with another cranky non-morning one

I'm not sure why or how it was decided in this universe of ours that morning people marry non-morning people. Maybe it's all a grand cosmic joke, maybe it's something else; all I know is, I wouldn't trade my non-morning person for anyone. I've grown rather fond of her sleepy-eyed look as she cuddles our son, and that first cup of coffee, and whimpers.

Yes, my daughter and I look on the two of them with amusement, toleration, and patience (well, patience most of the time—other times we just have to move them along). We do the best we can with them…

I have a picture of my daughter, sitting on the couch one early Sunday morning, reading the paper with me (her paper is upside down because she can't read yet), and she has the cutest smile on her face. You can somehow sense that there's no other place she would rather be on earth than that couch, that morning.

Somehow or other, I have come to understand that, if nothing else, a home with opposing viewpoints about mornings sure keeps life interesting.

If only life was always this peaceful (yes, I'd settle for even the occasional day).

Good Neighbors

Neighbors can be both good and bad, but when they're good, it's generally the people living there who make it that way.

In my neighborhood, there are all kinds of people we could discuss who are interesting, but today I want to focus on the neighbors at a fire station near us.

Now, my son is crazy for just about anything having to do with firefighters. He has fire-engine toys; firefighter hats, firefighter coats, firefighter boots, and—well, you get the idea.

Whenever we're driving and he sees a fire truck or rescue unit, he bounces so hard I worry that someday he is going to put a dent in the roof of the car. I mean, this kid is crazy for firefighters.

Oh, sure, sometimes I try to get him interested in the noble and exciting profession of writing and teaching, but he just looks at me like he has a crazy man for a dad. Ah, well.

Neighbors are important for the small as well as the big things they do

We all know, especially after the heroics of September 11th, of the tenacity and bravery of the nation's firefighters. But we also know that firefighters were doing that same kind of work year after year after year for centuries before that.

Long before September 11th, firefighters were going into burning buildings, being dropped into raging forest fires, and battling the beast to save lives and property. It was simply that September 11th *made* us take a new look and remember what "fighting a fire" was all about.

Firefighting is not about fires, it's about people. It's about nature, it's about families, and it is about saving the lives and property of neighbors.

But there is, and always has been, even more to the profession. There is more to it than search and rescue, paramedic service, and any other kind of "triage" the nation, or the community, needs. There is also the simple act of being a neighbor and all that implies.

For the want of a key

A few years ago, we went on vacation. My wife's parents had been visiting us and they decided to stay on at the house for a few days after we left.

One morning, her mom and dad walked outside and locked themselves out. There were doors and windows open in the back, but a fence prevented them from getting back there. What to do? What to do?

Well, what they did was go to the fire station near us and explain their situation. Did the firefighters in the station tell this retired, elderly woman to call a locksmith? Did they tell her that there was nothing they could do? No. What they did was follow her back to the house in the fire truck.

One of the firefighters then proceeded to hop the fence, go through the house, and open the door.

In other words, these neighbors solved her problem in the fastest, safest way available. My mother-in-law was, of course, very grateful and told them that her daughter would bake them a cake when she got back from vacation.

And my wife did bake the cake, and she and our son took it to the station. This made that kid happy, as did seeing the firefighters again when they drove the fire truck to the house to return the cake pan (is that cool, or what?).

The point of the story is this: it is the small things, as much as the large, that make good neighbors. Is it the job of these firefighters to climb a fence so someone can get in their house? Of course not. But they did climb that fence; they did take the time to help a retired couple from being locked out, or from having to drive around a strange area looking for a locksmith. To the men and women of Fire Station Number 7, thanks for being great neighbors.

Help! There's a Pregnant Lady in the House

First things first: my wife is pregnant. So, anything you read here today is absolutely, positively true. At least, most of it is true. Okay, some of it. And the reason I say that is because I may have been doing a little bit of lying recently. Okay, a lot. But I have reasons—good reasons for doing all this lying, namely, self-defense.

Some men will agree, and some women will disagree, with the following: Pregnant women are crazy. And I don't mean crazy like mental-institution crazy, I just mean your garden variety, take no prisoners, and make the spouse—male or female—climb the walls kind of crazy. But I mean that in the best possible way.

See, my wife is not the mean kind of crazy, at least most of the time. Oh, sure, there are times when she comes in the house and our son, the dog, and I can tell by how she puts the key in the lock what kind of mood she's in. But no, what I'm talking about is the little kind of crazy, the quiet kind of crazy.

Here's an example

Before my wife got pregnant, she used to sleep. She was a world-class sleeper, one of the best on the planet. Now things are, shall we say, different. She still sleeps, but in spurts, and gets up verrry early in the morning. I rise at five every day, and often, she's up before me. I used to be able to quietly get up, give the dog his breakfast, get my coffee or tea and newspaper, and have a quiet hour or so before the house came alive. Not any longer.

Lately, as the dog and I have come down the stairs, the first thing I see is her, reading or watching TV. She has been intruding on my quiet mornings. The dog doesn't mind; he loves something warm to cuddle up against after breakfast. So anyway, she sees me enter the room and in a cheery voice says something like, "Good morning, sweetheart." I just look at her and wonder who this person is and what she has done with my wife.

It's not that cheeriness is a bad thing; it's just that any conversation at five in the morning is rough to take.

Our son is not a morning speaker. He gets up after his alarm goes off, and I then go in his room and add a bit of fatherly encouragement—like, "If you don't get up right now, I'm going to pour cold water on your head."

So, he stumbles into the family room carrying his blankie and Labbie the stuffed Labrador and looks for a place on the couch to disappear into. Then his mother gives him a warm, cheery greeting. He looks at me rather painfully, but I remind him that there is not a mute button on his mother. He then just nods at me and curls up with the dog— the two of them trying to keep the coming day from appearing any faster than it is.

Another example—as if you needed one

Have you ever met a cranky person? I mean, a person who is not particularly mean, vicious, or cruel, but rather just cranky. Well, I am now married to just such a person. Oh, she didn't start out that way. No, no, at one time she was really very nice. Sure, she had her moments with individuals she thought were trying to cheat her or something, but overall, she was nice.

Well, the woman has turned cranky. Actually Cranky. Actually, actually CRANKY! She gets cranky at the dog, the neighbors (but not in person—we still have to live here), our son's teacher, my mother, sister, father, her mother, brothers, sisters-in-law, and father, and anyone who happens to be walking by the house at the wrong time. The only thing that spares the letter carrier is the fact that he comes at a time when she generally isn't home. I hope he appreciates it.

She also gets cranky at our son and, especially, me. Our son doesn't mind much; he just looks at me, kind of shakes his head, and dives for the nearest door with the dog that was already headed in that direction. Smart kid.

Collecting evidence to use against us.

Hospital Maternity Floors

We are giving birth. My wife is doing all the hard work, all I'm supposed to do is stand around and do whatever she wants, whenever she wants it, and however she wants it, and then please do it sooner because she is the one who has carried this thing around for nine months and has been sick and is now having to go through the pain of childbirth!

So, we're giving birth, and we've been doing all the correct, safe things. We've been going to birthing classes, safe baby classes, and breastfeeding classes.

We've read books, talked to the teachers, had other parents over to discuss natural birth and the use of a doula (someone who helps the mother go through the natural childbirth).

During all this, one of the things we expectant parents are supposed to do is go visit hospital maternity floors in the hospital where we'll be having our child. So, we did.

The Four Seasons should be so nice

The hospital where we're launching our daughter is on the coast; we live twenty miles inland. I can't wait for the labor pains to start—with my luck, I'll be driving down Interstate 8, during rush hour, with my wife in the back seat screaming that the baby is coming, and we're stuck in bumper-to-bumper, grid-locked traffic. Think maybe one of the traffic helicopters will set down and pick us up and take us to the hospital? Nah, I didn't think so either.

Back to the hospital. We make an appointment to see the floor, then we show up at our appointed time. During this tour, we give them some forms that we've had to fill out and they give the expectant mom some tests. But none of this is important. The important thing is the hospital room.

Each expectant mother is given her own private room. This room is done in muted woods and shades of soothing color. It is fairly luxurious, and this is the room that the mother will be in before birth, during birth, and after giving birth. It's all done from this one private room.

The nurses wheel in the necessary equipment when needed and then wheel it out when finished. Everything else is behind wood-covered panels and doors. I really like this place.

I'm not kidding about all this. It is extremely nice. I was thinking it was going to be a cold, sterile operating room with instruments from the 1800s (okay, that part is a bit much), but I know we've progressed a lot. Most of the mental pictures I have of these rooms come from television shows, and those don't look at all as inviting as these birthing rooms.

Well, I for one was absolutely amazed. Our daughter will come into the world in a luxurious suite, with hand-picked music playing in the background (Mom wants Motown), will not have to be taken anywhere else (first bath and everything is done in the suite), and will very quickly be snuggling up to Mom for her first meal.

After it's over, I will have been forgotten about as long as I've remembered to do what it is I'm supposed to do—take pictures and call the family.

How Many Diapers?

We've been getting ready to welcome a baby into the house. While unpacking something called a Diaper Genie, I got curious. Just how many of these things, these diapers, were we going to have to change? (Let's be honest here, Mom can change all she wants to; I was wondering how many of the smelly things *I* was going to have to change). So, I started doing a bit of research and crunched some numbers.

Those numbers didn't seem too bad until I began to add them up. Let's see, newborn babies use this many per day, toddlers use this many per day, times thirty days, times number of months, and—what? I mean, WHAT??????

Now, I admit that math has never been my strong point, but even I can use a calculator. And I did, over and over and over again. The numbers kept coming out the same.

Almost 10,000

Excuse me? Ten thousand diaper changes? Ten thousand times of undoing a smelly diaper, cleaning up…well, you know what, and then putting on another diaper, just so she can do the whole thing over again? Is someone out of their mind?

That 10,000 number is an estimate. It fits within the middle range of numbers the site gave. But let's face it: you know the actual number will be even more. Babies get sick, babies get diarrhea, and babies drink a lot of fluids.

As I looked at the cool blue numbers on the calculator's display, I began to feel woozy. Mountains of diapers the size of Mauna Loa Volcano would soon be appearing. I guess I should probably buy stock in whatever company makes Pampers—and there's another thought. What's best to use, cloth or disposable? Cloth is better for the environment; disposable is better for my home environment. Perhaps we'll do a mixture of both.

They haven't gotten it right yet

Diaper manufacturers are working hard at making an ever-better diaper. Unfortunately, they're still far from getting it. See, here's the thing: we still have to change it. We still have to go through all the messy steps to get a clean diaper on the now-clean baby. There must be a way around all that. Well, there is. I've invented a new, revolutionary way of caring for babies' bottoms and the stuff that comes from them. I call it *Roll o Diapers*.

Yes, *Roll o Diapers* will soon change the way the world looks at messy bottoms. How, you ask? Simple, you just sell diapers like paper towel companies sell paper towels. Have paper diapers on a roll and simply tear off what you need. We can have Scott diapers, Brawny diapers, or Viva or Bounty diapers. We can have the diapers that are the "quicker picker-uppers." Ha! Won't that be handy.

Okay, back to reality. Any day now, I'm going to have to start in on my part of those 10,000 diaper changes. I would like to think that the baby will appreciate it, but I know better. Babies don't and shouldn't have to appreciate the care they require. That simply comes from the love, and duty, of a parent. And besides, those 10,000 changes will pass before I even know it—or so says my mother.

But I do plan on getting even. When I get older, I intend to use a whole lot—*a whole lot*—of Depends.

Get ready, 'cause it's coming at ya.

Insanity Comes with Parenthood

There are many reasons that parents start pulling their hair, howling at the moon, and quietly crying in corners to themselves. The main reason is that we are silently, easily, unstoppably sliding into something called PI (Parenthood Insanity). Often, this PI is caused by our children, someone else's children, or just children in general.

Oh, sure. Kids are wonderful things. The future of humanity depends on them, after all (yes, it's a bit scary, but it's always been that way). That said, they will still push you ever more slowly toward the edge of running away. Here are just a few examples from a single day.

Example 1

This past week, we did the holiday barbecue thing. The day was beautiful, the barbeque was smoking, the drinks were on ice. It was going to be an easy, wonderful afternoon. We slept in, then slowly started getting everything ready. The barbeque was fired up, steaks and Boca burgers were tossed on the grill (the Boca burgers were for the vegetarians among us; yes, mostly me), my mother came over, and the day looked sublime.

You know that's not going to last, right? While we were eating, my son casually mentioned that he needed to get a haircut before leaving for fire academy. "Aren't you leaving at seven a.m. tomorrow?"

"Yeah."

"It's Easter Sunday."

"I know."

"Where will you get this haircut?"

"What do you mean?"

Sigh. "Do you really think there are many (any) places open for a haircut today?"

The blood started draining out of the poor kid's face. "Um, there aren't?" he asked

I just shook my head and assumed the exasperated dad pose (leaning back in the chair, hands clasped behind the head, quizzical look on the face). He started to panic.

I couldn't let that go on too long; I'm not (that) cruel, after all. I told him to start looking to see if he could find someplace open that might cut his hair. He started frantically going through websites and he finally found one open place—Salon on 30—and called. They told him if he came right then and gave a credit card number to hold the spot, they'd cut his hair. So, he gave the credit card number and we jumped in the car and took off. Quite a distance away from the house, but we (okay, he) had no choice. It was the only place he could find.

Why did I go along? What, miss out on this? Not likely.

Example 2

He was getting directions from the phone and a police officer saw that and pulled us over. Son told him he was just getting directions to go to the only place he could find to get a haircut because he had fire academy to go to. And the phone was not on his face

The officer let him know that "hands-free" means fully hands-free. Son knows this, of course. The officer let him off with a warning and the kid started breathing again.

We got back on the road and barely made it to the place by the 4:15 appointment time. But barely made it equals made it, and whew!

Neither of us had been to this salon before. It had a made-over warehouse vibe (because it really was a made-over old warehouse or business of some kind). The people there were friendly but not overly so—in other words, professional. They got him in right away and I started writing on my phone while waiting. They offered me a beer and started naming the brands. I stopped them at Pacifico. Why go beyond that?

Can a Pacifico help one write? I have no idea, but it probably can't hurt. And it certainly makes a breezy afternoon in a hair salon go by as one waits for their kid to get a haircut.

Example 3

And then came the price. Son got his first $60 haircut on Easter Sunday. His haircuts are usually about one-third that price. Or less.

His eyes started to pop out of his head when he heard the price, but I told him no worries, I got it. He was stressing enough as it was;

no sense adding to it.

I have to say that I rather liked the place—interesting décor, and they offered me a Pacifico while I waited. Plus, the kid did get a really good haircut. It wasn't cheap, but it was definitely worth it.

So: good haircut—that Pop paid for—and he didn't get a ticket. He had a pretty good afternoon. I had to ask why he waited until Easter Sunday to get a haircut—you know, a dad question—and he allowed that wasn't the best of ideas. I couldn't agree more.

I wrote a piece a few years ago about how tough parenting can sometimes be. Many people connected with that. In the piece, I discussed how I got to thinking about being a parent. Of course, this is usually the kind of thing you only think about late at night when you can't get to sleep. And so it was with me (then and now).

There are all kinds of parents: easy ones, tough ones, taskmasters, fun ones, boring ones, and every kind in between. I began to wonder about just what kind of parent I am. Am I mean? No. Am I tough? No. Am I fun to be with? Well, occasionally. Personally, I like to think that I'm a riot of fun to be with twenty-four-seven, but there are people around who might argue with that, so I'll let it go—for now.

Most parents try to do a halfway decent job. At least, we try to. But doing even a halfway decent job can be downright difficult—at times, nearly impossible. And that's to be expected, of course, since most of us are in the middle of parenthood insanity.

Bubble gum acid in a rose-colored slushie

The day dawned
hot and groggy
or
maybe that was me
Last night I dreamed about
    what, I don't know
But it must have been more than
the
mid-sized
half-pint
middle-aged
middle-of-the-road

midstream
mainstream
for
middle-weight half-wits
buying Slurpees at 7-Eleven

Kids, Rainy Days, and Sanity

It has been particularly dry in Southern California over the past few years. But lately, we've been getting wet again and people are noticing. Most of us love rain. People *really* love rain when there is a multi-year drought going on. And let's face it, can there be anything better than a rainy day, when the rain gently falls, nourishing the earth and every living thing? The kind of day where children of all ages joyfully and gleefully play to the sound of rain hitting the roof. Yeah, yeah, I know. It sounds wonderful, but the reality is much different.

Yes, the rain nourishes; yes, the rain may fall on your (probably leaking) roof; and yes, kids like to play. But, and you know this is true, kids soon tire of that rain. Pretty soon, they come to you and say, in that special whiny kid-voice that only a child can do, that they are bored. They are bored and expect you to do something about it.

Well, I'm here to help. I am qualified to help because I have kids like this at home, and right now, it's raining, and they want me to do something about the boredom (especially now that the Christmas and New Year holidays are over and the excitement has died). They want me to entertain them. Yeah, right.

In searching around for ways to keep my darling son and daughter from being bored and thereby driving me crazy, I was able to find a few helpful things. I am going to share those with you now.

Things for kids to do to keep them entertained (and occupied)

1. Sleep late.
2. Sleep later.
3. Wake up really, really slowly.
4. Polish the doorknobs. Hey, how often do you actually do this?
5. Have them call friends they have not spoken to in a long time and then tell them to hang up when that person answers (if the kid wanted to talk to the person, they would have. And kids love this

one—they can do it for hours. Just make sure they do not start calling your friends or people at random from the phone book). NOTE: Block caller ID before attempting this or people will be doing it back to you or will end up at your door with burning stakes. And who needs that, right?

6. Have them make your breakfast (wait, I'm choking from laughing).

7. Make them clean up the kitchen after making your breakfast.

8. Dry the dog that got wet outside in the rain and now smells like a sewer going through a garbage dump.

9. Clean their room.

10. Better yet, have them clean your room.

11. Wash the garage floor (sure, it is the garage, but they'll use a lot of energy on that grease).

12. Dust the inside plants.

13. Dust the outside plants (not the ones in the rain).

14. Bathe the dog, who got out again and got wet again and stinks again because that's what dogs do so well.

15. Bathe your cat. Hey, it's always fun to annoy a cat. NOTE: Tell your child to be careful of sharp claws from this hissing, spitting cat that wants to kill anything within reach. Usually, the cat will not kill the kid, it will kill you because it knows that the whole horrible idea was yours.

16. Give them money, put them in the car, gather a few of their friends, and head to the movies. This one is a win-win for everyone.

Okay, there you have fifteen wonderful ideas (and one really great one) that you can use to keep children busy, so they do not drive you nuts during a rainy day. Feel free to use whenever necessary.

A love affair with water

Personally, I love rain. There is nothing quite like the sound of it hitting the roof in the early morning. Being snuggled in bed late at night, with splatters of water hitting and running down the window is a sound reminiscent of old films, Key West, and drops falling from trees while kids take refuge.

Water is so crucial, so fundamental to human life, even the sound of it resonates deeply within us. Water is part of the cycle of life on Earth, part of what makes life possible, so much so that it seems even our soul is in tune with the very molecules that make up water. And yet, I live in a desert. Yeah, I don't know why either.

Now, I suppose that there are kids who probably don't like rain, kids who would rather be playing with a ball on a dry field. But what do they know of the wonderful secrets of rain? What do they know of nature's art? I'm sure that parents would rather their kids not get wet, laboring under the mistaken belief that getting wet or cold can make you sick (note: it is germs and viruses and the like which make people sick, not regular old temperature or moisture). Let's face it, these parents are just a bunch of wet blankets (excuse the pun), who probably haven't had a Popsicle in fifteen years. It's time to forget all the nonsense of practicality and just go for it. In other words, you become a kid again as you let your kids be kids.

Don't you wish you could be a kid again? Not forever, of course, but just for a day or two (hey, you still want to drive). Wouldn't it be fun to see the world as a new thing just one more time? Splash in a puddle and still be excited instead of angered? Stick your tongue out to taste a drop of rain?

Well, give it a try. Just for a minute, go back a few decades and remember. Think of the sounds, the newness. Be a kid again, one more time, in the rain.

Parenting Gets Harder with Time

Every day, at least once a day, I think about parenting. It comes with the territory of being a parent—go figure. This happened again yesterday when I was trying to fix a bike chain. Usually, parenting is the kind of thing you only think about late at night when you can't get to sleep, but not this time. Oh, no. This time, a chain set it off. Lucky me.

Now that Son is a teenager in NROTC and Sea Cadets, while still fighting math, and Daughter is trying to find her way through spelling tests and the trials and tribulations of being a growing girl, I am noticing so many new ways to make a mess of things.

Parents and kids

Most parents try to do a halfway decent job. We want more, but we'll settle for that. At least, we try to. But doing even a halfway decent job can be downright difficult—at times, nearly impossible. But only *nearly* impossible—it's never absolutely impossible. If it was impossible, none of us would be here, and since we are…

So, just what is a good parent? Note that I'm not talking great parent here. The PTA has some of those people, and personally, I think they're aliens from another planet. I see them occasionally at my kids' school and they are just flat-out scary. Those parents are even worse than the soccer parents, and you know how weird those people can be.

A good parent:

Is generally, mostly kind

Attempts to be patient no matter what the child has done, including setting the dog on fire and then letting it run through the house.

Remembers hugs (or at least tries to because the older the child, the harder it is to grab those hugs).

Is not opposed to inviting the neighborhood kids to come over and play and makes sure to have a basketball hoop, rusty or not.

Plays with the kids (or tries to for a minute or two until being banished).

Knows when to disappear and let the kids play by themselves (pretty much all the time in the teen years).

Can make a roaring campfire out of two sticks and one wet match (or convince the kids that taking KFC to the camp is more fun).

Can make s'mores blindfolded.

Knows every outfit for every season.

Likes to play with Barbie with his daughter—even gets his friends to join them.

Likes to play space alien with her son—even gets her friends to join them.

Thinks that a weekend with the kids is just about as good as it gets.

Finds out that children's films are not all ghastly.

Is glad the PTA moms call (not true, of course, but they can fake it really well).

Wishes the PTA moms would lose their phone number.

Wishes that the tables in kindergarten were made larger so that when they had to come for Parent/Teacher conferences, they wouldn't look quite so stupid all bunched up with their knees hitting their chin

Wonders why it is that they feel the same way when entering a classroom as an adult that they did when they were kids.

Thinks that their kids are bright even when they do stupid things (oh, please! You know you do);

Wonders how they could do such stupid, stupid things like put chocolate milk in the tropical fish aquarium.

Doesn't put the kid on time-out even when they ask you how old you are (but admit it—you want to really, really badly).

Doesn't put the kid on time-out after she or he told the teacher you said that you thought the homework assignment was silly or that particular teacher should be doing some other job instead of teaching (see how that goes over sometime!).

Is struggling to figure out where the money is going to come from to pay for the child's tutor, the child's soccer outfit, the child's music lessons (and don't get me started on cars, insurance, and braces).

Is struggling to figure out why the child needs a tutor—it must be that "other" side of the family.

Sometimes is forced to simply say no.

Sometimes says no again.

Sometimes says yes, even when they don't want to.

Says maybe way, way too often (but hey, it can buy a little time).

Loves their child when the kid has been very, very bad—knowing it's harder to love the problem child but knowing that child needs love more than ever.

Knows that the job never ends.

Couldn't imagine a day without that child's smile *or* frown.

Parenthood in all its many shapes and forms.

Six Months Old!

My daughter has now turned six months old and my oh my, how time seems to fly. She does so much more now than she ever could. For instance, she spits up, sits up, goes to the bathroom, spits up, sits up, goes to the bathroom, spits up, sits up…well, you get the idea.

Actually, what she does is a great deal more than that. I've broken her day down into steps so you can see just how much she does on a continual basis (the following is not in any particular order).

She:

Sits up

Spits up

Eats

Throws up

Sits up

Spits up

Eats

Throws up

Goes to the bathroom

Goes to the bathroom again

Sleeps

Takes a nap

Sleeps

Sits up

Spits up

Eats

Throws up

Sits up

Spits up

Eats

Throws up

Goes to the bathroom
Goes to the bathroom again

That's not all!

No, that's not all she does, because she also:

Smiles
Coos and squeaks and laughs
Says daddy
Smiles
Coos and squeaks and laughs
Says daddy (more or less)
Smiles
Coos and squeaks and laughs
Smiles
Coos and squeaks and laughs

She does a number of other things too, of course, but these are the vast majority of things my daughter.
does. She is a very vocal child—there are times when this is good and times when it is not, like 3 a.m. She is also getting mobile: now she rolls all over the place. She can't quite crawl yet, so she rolls everywhere she wants to go. The dog just looks at her with a bored expression on his face, but I like it.

She likes to laugh and that's a good thing because, what a coincidence, I like to make her laugh. I don't know why, but there is something very innocent and pure about the laugh of a six-month-old child. Her laugh hasn't yet become cynical, or bored, or cold.

She likes to grab hair—everyone's, including the dog who ignores it—and hold on. Sometimes, it can be a trial to get her to turn loose. Dinner is fun, although feeding her can generally be a very messy affair. She wants to eat, play with, and smear her food—and then laugh. By then, I'm usually laughing too (but not always after I've cleaned her up three times before half the meal is finished). And then I just give up and let her get as messy as she wants—figuring it'll come off in the bath. And so far, it has.

When I kiss her ears, she laughs, and when I hear that laugh, I know why the human race has to get better at being humane and loving with one another. Yes, I know that the likelihood of us all actually being good to each other is not part of the near future, but it is something to reach for.

So, what is going to happen during the next six months? I don't have a clue. Hopefully, she learns to crawl and walk and talk, and keep the family wrapped around her little finger.

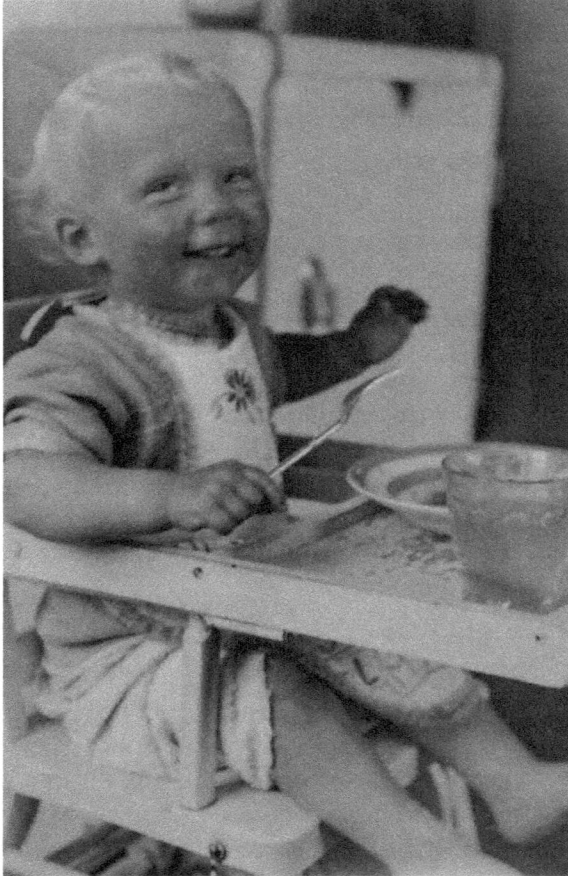

Thank-You Cards

A couple of weeks ago, my son had a birthday and there were the usual parties. Yes, I said "parties" because there was one with the family and another with his friends from school. Two parties for someone turning seven might seem a bit much, but what do I know?

Anyway, now that the dust has settled from all these parties, the time has arrived to write the thank-you notes. Let me just say that the child prefers getting the gifts to writing the notes. Much prefers it. And who can blame him?

Watching him at his little desk the other night fighting with his mom about doing it got me thinking about the whole thing. I have come to a conclusion: the time has arrived for us to stop the thank-you card.

Yes, I realize that the card companies and purveyors of books and columns on manners are hissing, those who tell us exactly what to do and how to do it are choking on their own smiles, and everyone's mom from coast to coast wants to burn me in effigy, if not in actual fact. Too bad. The time has come for a slight change in manners.

It's toys or clothes, not a lung or kidney

Yes, of course, there are times for thank-you cards. If the person who gave you the gift is not there to thank in person, or you open the gift later, then sure, send a thank-you note. If the person donated a kidney or a lung or some other crucial body part to you, then yeah, send a card. But if you are at a party, open the gift with the giver there and you then say thank you, that's enough.

At my son's party (both of them), he opened his presents during that slow time between eating lunch and then having cake and ice cream. We all sat around and watched him open these gifts. We all heard him very politely thank the person who gave him the gift (yes, he really does have good manners). Now, why does the poor child—and by extension, his parents—have to later send a card?

I'll tell you why: it's because card companies determined it was a good thing for their bottom line for us to do so. I don't mean to say that they were being greedy and sitting around a table trying to figure out ways to get more of our money. No, I'm just saying that when your business is selling something, you try to sell as much of it as possible. So, you advertise and tell us to be polite and send a card. And we insecure individuals (which is most everyone with a firing brain cell or two) do.

I have a proposal. It's simply this: let's stop the thank-you cards except in certain circumstances. If someone sends you a gift, then yes, send a thank-you card. After all, you do want to thank them, and they need to know that you received the gift. In other words, anytime that you cannot thank someone in person, send a card.

Anytime you don't open a gift when the person is there, a card should be sent. Wedding gifts, where the guests leave the gifts but they are not opened, are one example of this in which a note should be sent.

You get the idea. Simply put, if you cannot say thanks, then send it. Otherwise, just say your heartfelt thank you and both you and the giver will know that you have both appreciation and manners. And let the card companies come up with a new holiday or reason to buy cards.

Worried Kids

I have a question: how would you like to be a child in today's world? What must it be like to be eight, nine, ten, twelve, fifteen, sixteen years old and worry about all the things kids worry about today?

Sure, kids have always worried about things—and they usually worry much more than adults give them credit for. My father remembers the Depression and worrying about when the family might get the next meal. His father, my grandfather, was a barber who cut hair during the depression for twenty-five cents. They raised a few chickens for eggs and had a small garden, but things were very tough in Phoenix during the late twenties and early thirties.

Most people did, however, survive. It probably also made some of them stronger (while also making some of them paranoid, ever fearful, and weaker). My father and his brothers survived because of their parents and their own resourcefulness.

So, what do kids have to worry about in this day and age? And remember, an awful lot of adults will tell kids that "You've got nothing to worry about now! Why, in my day…" but kids do still worry; they probably always will worry because they have a wonderful propensity for feeling whatever the adults around them are feeling.

Let's look at just some of the things kids are worrying about now.

Just a very small list:

1. AIDS
2. SARS
3. War
4. Violence on television
5. Violence in schools
6. Violence in playgrounds
7. Violence in sports
8. Violence in the home
9. Drugs

10. Being shot while riding in a car
11. Kidnapping
12. Sexual abuse
13. Pregnancy
14. Cancer from any number of things
15. New school exams/exit exams/entrance exams/exams, exams, exams
16. Having an un-crowded school
17. Getting into college
18. Paying for college
19. Getting a college degree that will enable them to actually get a job
20. Getting a meaningful job
21. Getting a job
22. Getting a job
23. Getting a job
24. Getting another job because careers rarely last a lifetime
25. Going back to college to get up to date on technology
26. Technology
27. Having both parents around
28. Having both parents
29. Having any parent
30. Being able to retire at a good age
31. A Social Security office that still has funds for their retirement
32. Owning a nice house
33. Owning any kind of house
34. Paying for that house that costs in the hundreds of thousands
35. Global warming
36. Pollution run rampant around the planet
37. What the future will hold

Now, yes—I realize that most if not all of those things are also worries that we adults carry with us on a daily basis. But here is the important thing: those are worries that only adults should have, not our children.

How sad that we worry about guns when dropping children off at school. How even sadder that they have to worry about it.

Now, I'm not suggesting that kids should not have to worry about a thing. Not at all. I'm just thinking that kids should only have to worry about "kid" things. You know, things like which shoes to wear, what kind of popsicle to eat, whether or not to jump on a bike and race to the corner and back. They should worry about dating and not how "far to go" on a date, about what to eat and not about dieting, about the cute kid next door and not the "neighbor" next door. You get the idea—kids need to worry about kid stuff and leave the heavy stuff to us adults. Only problem with that is, too often, we adults mess it up. We make mistakes, get it wrong.

Not that perfection is possible, of course, but I think most adults would like to do better than we do. And most of us try, and try, and try, and keep on trying. Perhaps someday we'll get it right—and then our kids will too.

Until that day comes, just keep in mind something my father used to say when I was a kid: "Hey, I'm an amateur at this too." And he was right—he was an amateur father and I was an amateur son—it was the first time at being either one for both of us. We got better at it, of course, just in time for me to be the amateur father.

A world with too much worry for kids and other living things.

When Things Go Wrong, They Really Go Wrong

What is it with kids and illnesses, and why does every kid in the household have to get something at the same time? Yes, I'm sure that it probably isn't always that way—but it sure seems like it sometimes.

The other day, our son decided to get a raging toothache at, naturally, 4:45 p.m. I had just picked him up at my parents', where he'd spent a few mellow hours, and on our way home, he told me he had a really, really, really bad toothache.

So, I changed direction and went straight to his dentist. At 5:02 p.m. they were closed, but a nurse saw us, came to the door, took a look at Ryan, and let us in. The dentist had left, but they reached him on his cell phone down the street where he was putting gas in his car. He came back to see Ryan—I like this guy! They determined that he had a tooth infection, gave me a prescription, and we went home.

We're not even started yet

When his loving and (most of the time) patient mom came home, I went to the drugstore, filled the prescription, drove to a grocery store and bought soup, and went home. He ate a bit of the soup but pretty much just took it easy. A bit later, the Children's Tylenol kicked in, the kid-directed TLC kicked in, tiredness kicked in, and he finally fell asleep. We were good for the night. Yeah, right.

Daughter, who had gone to bed quite happily for a change, started throwing up. I'm holding a small plastic trashcan under her, because that's what was closest at the time, and she's managing to hit it occasionally. The rest of the time, she's spraying me. The thing is, you have to just stand there and watch as it happens. There's not much you can do about it, she's just two years old, after all, but you sure do hate to see it.

When she finally finished, there was puke (yes, there are a lot of more sanitized words, but that's simply the best one at the time) on her, the rug underneath her, all over my hands, arms, clothes, shoes. Oh yeah, it smelled great in that room.

Wife cleaned her up and I tackled everything else. I took the bedding and rug out in the back, shook them off down the hill (sometimes it's great living on a canyon) and then squirted them off with the hose, and then finally stuffed them in the washing machine.

You feel so sorry for them as they're going through all the paroxysms of puking, shaking, and gagging while at the same time you're doing a bit of gagging yourself because there is warm, body-temp chunky barf all over your hands and arms. It was a night, all right.

From barf to toothache

So, now on to Son and the toothache: We took him to the dentist a bit later the following morning, after which he proceeded to lie down and watch TV because he had an infected tooth pulled and stitched and wasn't feeling all that hot. At the same time, spacers were put between other teeth (in preparation for the braces going on), and next week, they're pulling out three more teeth (which aren't, thank goodness, infected) to make room for the adult teeth as they come in.

Oh, the pain

I'm sure he doesn't hurt a whole lot, but he's a kid; and while he can be terrifically brave about some things, tooth pain just isn't one of them. And who can blame him? A lot of grown-ups I know aren't all that brave about it either (heck, some people are so afraid of dentistry that they avoid it for years, and that's a shame because their over-all health can suffer from that).

My father once told me that having two kids is not twice as hard as having one—it's four or five times as much. I, naturally, didn't believe him—didn't think he knew what the heck he was talking about. Well, he did know, was right, and I'm finding out the hard way, one injury at a time.

I wonder if there's any way that we could somehow get the kids to take turns? You know, one kid sick one week, another kid sick the following. This would make it a whole lot easier. Not that I necessarily need everything simple, but if it's possible…well, why not?

Why do you suppose that two kids are four or five times harder than one? Do they get together and gang up on parents? Do they decide to make life difficult for us? I'm not sure, but I don't think so. Hey, my two can't agree on anything at all as it is, much less work together. The last time they really, truly worked together on something was Christmas, and even then, they both still fell asleep waiting for Santa Claus because they couldn't trust each other enough to let one sleep while the other watched.

But that was last week, and this is this week. Those pains and troubles are starting to fade as new ones take their places. Only thing is, I'm scared to death wondering what's coming up. With those two, you never can tell. I love them endlessly, but they do keep life hopping. Which, I suppose, is probably a good thing. I know I wouldn't trade it for anything (except maybe a few hours' sleep).

Moms and Dads

Did your parents have different parenting styles? From what I have been able to tell, from either talking to parents or just observing how my wife and I parent our own child, I must conclude that no two people have the same parenting style, especially moms and dads.

The problem is, no one has been able to name these styles and show the differences. That is where I come in. As a public service (another one of my many) I am going to, once and for all, in black and white, show just how parents differ in that great old chore of parenting. And to make it easy for the guys, I am going to use a simple list. First, I will name the problem and then show how moms and dads deal with the situation. If you see yourself in this list, do not blame me, blame one of your parents. That's what society has them for, after all.

His and Her Parenting Styles

Problem: Crying child with no evidence of blood
Her Solution: Run to child
His Solution: Do you hear anything?

Problem: Crying child with blood
Her Solution: Grab tourniquet
His Solution: Look for Band-Aid

Problem: Child asks for money
Her Solution: Digs through purse
His Solution: Ask your mother

Problem: Child wants to borrow car
Her Solution: As soon as I finish with it
His Solution: Ask your mother

Problem: Child wants to start dating at twelve years old
Her Solution: NO
His Solution: Daughter—NO; Son—Okay, but you can't take the car

Problem: Daughter wants to bring her boyfriend over for New Year's Day
Her Solution: Yes, we would love to meet him!
His Solution: Okay, but he better like the same football team I like

Problem: Son wants to be an artist instead of the sportscaster you dreamed of
Her Solution: Give him time to find his medium
His Solution: What?

Problem: Likes jazz fusion music
Her Solution: Lets him play it in her car
His Solution: What?

Problem: Child asks their first question about sex
Her Solution: Ask your father
His Solution: Ask your mother

Problem: Daughter wants to join a motorcycle gang
Her Solution: Over my dead body!
His Solution: Okay, but only under two conditions. One, you keep your grades up, and two, he comes over here and fixes my car.

Problem: Daughter wants to become a weightlifter and bodybuilder
Her Solution: What?
His Solution: What?

Problem: Children finally get older and team up against you
Her Solution: Move to Palm Springs
His Solution: Move to Denver

As you can see from this *very* incomplete list, there are huge differences in the way parents do their job of raising kids. In fact, when you think about it, it is amazing that kids get raised at all. But luckily they do, and generally without too much damage to either the kids or the parents. Mostly.

The Frivolous, Mundane, and Yes, Boring

According to my kids, most things in life are frivolous, mundane, or boring. Mostly boring. Especially boring.

A while back, I decided to write down everything they said was boring. Here is the partial (yes, partial) list:

1. School
2. Washing our dogs
3. Their mother's car
4. Dinner last night
5. Dinner the night before
6. Dinner every night this week
7. All dinners that aren't eaten at Corvette Diner, do not include pizza, or might remotely be considered healthy
8. The kitchen
9. Her bedroom color
10. Her bedroom carpet
11. Her bedroom blinds
12. Her bedroom
13. His phone
14. Homework
15. Homework
16. Homework
17. Homework
18. Homework
19. TV because there isn't anything on that's good
20. Any music she/he didn't choose
21. My shoes

22. My shirts
23. My socks (socks? They're socks—they're usually boring)
24. My haircut
25. Me
26. Their mother
27. The lawnmower
28. Using the lawnmower
29. The lawn
30. Flowers
31. Gas stations
32. Putting gas in the car
33. Getting a haircut (him but not her—she loves it)
34. Putting dishes in the dishwasher
35. Cooking dinner
36. Cleaning up the:
     Kitchen
     Patio
     Living room
     Dining room
     Bathroom
     Their room
     The garage
     A window—any window

Did I mention that my kids do not much care for cleaning things? I'm sure they believe that cleaning is a magical thing that happens automatically. I'm not sure why they think this—other than, perhaps, it's hereditary. I'm sure I thought the same thing at their age.

In fact, everyone I know thought the same thing until they moved into their own home for the first time. Talk about an eye-opening experience.

It's not just the cleaning that was so jarring. We all, in the depths of our minds, knew things need to be clean. No, the jarring aspect of moving into our first place was shopping for cleaning supplies.

Do you remember shopping for cleaning supplies by yourself, for yourself, for the very first time? That was both liberating and slightly scary. You think, *Will I have enough money? Will I get the right things?*

And as you shop while thinking those things, you also have running through your head, *I'm an adult. This is so no big deal. I'm good. Oh, yeah, I'm good.*

But whether you remember it or not, you also gave a slight, "Whew!" when you put the items in the car. You made it and you didn't embarrass yourself too horribly. Unless, of course, you did (and you lived through it anyway).

After getting home, you put everything away and looked around your little apartment and thought, *Okay, now I really do need to do something about this mess.* And you started cleaning.

All the things you learned as a kid started to pay off. You got the bathroom clean, the kitchen bearable, the rest of the house at least non-toxic. And you were proud. And that was cool.

That was the first time you cleaned your own place. Every single time since then has been, what? Yes, boring.

You were right!

Yep, you were right all those years ago when, as a kid, you said how boring it was to clean the house. You were right, and now you have the proof.

Unfortunately, now comes the big, "So, what?" Yep, you were right. It was boring and it is boring. But the place still needs to be cleaned. And you are the one who is going to have to do it. Well, unless you go to college and get a degree in a growing field and can get a job that pays well enough to hire someone to clean the place for you.

Is school still boring?

The Many Faces of Dirt

There are few things that very young kids, particularly boys in my minuscule experience, like better to play in than dirt and mud. I'm sure girls probably enjoy the finer points of dirt as well, but being a man and having a son lets me speak primarily from a male perspective. So, this column addresses boys and their fascination with playing in the dirtier things of life.

There is not a puddle on earth that my son has not jumped in should it have appeared in his path. Indeed, he will walk (run) out of his way to jump in a puddle of water, and the muddier the water, the better. It doesn't matter how dressed up he is, how shiny his shoes are, how important the occasion is—if there is muddy water in his path, he dives in.

As a parent, we start to become eagle-eyed, ever on the lookout for the puddle that will erase all the time and effort it took to get him cleaned up in the first place. It becomes a game of wits as parent and child fight to see who eyes the water first. As the parent, you know that if the boy sees it first, he is headed for it at an unstoppable speed. He knows that if you see it first, you will detour him around the puddle far enough to make it impossible for him to jump in.

Dirt, dirt, and more dirt

And what after the water? The dirt, of course. Ah, the dirt, so many kinds of dirt, so many textures, so many ways to get it all over you.

1. You can just dive in, scruff the shoes around a bit, and see how much dust you can raise.
2. Ease into the dirt, being cautious and letting the dirt happen gradually.
3. Avoid the dirt entirely—this is not an option most boys entertain unless a parent is nearby. Very nearby.
4. Check out the dirt, grab a hose and add water.
5. Add more water.

6. Keep adding.

7. A little bit more.

8. "Turn off that hose, water is running in the back door!!!"

9. Okay, just right. Now jump in.

10. "You better not be in that mud with your shoes on!!!"

11. Now take off shoes.

12. "Remember to take your socks off too!!!!"

13. Take socks off.

14. Squiggle, wriggle, and jiggle around in that mud as much as is humanly possible.

15. Do it some more.

16. "You're not getting dirty, are you?"

17. "Did you hear me? I asked you if you were getting dirty!"

18. "I'm coming out there!!"

19. "I'm not getting dirty…"

20. "Then why did I hear the water running?"

21. "I don't know."

22. Now you can make mud pies, mud animals, mud soldiers, mud balls for throwing, and—well, you get the idea.

23. When you can't get any dirtier, get out and sit in a chair, preferably a chair with cushions.

24. Get ready to do it again.

Parents have a couple of choices here. 1. Yell and tell them to get out of the mud. 2. Get in with them. 3. Sit back, have a drink, listen to some music, and try to keep the kids from ingesting too much of the stuff.

What is it with kids and dirt?

To All the Single Moms and Dads Who Do the Impossible Every Day

First, there was our son, who is now eight; then, a little over a year ago, our daughter was born. Now that I have spent a year with two kids, I have to give every bit of respect and awe to the single moms and dads who are raising kids by themselves.

My wife and I have a crazy enough time as it is—even with two of us. I don't have any idea at all how a single parent manages it. More than that, a single-parent household generally has only one income (child support rarely even comes close). How do they manage it?

The day

Here is an example of one of our average days: We wake up, take showers, and get dressed (while getting coffee and feeding the dog). Then we get the kids up.

Son staggers into the family room, collapses on the couch, his hand reaching out for milk, and turns on cartoons. He slowly, very slowly, begins to gain enough consciousness to look the day in the eye (we learned long ago to set his alarm early enough to allow for this).

While his heart starts to beat, we're making lunches, cooking breakfast, making lists, and deciding who will pick everyone up from school. Then Daughter begins to stir. We hear her turn on her crib music from the monitor we have. She's letting us know that she wants up.

I then usually get her bottle ready, go in and get her up, change her diaper, and bring her in. Michelle then feeds her.

While Michelle is feeding Daughter, I get Michelle's breakfast ready, give it to her, get Son's breakfast and give it to him, and try to find time to pour another cup of coffee.

Now the fun starts

Son, eat your breakfast.
Son, eat your breakfast.

Son, eat your breakfast.
Son, eat your breakfast.
Son, eat your breakfast.
Son, eat your breakfast.
Son, eat your breakfast.
Son, eat your breakfast.

He finally eats and now must get dressed.
Son, get dressed.
Son, get dressed.
Son, get dressed.
Son, get dressed.
Son, get dressed.
Son, get dressed.
Son, get dressed.

While all this is going on, Michelle has taken Daughter in to get *her* dressed. Daughter comes out and now starts her breakfast. Well, Daughter doesn't want breakfast this early. So, she just has a small snack (she'll eat breakfast in about an hour). This snack she shares with the dog, leaves on the carpet, and generally doesn't want until I throw it away because, after all, she has shared it with the dog or put it on the carpet.

Michelle is now scrambling to get her briefcase, her car keys, her phone, and her calendar. Then she kisses everyone goodbye and heads off to work.

I gently shut the door behind her, look around, and heave a sigh. Daughter is climbing on Son, Son is trying to get her down, and the dog is trying to steal a cookie.

Now what?

As I pass Daughter on my way to get a (hot) cup of coffee, I smell the unmistakable aroma of a dirty diaper. Okay, a very dirty diaper. I pick her up, we go into her room, and I place her gently upon the changing table. She's laughing, reaching for anything she can find to play with, and I'm struggling to unsnap the first layer of her clothes.

Then I realize that they aren't snaps, they're buttons. Okay, I start unbuttoning her. Then I get to the snaps underneath. And now she's really squirming. But we finally get everything undone and reach the diaper. Finally! We struggle a bit with the actual diaper now, and the actual poop in the actual diaper, and the actual diaper wipes for the actual bottom covered in the actual poop.

But it's all clean now. Thank goodness.

We grab the tube of diaper rash cream because she has a diaper rash and spread that on. And only now can we get a new diaper and fit her clean little bottom into it. And button up the dress, and smooth everything out, and stand her on the floor, and go look for her brother because we have to get out of the house or he's going to be late for school, and if I have to tell him that one more time, I'm going to scream!

We finally get everything together, get it all in the car, and lock the house. Kids get in the car, we get ready to leave, and Son informs me that he's forgotten his school project.

Turn off the car, close the garage door, run in the house, scoop up the project—and Daughter's diaper bag that I forgot—and head back to the car.

We get to Son's school and I drop him off, then on to Daughter's school. I take her in, get her settled, and slowly walk back to the car, ready to begin my day. Now, if I can just remember where I left my briefcase.

Nope, sorry, I just don't know how single parents manage to do it all. I am in awe of them, I salute them, and I hope that someday their kids will appreciate the amazing job those parents did.

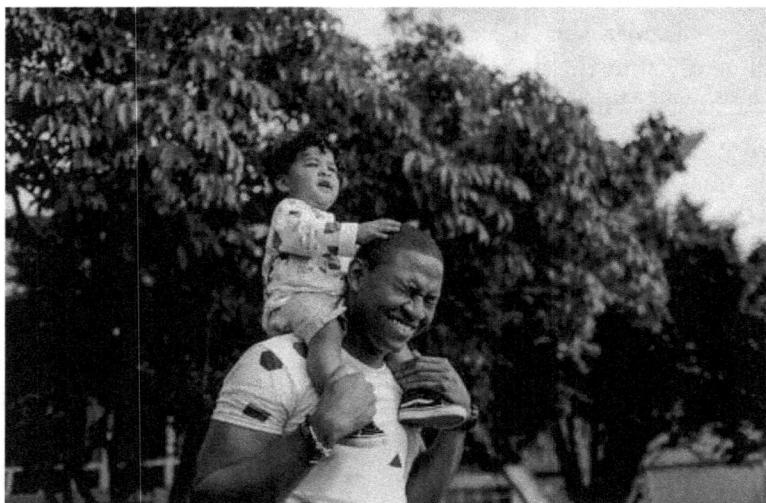

Playtime…it makes the difficult things possible.

The Universe Looking Back

Late at night in bed, as I try to let sleep wash over me, I am naturally given to recall the events of the past couple of weeks—those weeks in which my daughter was born and our family life was forever changed. Looking back, the one memory that stays with me the most, the one that keeps replaying itself over and over again, is that instant my daughter opened her eyes for the first time…and what she saw was me.

What happened next that mid-Monday morning in a San Diego hospital was essentially this: I looked into my daughter's eyes the instant they opened and saw it all.

I looked into two tiny eyes and saw the universe. I saw everything that has been and will be. It was all there, and more. There was the future and there was the past, there was despair and there was hope. There was laughter and sorrow, poverty and wealth, health and sickness.

But it's just two little eyes

I have told people about this experience of mine, and they all nod their heads, smile quietly, and think to themselves, *Another new dad!* And perhaps they're right—perhaps this is something that happens to every new parent. In fact, I would bet that, in some ways, it actually does occur. So, I'm certainly not claiming some sort of new "for the very first time on the planet" experience.

The experience was, however, new to me. And, in many ways, this kind of thing keeps happening with my wife and me—this kind of *new* thing since our daughter was born, things that have never happened before and will never happen again in the same way. But this *exact* thing had never happened before and, with her, never can again.

Looking into new eyes for the first time—before anyone else does— is something I cannot even begin to describe; there are no words for that feeling or those emotions. Perhaps one of the reasons that there are no words is because that moment has never existed before (at least with my daughter and me). How can one describe something that has not existed and can never exist again?

But now that moment does exist—it happened—and every day, I

reach for some good way to describe it. So far, that "good" way hasn't made an appearance. Even writing this short piece about it has taken days. And I don't know why...

How many billions of individuals have been born since the dawn of humanity? Wikipedia says approximately 100 billion. And for each birth, someone was there to look into the baby's eyes for the first time. And yet, somehow, it was unique, it was special—it was, indeed, magical.

Is there something magical about children? Or is it nothing more than our desire for the human race to continue that imparts magic into them? Are we reading more into it than there should be? Probably. But we nonetheless do it, have always done it, and probably always will do it. And I don't know why...

All I do know is this: somehow, someway, I saw everything—the physical and spiritual universes, the distant past and the far future in those eyes. I saw ancestors that are no longer walking among us and descendants that will not walk among us for centuries. I saw my grandmother and granddaughter. I saw everything in those two tiny eyes.

Seeing all that has somehow changed me. Made me a different person than the person who drove my wife to the hospital at 2 a.m. on that quiet Monday morning. Interestingly enough, I'm not yet sure exactly how I've changed; all I know is that the change occurred because I saw a universe in two tiny eyes.

A child opens her eyes and we see the universe.

Dad! The Murano has a flat tire!

There's nothing quite like a flat tire to start the day. Well, okay, maybe boiling in oil. It's just that when you look at the tire, and there it sits all flat and not at all the way it's supposed to look, you get this sinking feeling in the pit of your stomach. You know the day is going downhill from there.

It's been a long time since I've changed a tire. But a skill once learned is seldom forgotten, and there I was, yanking the jack out of the back of the Murano. After I found the jack in the back of the Murano. After I got out the owner's manual and looked up the location of the jack in back of the Murano.

Ah, okay, it seems that the rear floorboard comes apart in three pieces instead of just the one I was yanking on, and it's the right piece that covers the jack. Got it.

Placed jack under the car in the designated spot, according to the placard placed on the underside of the spare tire cover. Started jacking.

Son says, "Uh, dad, is that the right tire?"

I look at it. "No…no, it's not. Thanks for noticing."

No sense in exploding now. I let the car down and move the jack. Why did I jack up the rear tire instead of the front one that was flat? Because I was trying to put the jack together in a place that was close to the placard that told how to put the thing together. And then I just started jacking. I'd love to say that I won't make a silly mistake like that again, but I know me better than that.

Son is owed something big because if I had jacked up the car all the way and then removed the wrong tire, well, the sound of tire iron on Murano would have been heard in Las Vegas.

I moved the jack and started jacking once again. And jacking. And jacking. I'm not sure who designed the jack for the Murano, but I am sure this person should be sent straight to a Saharan desert for a year or two. Not that it was difficult, not at all. Just place jack in the *correct* location, insert bar into jack, insert extender into bar, and begin cranking; for each turn of the bar, scrape knuckles once. And yes, I had it put together correctly. I checked the manual. Twice. Turn, scrape. Turn, scrape. Turn, scrape.

"Son, go get some Band-Aids."

"Where are they?"

"Same place they've always been. The same place they were yester-day when we got a Band-Aid for your blister. Now GO GET THE BAND-AIDS!"

"Okay, Pop. Sheesh." I'm not sure I'm going to make it through his teen years.

It's on!

Finally got car up, tire off, and spare tire on. Son and I wash up, he and his sister scramble for backpacks and lunches, I grab a Coke, and we head off to school only thirty minutes late. Not bad, not bad at all. After I dropped them off, I drove to Firestone to leave the tire to be fixed, "provided it can be fixed, and do you want to replace the sensor in the tire that might have been ruined?"

"What sensor?"

"The sensor that tells you if the tire pressure is low." He then looked at me, said, "Just fix the tire, got it."

So, I left the tire and drove home, thoroughly annoyed at the entire morning. Just about then is when many people come up with a refrain that goes something like this: "If they can make microwaveable cup-cakes, why can't they make a tire that won't go flat?"

Who knows? For now, we just have to get out the jack (but not me—from now on, I'm calling AAA no matter how late the kids are to school).

I hate tires.

Red Civics & Blue Civics

So.
Yesterday, my son packed the Honda Civic
        and headed to The Girlfriend's house.
I was feeling a bit sentimental about it 'cause dads get to.

Then.
I got a call about an hour later.
"Dad!"—uh-oh, I knew there was a problem—"I've been in an accident".
Are you okay?
"Yes"
What happened?
"I hit a car on the freeway because the traffic stopped, and I couldn't"
A rear-ender
        my eighteen-year-old son's red Civic hit a twenty-something
        girl's blue Civic.

        I'd be upset but the irony of it
        the cosmic perfection of it
        is just too good.

Red Hondas and Blue VWs

Today, I watched my son head north in his old red Honda Civic
Headed for a long weekend with
     a girlfriend
She's cool, that girlfriend
Funny, attractive, athletic, intelligent, sassy as hell

Once, I watched my dad in the rearview mirror as I headed north
in my old blue VW
Headed for a long weekend in Daytona with
     The girlfriend du jour

Years in between dissolved and the son became the father
watching the son who would become the father
and the father went to exit stage left

And the father is waiting his cue to exit stage left

Look at Your Hands; What Do You See?

On a quiet Tuesday evening a few years ago, I was sitting with my father in his room at San Diego Hospice. He hadn't spoken in a day or so, and I was watching his face and hearing him breathe and just staying close. As I sat there, I saw his hands. Hands I have seen my entire life. This time, they were older; this time, they had more wrinkles; this time, they were paler. This time, they were little more than skin and bones—not the strong, muscular hands I had known. But they also showed the travels and travails of a lifetime.

His hands showed hard work on the salty, slippery decks of Merchant Marine ships during World War II. His hands worked on those ships as an able-bodied seaman during war years when they sailed the Pacific with lights-out in the black of night, evading enemy ships and planes and taking food and medicine to troops and civilians in the Pacific Islands, Northern Europe, and beyond.

More than that, however, his hands showed a lifetime of work, decades of golf, years gripping a wheel and bandaging up kids' knees. His hands showed a lifetime of living.

That's what's so great about our hands. Facelifts can remove wrinkles. Contacts and eye surgeries can improve sight and let you toss glasses aside. Peels, and sanding, and reductions and lifts can change so many things about us, but our hands, well, our hands tell the truth. Our hands tell about every diaper we've changed, every tear we've wiped, every car battery we've charged, every meal we've cooked, and every nail we've pounded.

A life written in our palms

In our hands, we can see every other hand we've held, every animal we've petted, every snowball we've made, every coconut we've opened, and every ice cream cone we've hung onto. Look at your hands. Hold them up. What do you see? Whose life do you see?

I look at my hands and see them holding on to a water-ski rope. I see them in gloves holding ski poles. I see them holding my daughter for the first time—just a few minutes old. I see them wrestling with peanut-butter jars, trying to turn screwdrivers, and gripping pliers, squeezing for that last ounce of pressure.

I see them arm-wrestling with my son, helping him build models, bicycles, and so much more. I see them calming him after he broke an arm at school.

I see them wiping my sister's brow as she lay dying. I see them wiping my father's brow as he lay dying. I see twelve-year-old versions of them, holding a shovel and helping my father bury a pet somewhere in the Sonoran Desert of Mexico.

I see them trace the ear of a high school girlfriend. I see them putting a wedding ring on my wife. I see them bandage kids' scrapes, clip dogs' and kids' toenails. I see these big old hands ever so slightly grasp the brush of clear, or pink, or pale pink, or clear pale pink fingernail polish and polish the tiny nails of a six-year-old daughter (something I've gotten pretty good at, by the way).

Take a minute or two and look at your hands. What do you see? These are the hands of our lifetimes. These are the hands of many places, many stories, many individuals, many joys, many tears. They're my hands and your hands, my story and your story. Look at your hands and remember one of the majestic, one of the funny, one of the sad, one of the heartbreaking, one of the humorous stories of your hands…and your life.

These are the stories of us—written in our hands.

Reflections on Fatherhood:
Embrace Your Surprises

My dad lived to be eighty-eight years old. During those decades, he would occasionally say something to me that I never really understood until I had kids. And it was simply this: "I'm an amateur at this too." He was so right. We're all amateurs no matter how many kids we have, because each child is unique. He was an amateur father with me, I was an amateur son with him. We muddled through. Here's the best thing I know about muddling through: Embrace your surprises.

My dad lived through things I cannot even imagine. He grew up during the Depression wearing government-issued clothes of which he was so ashamed it left scars that stayed with him his entire life. He was in the Merchant Marines during WWII. He was a pacifist who nonetheless saw the horrors of WWII and the necessity of helping those suffering because of it. He served on ships taking food and medical supplies from South America to India, China, and the Philippines. He was a strong man with a cotton-soft interior that I thought was pretty cool.

Fatherhood. I always had mixed emotions about fatherhood.

My wife and I always knew we were going to adopt a child. We were professionals, we had health insurance, we were dedicated, and we could do this. Adopt a child, absolutely. So, we did all the paperwork, went to the classes, had the inspections, and we were good to go. Then we waited a while, got on with our lives. One day, the county called. They had a child, and were we interested in learning more? Sure, we said. Well, he was a little failure to thrive, a little language issue. That's no problem.

The day we met our son, he came running over to us, hugged us, and we were a family from that second. The county was very cool—they were going to try to push it so he could be with us by Christmas. Son came to our home on Christmas Eve, and we'd only had a week or so to prepare. We put a boy's bedroom together in a day. He came to our home on Christmas Eve, and I was an amateur. And he didn't care.

Our daughter was born a few years later—she apparently wanted a brother in the house first. She came to us in early February, and when she was born, the attending held her up for me to see and Daughter opened her eyes for the first time, and I looked into them and saw eternity. She looked into mine and offered her version of a smile. I was an amateur. And she didn't care.

Reflections on fatherhood. I don't know anything about fatherhood. I know about diapers, feedings, lack of sleep, owies, blisters, softball and soccer, homework, and getting rid of things that go bump in the night. I know about driving lessons, and outgrown clothes. I know about the start of dating, the intricacies of school friendships, little girls and their friendships…little girls and their friendships…and I don't want to solve for x, you solve for your own x. I couldn't do it the first time, and now I'm teaching you? Go ask your mother!

On a trip to the Grand Canyon, we drove through Phoenix. My father grew up in Phoenix in the 1930s. One hundred and ten degrees in the summer, no air conditioning. Dirt poor. He and his brother used to crawl under a fence in the back of a junkyard, steal a piece of iron, put in in a wagon, pull it to the front of the junkyard, and sell it, and if you do that enough times, you can collect a dime and go see a movie in an air-conditioned theater.

We drove by the little house he grew up in, and we drove by the school he attended. It was closed, had been closed for years. Falling apart, graffiti on the walls, and out in front was the flagpole. We took a photo of my son standing on the base of the flagpole his grandfather had faced when saluting the flag so many decades earlier. The interdependent web of all existence of which we are a part.

My father's father, my paternal grandfather, died when I was two years old, and I never knew him. But I have one thing of his. I have a small battered suitcase with barber tools in it. The man was a barber, "shave and a haircut, two bits." And somehow, the kids were mostly fed. My mother's father, my maternal grandfather, helped build Hughes's Spruce Goose, worked on railroads, and somehow, the kids were well fed.

One grandfather I never knew, the other was a hero of mine. He used to let me drive his old Dodge truck and pound nails in the dirt he later had to try and pull out. One I knew, one I didn't. We're all amateurs.

75

A few years ago, my father said that he had something to tell me. He told me about his first marriage, a painful war marriage that was doomed from the start. My dad was on ships and rarely home. It was what it was. He mentioned that there was a child, but he never looked for the child because during a bitter divorce, his wife told him the child wasn't his.

I met that child a couple of weeks ago. A man now, of course, older than me, who lives in Washington state. He's had a good life but mentioned that when his mother died a few years ago, he found his birth certificate going through her things, and it was my dad's name on that certificate. He decided that finding his father was something to add to his bucket list and one day started looking. He found my dad's obituary. He was too late, but he eventually decided to seek out any siblings. He found me and we had a good meeting. I had a great father and my half-brother had an absent one because of a bitter divorce. Dads, don't let your own pain move to a new generation. Embrace your surprises.

We're all amateurs. We live through the highs and the lows. The highs of the birth of a child, the highs of the hug of a child, the highs of the hug of a father, the lows of giving pain to a father. The hardest thing I have ever done in my life is to look in my father's eyes and tell him that his daughter had just passed away. Embrace your surprises.

Reflections on fatherhood. I'm an amateur father and son and brother. But I'm learning. I know that this doesn't have to be as hard as we often make it. We fathers are all amateur fathers, but that doesn't mean we can't be great amateurs. Embrace your surprises.

The Final Wave Goodbye

My father was far into his eighth decade when he passed away. In addition to the cancer that took his life, he fought ever-worsening macular degeneration, hearing impairment (he wore two hearing aids turned up so loud, they squealed most of the time), and weakness.

He saw the best doctors and bought the latest gadgets to help his sight, but there wasn't a cure for macular degeneration.

He was sublimely unhappy for the last few years. My father was an active guy his entire life. Born in Illinois, he grew up in Phoenix during the Depression, and then later, living in Los Angeles, he became tough. He was a champion weightlifter on the western seaboard before enlisting in the Merchant Marines in World War II.

He circled the earth numerous times, often in blacked-out ships, dodging torpedoes and avoiding bombs. He was a pacifist but recognized that sometimes pacifism just may not work. So, to help the Allies, he spent the years on generally unarmed ships delivering supplies.

He was in the Philippines, the South Pacific, South America, Northern and Southern Europe, and many more places that needed all the things required to keep armies moving.

After the war, he settled down, married my mother, and started a real estate and construction business. It was successful, but more than that was how he continued to live his life. He and a friend and brother drove from San Diego to the tip of South America. He went on a safari to Africa (the only shooting he did was in the form of photos). He sailed a yacht from the West Coast through the Panama Canal to Florida.

Like so many people of that era, he was changed. WWII changed him from a kid to an adult in a hurry. And he kept on changing. After the war, he went from an Eisenhower conservative to an Obama moderate. I've always liked that about him—he would argue, passionately, unless shown something better, and then he could change.

My father passed away. It is unbelievably hard to write those words. And yet, that is what he wanted. Not that he wanted to leave; it's just that he was tired. Tired of not hearing, tired of not seeing, tired of being weak, and tired of being dependent on my mother, on me, on so many others.

Hank Beauchamp was a member of what Tom Brokaw and others call "the greatest generation." A World War? Just tell them where to go. A depression? They'll scrounge. A recession? They'll find some kind of work to do. An illness? Well, an illness is another matter. An illness is something they aren't familiar with, don't know how to deal with, can't always fix.

And so, my father departed. He didn't want to go but was ready.

A few years ago, my wife and kids and I took a trip to Lake Tahoe. We went through Phoenix to see if the house where my dad lived as a kid, and the school he attended, was still there. They were.

The house was old but being lived in, but the school was closed and abandoned. We snapped a photo of our son leaning on a flagpole in front of the school. It wasn't all that hard to see my dad on that same schoolyard eighty years ago, surrounded by laughing kids, playing, before being called into class.

Baby to child, child to kid, kid to adolescent, adolescent to young man, young man to adult, adult to old man, old man to family memories. May the memories be good, may the memories be kind.

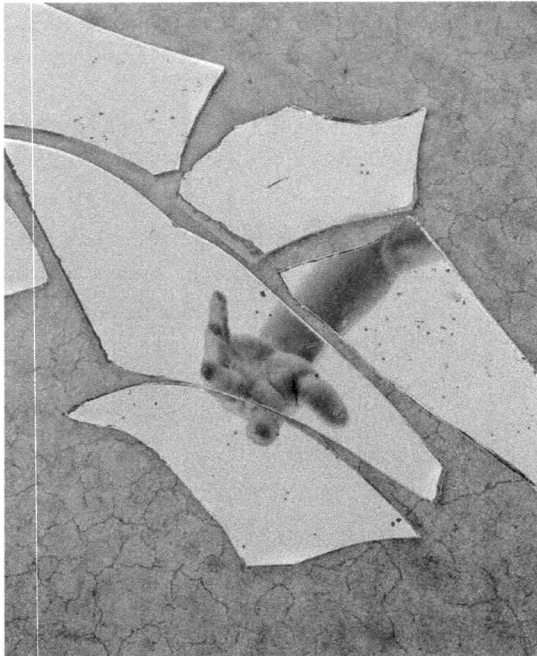

CHAPTER TWO

Resembling Coherency

Yes, I realize that some people are going to look at the title of this section and think, *Resembling coherency? Isn't coherency an absolute?* Well, yes and no. Sure, a thought or a communication is usually coherent (barring all the things that get in the way), but occasionally, I'll have something that more *resembles* coherency than actually is. And yeah, I get that I'm playing a semantic sort of game with the word, but it's a good way to describe these pieces.

I'd love to put RESEMBLING COHERENCY on my license plate because, often, I encounter drivers who seem to be semi-coherent, but the state won't let me. Too many letters, they said. Which I'd know if I read the instructions, they said. Hmph.

Anyway, I suppose I think of the thoughts behind some of these essays as resemblances of coherency. I'm sure I was fully coherent when writing them (well, pretty sure), but in retrospect, I can see how *resemblance* may be closer to the truth.

Where Does Your Craziness Appear?

Are you crazy? Yann Martel, in *Life of Pi*, says, "All living things contain a measure of madness that moves them in strange, sometimes inexplicable ways."

If that's the truth, then we're all just a bit crazy, some of us obviously more than others. So, the next question is, how crazy are you?

Well, let's see. We can design a test that will tell us just how crazy we are. Are you brave enough to take it?

Questions that *may* let you know how crazy you are

1. You decide to go on a diet while going through McDonald's drive-through—for the twelfth time this month

2. You decide to get married because it seems right

3. You decide to get married for a second time

4. You forget your spouse's birthday—year after year

5. You think the government is out to get you (unless they are out to get you, in which case, you're not crazy at all, just cautious… probably)

6. You think that ice cream is a health food

7. You think that hamburgers are good for you because they do, after all, contain protein

8. You drink twelve Diet Cokes a day

9. You believe what politicians tell you in an election year

10. You believe what politicians tell you anytime because they are, after all, only there to help you

11. You think that cities need bigger ballparks rather than bigger libraries

12. You will eat a cookie with ten ingredients in it

13. You buy a one-year-old car with a new paint job without considering it may have been in an accident…or a flood…or buried in a snowbank

14. You keep going out with the kind of people your mother warned you about

15. You are really, really sure that the Centers for Disease Control is out to get you

16. You think reading is a waste of time but will spend hours in front of a TV set watching reruns of old sit-coms

17. You watch the Cooking Channel while eating take-out fried chicken

18. You believe that exercise is bad for you because muscles weren't made to work that hard

19. You keep going to a restaurant that made you sick once because they have two-for-one days

20. You refuse to buy clothes in the correct size because if they're too small it will be good incentive to lose all that weight you've been really, really wanting to lose for years

21. You look for old boyfriends or girlfriends online

22. You think your kids actually listen to every word you say

23. You think your spouse actually listens to every word you say

24. You think that anyone actually listens to every word you say

25. You think that having kids and pit bulls in the same house is a good idea

26. You work on your own car

27. You work on your own computer

28. You think that your kids will like the same music you do

29. You keep switching cell phone companies and plans looking to find the perfect one (cheapest)

30. You talk on your cell phone while standing in a line, driving a car, at a restaurant, while buying something, waiting in a doctor's office, etc., etc., etc.

31. You have a cell phone, a sat phone, three e-mail addresses, and a website—and you're sixteen years old

32. You're sure Elvis is still alive

33. Every year, you take a vacation, and wherever you go on this vacation, you look for Elvis

34. You're absolutely positive that you've seen Elvis at least three times

(twice at a Denny's Restaurant and once at the County Fair eating cotton candy)

35. You bought a car that the seller told you was once owned by a film star (but wouldn't tell you the name of the star)

36. You buy a new cell phone every six months because, "Well, gee! It works better than the other one, which was so old! I can't believe you didn't know that! And this one has different colors you can put on the face and everything!"

37. You refuse to get a cell phone and then have to look for hours for a payphone every day, which are pretty much nonexistent these days

38. You live in a family where your wife texts you, you call her cell phone on your cell phone to discuss who's picking up which kid (oh, wait, that's my family—never mind)

And there you have it, thirty-eight definitive ways to help you determine if you are crazy. You can score it yourself, any way you like. I thought about taking it myself (and since I wrote it, I figured I had a pretty good chance of coming out okay). But then I decided not to; after all, why push one's luck?

It's only sanity...

Something Is Gonna Get You and It Won't be Pretty

Planet Earth is a dangerous place to raise kids and other living things. Have you ever taken a good look at all the things that can mess with your life? There are things out there that play havoc with our bodies, our minds, our emotions.

One day (okay, it was a bit slow and I was bored—just never mind), I decided to take a brief inventory of all the things that we must watch for, be careful of, avoid, and remember to do. Well, that list got far too long for me to want to remember. So, I gave up on that idea and instead just listed a few of the things some friends and I could think of over dinner one night. Funny thing was, the more we drank—I mean, ate—the longer the list got (again!). So, I cut out a bunch of it, and what follows are simply the highlights of the list that every grown person should be deathly afraid of. Or at least think about occasionally between innings or during commercials.

You've been right all along—they are out to get you

If aspartame doesn't cause you death, great bodily or psychic injury, or a warped personality, the following will:

Global warming

Artificial food ingredients

Counterfeit drugs

French fries

Hamburgers

Fried anything

Air pollution

Water pollution

Asbestos

The sun
Makeup
Alcohol
Tobacco (in any form)
City water runoff
Africanized killer bees
Africanized killer ants
Lead (in food, paint, gas)
The whole damn AMA
New diseases
Old diseases
Gang violence
Violence in schools
Violence
Car hijacking
Tainted beef, poultry, fruit, eggs
Toxic people
Hyper-macho coaches
Hyper-macho cockroaches
Landfills
Freon
Styrofoam

Don't give up yet—we're just getting started

Plastic
Trans-fats
Cholesterol
Caffeine
Food coloring
Food flavorings

Not wearing seatbelts

Wearing seatbelts

Synthetic clothes

Synthetic food

Synthetic fiber

Synthetic medicine

Synthetic anything and everything

Pit bulls

Idiots who say things like, "Guns don't kill, people kill!"

Electric fields

Magnetic fields

Living under electric transmission lines

Voting for liberals who want to give the whole country away to godless commies

Voting for conservatives who would rather let someone starve or go without clothes or an education in order to buy more bombers

Voting

Not voting

Politicians

Back-room deals

Hang on—we've got more to go

In-laws

Out-laws

Laws in general

Lack of laws

Too many laws

Hepatitis C

Athlete's foot

Auto-immune diseases

Mad cow disease

Gum disease

STDs

Any disease

Every disease

The Centers for Disease Control

FBI

CIA

Your government

My government

Any government

No government

Racism

Sexism

Ageism

Any "ism"

The ADA

Lack of the ADA

Obesity

Childhood obesity

Societal ills

Population increase

Nuclear proliferation

Nuclear power

Lack of nuclear power

Don't forget the germs!

Germs on:

Doorknobs

Light switches

Seats

Movie theaters

Drinking fountains

Faucets

Tables

Shopping carts

Entire public restrooms

Food

Kitchen counters

Restaurant tables

Oh, the hell with it—there are germs everywhere and they are all out to get us (yes, the germs are getting personal)

Enough already!!!

And finally, one last thing to be afraid of: Pennies! Now, come on, aren't you honestly tired of pennies? Most pennies are in children's banks, in drawers, in car seats, on the ground. And when they're on the ground, most people won't so much as bend down to pick them up. By getting rid of pennies, the Treasury will save millions of dollars minting and replacing them and we won't have to carry the useless things around.

That's really why you should be afraid of pennies: they're just bloody annoying. And something annoying can raise your blood pressure, which can help kill you. True, it's a bit of a stretch, but what the heck—deal with it. Hey, just be careful out there.

Scared yet? If not, you haven't lived enough.

Want to Be Invisible? Just Live Long Enough to Get Old

There are both good and bad things about getting older. One of the best things is that you experience enough to get at least a bit smarter. One of the worst things about getting older is you become invisible.

I remember my father would occasionally say that he hated the fact that people didn't see him after he started getting older. I, of course, since I was young, didn't have a clue as to what he meant.

Now, I understand it.

The arrogance of youth was, up until a few years ago, simply a silly little saying—it had no relevance whatsoever. Well, youth does have arrogance to it. When we are young, we think we can do anything, conquer any obstacle, and overcome any challenge. We know it all and we don't suffer fools—or the elderly—gladly.

It would be easy to say that we were ignorant, but that wouldn't necessarily be correct. We simply hadn't lived enough, seen enough, done enough to realize that we just might possibly be wrong. We learned that many times over the older we became, unfortunately.

Taking stock of life

Now, I have started to be more aware of things, to take stock of things, to attempt to understand things a bit more than ever. I have realized that I don't know it all, won't know it all, can never know it all, and that I should just get over it and move on.

Fair enough, but there is still that "invisible" thing that just won't go away. Why do we ignore the aged? Are we so afraid of aging that we simply must ignore the evidence of it? Are we so in terror of losing the strength, the mental acuity, the sexual abilities, the passion for life that we have that we tiptoe around what is staring us in the face? Perhaps…perhaps.

The worst part of aging

1. Forgetting how we got this old
2. Forgetting where we left the keys and often losing the right to drive
3. Forgetting where we left all sorts of things
4. Forgetting
5. Less strength, agility, eyesight, hearing, taste, sensations of touch, ability to smell, less...well, less of pretty much everything
6. Less ability to be "child-like"
7. Less ability to forgive
8. Less desire to forgive
9. Less desire for most things
10. Losing the need for spontaneity
11. Losing the need to break out in song, in joke, in passion
12. Just less, less, less
13. Our bodies forsake us
14. Our muscles forsake us
15. Our worry about money and income is constant
16. You forget how to use the turn signal

The best part of aging

The above sixteen items being said (and believe me, there are LOTS more), there are good parts to aging. Some of those are:

1. No one asks for your ID
2. You will occasionally meet some very nice people—individuals who will help you with something and smile while they're doing it
3. Membership in AARP, which can save you all kinds of money on things, has terrific travel tips, and does countless things for aging individuals
4. Saving money with "senior specials" and other discounts targeted to the aging

5. You no longer have to prove yourself—whether at work, in friend-ship, in sports, in business, in—well, pretty much anything
6. You get to sometimes see the forgiving side of people (while also too often seeing the unforgiving side)
7. You don't have to worry about your "figure"
8. You don't have to worry about being strong
9. You don't have to worry about being sexy
10. You don't have to worry (quite as much) about your kids

This list, while containing things that are generally correct, is nonethe-less written a bit tongue-in-cheek. Actually, there is very little "good" about aging. Sure, there are some side benefits, but most individuals would probably trade those in a second to get a few decades back.

There is very little that is good about seeing one's body deteriorate, seeing one's family and friends die, seeing strength slip away, noticing how difficult it is to remember things, watching as health slowly van-ishes, and realizing that every day we are more and more susceptible to any number of life-threatening diseases, injuries, and accidents that we would have shrugged off just a few years ago.

No, aging is certainly not for the faint of heart, and to add insult to all that injury is the thing that irritated my father the most, being invisible to so many people.

Son, Here Are a Few Things I Think You Should Know

Okay, kid, this is the deal. I was sitting in the backyard the other day, watching you and the dog playing. As the two of you were going at each other with wild abandon, I got to thinking about all the things you still need to learn. And I'm not talking here about the knowledge you'll get from school.

No, this is the knowledge that only comes to a person in two ways. One is hearing it from someone else and the other is simply experiencing it. Since I cannot give you most of what you will experience, my help here, then, is simply telling you a few things I've learned over the years. I hope it helps.

Important things to know

- Treat your friends with respect
- Treat your enemies with even more respect
- Never pass up a chance to go to the bathroom
- Differences are good—celebrate them
- Bad actions do not make a bad person
- Bad actions do not make a good person bad
- Always check the oil in the car
- Just because someone in a position of authority says it does not mean it is true
- Just because I wrote the above does not mean you should not listen to those in authority; it is your job to know when to listen and when to act on what you hear
- Yes, you probably can make it, but stop for gas anyway
- Never stop for the night with an empty tank of gas; you do not want to get an urgent phone call telling you that you need to be somewhere immediately and then have to wait in a gas station or, worse yet, by the side of the road

- Read the owner's manual
- Asking for help does not imply weakness or stupidity—it implies calmness, rationality, and the brains to know that no one can do it all
- Be good to animals, but never be better to an animal than you are to people
- Find a hobby and pursue it
- Be good to your family—they will help you even when no one else will
- Never pass up a chance to travel because it may help save you from a narrow view of the planet
- You do not know it all and never will know it all
- The above is not an excuse for doing something irrational, it is simply a fact
- Everything you do will influence someone else
- If nothing else, at least remember this: try to live your life so that when you fall asleep at night, there is never something you are ashamed of
- The above said, no one gets through life without some shame— and that's good because it can help you remember to treat people with dignity
- Always treat people with dignity

And now I am going to quit giving advice. Your life is your life—live it well.

Some Things a Parent Just Has to Do

We always hope that schools are teaching our children the things that they will need to know to get along in this big, wide world. Well, there are some things that no one can teach our kids but caregivers, be they parents, older siblings, or other family members (the good ones, not that weird aunt who uses "snuff"). I have come up with a list of just such things. I'm sure you have some equally important items that you could add—well, feel free. But, for now, this is mine.

Things your kids should absolutely, positively know

- Put on a sweater or jacket when it's cold
- Be nice to your sister or brother; someday, you all will be the grown-ups
- Always check the oil in your car's engine
- Always check your fuel gauge
- Don't chew with your mouth open
- Be nice to your sister or brother; someday, you will want your kids to be nice to you
- Be nice to your parents and apologize when you need to—someday, you may not have the opportunity
- Remember to vote, and when you do, really think about who you're voting for—don't let TV ads influence you
- Brush your teeth (and you know why)
- Don't overeat
- Don't undereat
- Don't nag at people (like I'm doing right now)
- If the dog looks mean, leave the thing alone
- If the cat looks mean, leave the thing alone
- If the person looks mean, leave the thing alone
- Don't buy an ugly car

- Don't buy a car just because it's not ugly
- The same as 16 and 17 above could be said for pretty much anything else you could buy
- Don't pay too much for a house
- Don't pay too much for a car
- Don't pay too much for anything
- Take a vacation at least once a year—it will help you be a better person
- Don't go to the same old place when you do take those vacations—explore the world, it's a very cool place
- Get news from more than one source
- Read more than one newspaper and magazine
- Try new foods
- Listen to new music
- Make a new friend, but never forget your old ones
- Call someone every day who is not expecting a call
- When there are warning signs out, believe them
- Buy the cheapest house in the best neighborhood, never the other way around
- Good oil is worth the small extra price (this counts for car oil, olive oil, and any other oil you can think of)
- Never be afraid to find a new doctor if you're unhappy with the one you have
- The same thing goes for car dealers
- Always, always, always get three bids before having anything done that costs more than two hundred dollars
- Yes, really use the damn recycle bin
- Don't get mad at the police officer for giving you a ticket when you know you weren't supposed to be going that fast in the first place
- Comfortable shoes are worth the money
- Same thing for underwear
- Buy the insurance; it will save you money someday
- Don't buy more insurance than you need—a lot of people waste an awful lot of money this way (especially the elderly)
- *Consumer Reports* is a valuable magazine to read

- When you need information, go to the original source—a good thing to remember for all of life itself
- Never believe gossip
- But while you do not believe gossip, don't close your eyes to the obvious
- Kiss someone under the stars
- Do number 46 more than once—your life will be much better
- Hug your family
- Remember that work isn't everything
- Remember that work is not a bad thing

Okay, there you have fifty things that every parent should tell their kids, fifty important, worthwhile, crucial things. And it's even better if you tell them while eating their favorite dessert. You'll have more fun that way too.

Making It Safe

Our daughter is now over seven months old. She has rolled around for quite a while, but now she is rolling and scooting and starting to crawl a *lot*. This means that we are now confronted with that age-old problem that all parents face; namely, keeping the baby safe from herself. This is not an easy thing to do.

Daughter wants to explore. If there is something within reach, she wants to touch it, and if it can be picked up, she wants to pick it up and, most likely, put it in her mouth.

So now we are in the process of updating the childproofing of our house. And good grief, there are a lot of ways for a child to get hurt. For instance, there are:

Table legs

Table edges

Table corners

Tables

Slick floors

Lamps

Lamp cords

Electric wall sockets

Wooden chairs

Kitchen counters

Stove burners

Hot oven doors

Drawers to pull out

Things in those drawers, such as utensils

Kitchen cabinets

Things in those cabinets, such as pots, pans, soaps, cleaners, polish, and other assorted chemicals

Hard edges on bathtubs, bathroom counters, toilets

Soaps, shampoos, makeup, and grooming supplies such as hair spray, deodorants, and lotions

And let's not ignore the razors, scissors, and other sharp things in the bathroom

Bedrooms should be safe, but when you're small, there are all sorts of things there, like bed frames, dresser and night-stand edges, lamps and lamp cords, phone charging cords (plus any landline cords as well—heck, I've got eight of those things in the house), plus cords from copiers, computers, clocks, stereos, toys, and a whole lot of other things.

Fireplace
Doorknobs
Windows and other glass
Sliding-glass doors
Staircases

Floor lamps or anything else on the floor that can be pulled over when the child tries to stand up

How about the garage? What's in your garage? Often, there is oil and other car fluids, tools, stuff stored all kinds of ways, and more hard edges than can be counted.

Do you have a patio?

Are there lawns, or flowers and other plants? What is the child allergic to or putting in their mouth?

Is there a swimming pool? If so, is there a fence around it? Is the gate in the fence locked? Or, with a small child, even an inflatable pool with a few inches of water is enough.

Look on the side of the house—is this where you're storing shovels, rakes, or other gardening tools? Is there fertilizer there? Are there old toys, old lawn furniture, or old rusty anything there?

Where do you have your garbage? Is it clean around the garbage containers?

How easy is it for a young child to reach the street—either from the backyard or the front? But primarily, is the backyard fenced? Will it keep the kids in and stray animals out?

Do you live on a hill or a cliff? Is there a strong fence to keep the kids away from the edge?

Do you have a second-floor patio? Are the railings made so that a very small child would not be able to slip between the wood slats and tumble out?

Are there ladders leaning up against a wall anywhere—inside or out?

Can the child walk—or fall—into a cactus?

How easy is it for drivers coming up your driveway to see a crawling child in the way?

What is there outside so colorful or noisy that it might attract a child?

Are there neighbor dogs that are digging under your fence to get in?

Any sprinkler heads to trip on?

How strong is the patio furniture? What are the spaces like between any webbing or wooden slats?

Isn't it amazing just how many things exist that are dangerous? This list hasn't even begun to touch on the actual number of ways our kids can find to hurt themselves.

If you want a real eye-opener, get on your hands and knees sometime and crawl around your house. You'll be amazed at all the things you see that are potentially very dangerous.

So, as parents, we do what we can, when we can, in every way we can to protect them. And then we say a little prayer and hope for the best.

It's Too Easy to Be a Thief

We've all seen the scams being sent around via e-mail that discuss getting money out of South Africa. All you need to do is send them good-faith money and your bank account numbers. In turn, they're going to give you millions for helping them get money out of the country illegally. That scam is just far too easy.

It used to be that being a thief was hard work. It wasn't as hard as pouring concrete in the summer, which is why some people turned to crime, but work was still involved. You had to rob someone, make a getaway, hide out for a long, long time, find someone to "launder" the money for you so it couldn't be traced, and you were constantly nervous.

Today, being a thief is so much easier. There is mail fraud, telephone solicitation, door-to-door scams, and best (or at least quickest) of all, the ever-increasing e-mail scam. Now you can try to rob thousands or even millions of people at the same time—it's theft, fast-food style.

I have received, over the past few weeks, the following scams that were trying, oh-so-earnestly, to help me in one way or another.

Recent scams

1. Viagra, cheap
2. More Viagra, even cheaper
3. Something that they said worked even better than Viagra, didn't require a prescription, and was safe!!!!
4. Breast and/or erection enhancement
5. Lose fat
6. Lose more fat
7. Lose fat quicker
8. Lose fat the quickest way ever
9. Body sculpting from a pill
10. Buy land for $1 an acre
11. Unclaimed money
12. Unclaimed property

13. Cheap adoption records search
14. Find that long-lost love
15. Buy government-seized cars for $1
16. Buy government-seized boats for $1
17. Buy government-seized art for $1
18. Buy government-seized planes for $1
19. Buy government-seized homes for $1 (see a pattern?)
20. Sex-change operations
21. Find a wife
22. Find a husband
23. Find a partner
24. Find buried treasure
25. Cheap vitamins
26. Cheap vitamins that will enhance your sex drive (and are cheaper than Viagra and work even better! Work for women too!!)
27. Pills that guarantee a longer life
28. Exercise equipment that is easy to use
29. Exercise equipment that doesn't feel like exercise
30. Exercise equipment that will take inches off your waist, legs, arms, neck, and stomach without you even working up a sweat
31. Places that pay top dollar for used exercise equipment
32. Investment opportunity of a lifetime
33. 50 percent monthly return on your money, guaranteed
34. 100 percent monthly return on your money, guaranteed
35. 200 percent monthly return on your money, guaranteed
36. Learn the secrets of the wealthy
37. Earn millions without ever leaving your home
38. Great job opportunities
39. Great travel opportunities
40. Go to college in your spare time (free!)

The list could go on for pages, but you get the idea. Over time, if you use a computer, you have probably seen hundreds, if not thousands, of similar promotions. They are designed to make someone rich; unfortunately, that someone is them and not you.

Of course, if you don't spend your money on worthless stuff, you'll have it to spend on something worthwhile. Something like, oh, I don't know, a boat, for instance. Now, that's worthwhile. But again, that's just me.

The world is out to get you, one byte at a time.

Be Like Water

How do you want people to perceive you? How do you perceive yourself? Are you the strong, silent type? Are you boisterous? Do you rant and rave at the slightest provocation? Do you smile at life and all that it brings you?

Much of life is in perceptions. Certainly, we want others to perceive us in a certain way. But we also want to perceive ourselves as a particular kind of person. What kind of person are you? What kind of person are you *really*?

I read a simple sentence a while back. I cannot remember where I read it, but it stuck with me. That simple sentence says a great deal. In fact, it pretty much says everything there is to be said about how we can act so that people perceive us well. But more than that, it also says a lot about how we can best perceive ourselves.

That sentence, that oh-so-simple sentence is nothing more than this:

Be like water...

Say, what? Think about water. What is water like? It's soft, fluid, and extremely strong. Given enough time, it will carve away rock to the extent that the Grand Canyon will be created. "Be like water" simply means that one should be strong, patient, and never ceasing.

But water is also soft. Run your hands through a warm puddle of water, let a spring trickle through your fingers, feel the warm softness of a hot tub. "Be like water," then, also means that it's okay for a person to be soft, warm, flowing, and surrounding life.

Finally, water is also fluid. Do what is necessary in life without always fighting. One can often make more headway going around a problem. The term "go with the flow" really does mean something.

Be like water...

Interesting, yes? Be like water. Think of all the problems you may have had lately. Might any of them have been fixed had you been more like water? Look back on your life. How could you have made any part of your life richer, happier, and less stressful, had you been like water?

Start using "be like water" as a mantra. Think on it, act on it, and reflect on it. As you go to bed tonight, say it to yourself a few times over and over.

Be like water...
Be like water...
Be like water...
Be like water...
Be like water...
Be like water...
Be like water...
Be like water...
Be like water...
Be like water...
The next time you have problems at work, say the words.
The next time you have problems at home, say the words.
The next time you have problems with your kids, say the words.
The next time you have problems with your spouse, say the words.
The next time you have problems of any kind, say the words.

Will simply saying the words help the situation you find yourself in? Probably not. But saying them might help your outlook on the problem. It might help how you perceive the problem. It might slow you down enough to make a better decision than you would have, had you rushed to solve the problem too quickly.

In other words, be like water.

Getting Healthy Because Someone Said It Was a Good Idea

Most of this information was sent to me by a friend, and somehow, it all makes sense. At least, I think it does. Nonetheless, don't use any of it for medical advice—you know how "truthful" some of the stuff you hear from friends or get over the Internet can be (or especially if you read it here). Anyway, I hope this helps with all those pesky health issues you might be having.

Answering those silly little health questions:

Q: I've heard that cardiovascular exercise can prolong life; is this true?

A: Your heart is only good for so many beats, and that's it...don't waste them on exercise. Everything wears out eventually. Speeding up your heart will not make you live longer; that's like saying you can extend the life of your car by driving it faster. Want to live longer? Take a nap, or two, or three. Or sleep late AND take a nap—why take chances?

Q: Should I cut down on meat and eat more fruits and vegetables?

A: You must grasp logistical efficiencies. What does a cow eat? Hay and corn. And what are these? Vegetables. So, a steak is nothing more than an efficient mechanism for delivering vegetables to your system. Need grain? Eat chicken. Beef is also a good source of field grass (leafy green vegetable). And a pork chop can give you, give or take, 100 percent of your recommended daily allowance of vegetable products.

Q: Should I reduce my alcohol intake?

A: No, not at all. Wine is made from fruit. Brandy is distilled wine, which means they take the water out of the fruity bits; you get even more of the goodness that way. Beer is also made out of grain. Naturally, you may want to go easy on these "concentrated fruit and grain products" because there can be some, shall we say, side effects, but nothing is perfect.

Q: How can I calculate my body/fat ratio?

A: Well, if you have a body and you have fat, your ratio is one to one. If you have two bodies, your ratio is two to one, etc. Sure, you can get one of those caliper thingies, but hey, spend the money on something better—like a hot-fudge sundae from 31 Flavors, so you can get all the necessary daily calcium.

Q: What are some of the advantages of participating in a regular exercise program?

A: Can't think of a single one, sorry. My philosophy is: No Pain… Good! Now, if you like looking at slim bodies, then sure, join a health club and gawk all you want (although you'll probably get thrown out of the place rather quickly if you do it too much). Nope, sorry, I'll stick with the No Pain Plan.

Q: Aren't fried foods bad for you?

A: YOU'RE NOT LISTENING! Foods are fried these days in vegetable oil. In fact, they're permeated in it. How could getting more vegetables be bad for you?

Q: Will sit-ups help prevent me from getting a little soft around the middle?

A: Definitely not! When you exercise a muscle, it gets bigger (remember high school gym class?). You should only be doing sit-ups if you want a bigger stomach. Who needs that? Personally, I don't have any use whatsoever for a bigger stomach, so I quit exercising years ago. My stomach isn't as small as I'd like just yet, so I plan to not exercise even longer, but not exercising is a program I can stick with.

Q: Is chocolate bad for me?

A: Are you crazy? HELLO…Cocoa beans! Another fruit! It's the best feel-good food around. In fact, it's one of my very favorite health foods. I eat different kinds of chocolate whenever I get the chance—which is often…very often. As a matter of fact, I'm expecting my Hershey's Gold Card any day now.

Q: Is swimming good for your figure?

A: If swimming is good for your figure, explain whales to me. Hmmmm? Didn't think of that, did you?

Q: Is getting in shape important for my lifestyle?

A: Hey! "Round" is a shape! In fact, round is a great shape—it's the shape of coins, of suns, moons, planets, cakes, pies, eyes, and more coins. Like I said, round is a great shape—enjoy it!

Well, I hope this has cleared up any misconceptions you may have had about food and diets. With magazines, television, the Internet, and nosy friends, there is so much misinformation out there, it's pathetic. We simply need to do what we must do to feel good, be "relatively" healthy, and just let it go. And, finally, remember: Life should NOT be a journey to the grave without some fun involved.

How Comfortable Is Your Comfort Zone?

What gets you out of your comfort zone? A middle-of-the-night phone call? A flat tire? A new job? Countless things can yank us out of a comfort zone. But first, just what in the hell is a comfort zone? What does one look like? Some people say they look like these:

A person—when you're with that person, you feel safe, serene, and comfortable.

A chair—perhaps an old recliner is your comfort zone, the place where you feel the safest.

Your home—you walk in, kick off your shoes, and the world seems far, far away.

Your car—you're by yourself listening to music—or the quiet—and just reveling in being with yourself.

Perhaps your comfort zone is not being within shouting distance of a conservative or shouting distance of a liberal.

Perhaps your comfort zone isn't a place or a thing at all but simply a state of mind—the state where you feel at peace, in harmony, wrapped in warmth and comfort.

Going back to the original question, what happens when, for whatever reason, you're dragged unceremoniously out of a comfort zone?

What causes a breakdown in your comfort? Is it a bad dinner at a restaurant? Is it the high price of fuel? Is it the high interest rate on MasterCard? Is it the low interest rate on savings?

Or is it when you exit the freeway? As you get to the end of the exit ramp and will have to stop and wait for the light to turn green, you see a person who may not have showered in a few days or weeks. Their hair is matted and long, their clothes are dirty and stained; their shoes have holes so large you can see them from your car. Is being parked next to this person and seeing a sign they're holding while you wait for a light to change what pulls you from your comfort zone?

It's not personal...or is it?

I may have just left a classroom where the class went wonderfully well. I taught something, and they got it! And then they ran with it and wrote all sorts of papers that pushed their understanding and creativity to the limits. Hurray for them! And now it's evening, and I'm tired from teaching and grading papers, and having meetings, and writing a newspaper column, and working on a book. I'm tired but exhilarated. I'm feeling great—the day went well, and all is wonderful with the world.

I get in my car as dark is settling, Corinne Bailey Rae about to come from the speakers, and I can't wait to get home and hug the kids. After a few quiet miles, I get off the freeway, and as I approach the end of the ramp, I see that person with a sign. And I see that I will be the car parked next to that person with a sign. I do not want to feel "Ah, gee, not tonight," but I might.

I can't help but remember something a grandmother said to me when I was with her in her car and something similar happened. She said, "Ah, the person just wants the money to buy whiskey." I remember even then thinking, *So, what?* If a person so needs something to stand out here for hours begging for change from strangers—and taking the abuse from some drivers that comes with that—then they probably really need it.

But I didn't say anything to her, and somehow, some of her discomfort zone apparently seeped into me. Doesn't come out often, but occasionally, it peeks around the corner.

I was with a friend when we were in this same position getting off a freeway and he said, "Oh, not again. I give to the Red Cross, I donate blood, I recycle, I vote, I don't drive a gas hog. Come on, how much?"

People asking for help can take us out of our comfort zones in a hurry. Maybe it's because we're face to face with another human being, one who may not be quite as pretty or clean or as heartwarming as one in a telethon. Or, do those kids yank you from your comfort zone too?

According to the National Alliance to End Homelessness, there are approximately 553,742 individuals who are homeless on any given night in the U.S. The U.S. Department of Housing and Urban Development (HUD) estimates that 39,471 veterans are homeless. And while we may want to think that most of those individuals are homeless because they are lazy, or simply don't want to work, we know that the reality is that people are homeless for many reasons.

Some are homeless because of abusive marriages and they've gone into hiding, or because they were thrown out of their house with nothing or are running scared from horrendous situations. Some are mentally ill, and some are too young to escape horrific situations. The reality is, there are homeless people, but it's too gruesome for some of us to think about—it's too far out of our comfort zone.

So, what do we do? How can we get beyond our comfort zone? Well, first, we must recognize that it exists. Then, we have to see the need to break out of it—and there's always that need—if not for the person, then for the human race or simply ourselves. Then, we have to *want* to break out of it, accept feeling a little edgy. Moving a world means being a little less comfortable.

If I Only Knew

We have many teachers throughout our lives. Parents, school instructors, college professors, aunts and uncles, religious leaders, and friends are just a few of the individuals we learn from during our time here. But, of all the people from whom we learn, our parents probably teach us the most important things. They teach us how to live.

There are some things, however, that our parents fail to teach us—things that are exceptionally important. And that's what this list is all about. The other day, I started thinking about all the things I wish my parents had taught me while I was growing up, and it seemed that there were quite a few. Here are some of the more important ones.

Things my parents forgot to teach me

1. The worm that the early bird ate probably made it sick.
2. Patience is great but patient people are rarely in charge.
3. The car never needs gas until you're late.
4. The trash never needs to be taken out until you try to throw something away.
5. Pets know when you are carrying something very hot.
6. Your child will always know exactly what to do to annoy you the quickest.
7. You will always answer the phone when the person on the other end is someone with whom you don't want to speak. And yes, caller ID can help in that regard, but do you *always* look at the screen before picking up the phone?
8. You will always take your pet to the most expensive vet in town—no matter which vet you take it to.
9. You will always take your pet to the most expensive groomer in town—no matter which groomer you take it to. Don't take your pet to a groomer? Good for you; we need dirty, smelly pets running around.
10. No matter how many times you say to yourself, "I think I can," sometimes you just can't, so quit trying because you're bugging

the rest of us.

11. The time you will look the stupidest will be around one of your child's friends.

12. No one can roll his or her eyes at you better than your child—or one of your child's friends.

13. No one rolls his or her eyes at you more often than your child.

14. There is always another tool you need.

15. The store is out of that tool.

16. The tool is on backorder.

17. The store will never be able to say when the tool is due to come in.

18. You will always find that tool at the very next store you walk into, even if it's a bakery.

19. You can never stop a special order or get a refund.

20. They will lose your special order anyway.

21. No one can laugh at you behind your back quicker than a new grandparent. Unless it's your child.

22. There may be teenagers everywhere, very responsible teenagers, but never when you need a babysitter.

23. The one time you don't smell the milk is the one time it has soured.

24. No one will ever like the music you like quite as much as you do.

25. The film is never as funny as you remember it.

26. The restaurant is never as good as you remember it.

27. No car will ever feel better than it does the very first time you drive it home.

28. The one time you need to look brilliant is the one time you won't.

29. Check your zipper before a job interview.

30. The only time you won't have your wallet with you is when you A) need it to pay for something, or B) when you need it to get your driver's license to give to the police officer who has just stopped you.

31. The only time your dog really did eat your homework is when the teacher decided there wasn't time to collect it.

32. No one who ever expects to get out alive should take a kid to a toy store just before Christmas.

33. No one is nicer than a kid just before Christmas.

34. Number 33 above is true even if the child no longer believes in Santa Claus (or ever did, for that matter).

35. No one can roll their eyes at you better...oh, wait. Sorry. I already said that one, didn't I?

As you can see from this woefully short list, there are many things that I'm wishing my parents had taught me. I would almost think that they had failed in their job, were it not for the sneaking suspicion that they really did tell me all those things and I, being the kid I was, simply didn't listen.

Are you teaching these things to your kids? If not, you'd better start. You need to prepare them for the rough, as well as the smooth, times ahead. Remember, at some point in the future, it will be they who wonder if they told the nurse about you needing more pain medicine.

Parents just have to hope that some of it sticks...

So, Change Already

I have a simple question: What are you doing today that will affect your life tomorrow?

Pretty much everything we do will have an impact on our lives in the future, of course, but some things can ultimately bring about profound differences.

For example, you know that if you inhale one pack of cigarettes per day, you will eventually pay for it with health problems. You know this; we all do. Yet we continue to buy Kools, Salems, Marlboros, or one of the dozens of other brands of cigarettes sold by the billions every year. So be it.

Question is, what are you doing? Look at the list below and see which of these things look familiar.

I admit it, I...

Smoke tobacco

Chew tobacco

Drink alcohol to excess (note the "excess" there—apparently, the occasional glass of red wine may be beneficial)

Overeat

Eat the wrong things (Hey, even if we don't overeat, if we're eating the wrong things, stuff like fatty meats, or processed foods with too much cholesterol and fats, it can be bad for us.)

Ingest pound after pound of sugar—especially refined sugar! (Okay, I admit it, this is definitely me. I'm a sugar junkie. I think I must have a "sugar gene" in my genetic makeup because my mother is a sugar junkie as well. I'm pretty sure I inherited it directly from her.)

Blame other people for my problems (see above). Let's face it, no one likes to admit they are making stupid choices, so we like to blame others for them—it's easier...much, much easier.

Get behind the wheel after "just one beer." Even if it really was just one beer—and your blood alcohol is below the legal limit—it will still impair your judgment. You are still a bit slower to react, still a bit slower to make a decision. That "bit" is often what decides whether you, or someone else, lives or dies. Do you want to die or kill someone for a lousy beer? Want a beer after a hard day at work? No problem, just buy it, put it in the trunk, and wait until you get home. And then stay there after you drink it. Hell, invite me over; I'll bring a case.

Abuse drugs (yes, even the pain medication the doctor prescribed)

Don't exercise enough—are you one of those people who cruise around and around the parking lot looking for a closer spot? Do you plan on joining a gym, but they cost too much? And yes, you could go to the YMCA and work out, but the times aren't right, or the locations aren't perfect, or…

Avoid physicians

Avoid dentists

Avoid anything at all that's even remotely unpleasant (Oh, please—you know you do. We all do.)

Avoid facing reality (What? Like it's going to go away?)

Yell and scream at people

Spend too much money

Buy the wrong things when spending all that money

Don't listen to people

Don't listen to yourself

Act too quickly

React too quickly

Don't apologize enough

Demand too many apologies

Okay, it's time

Okay, you've probably seen yourself doing at least one or two of those things.

How many ulcers are you giving yourself?

How much are you raising your blood pressure?

How many injuries are you causing yourself? How will those injuries change, and get worse, as you age?

How many divorces are you causing?

How many psychologists and psychiatrists are you keeping busy?

How much stress are you dealing with and how much stress are you making others deal with—including your family? How much stress are you giving your own kids? Is it really necessary?

What are you going to do to change? And this change has nothing to do with making other people's lives better; rather, it has to do with making your *own* life better. The simple answer to that, of course, is to simply quit doing all the bad stuff. Quit smoking, quit drinking, quit overeating, eat healthier, take your medicine, see doctors, spend less, and on and on.

But we all know that it's just not that easy. If it were easy, we would have done it a long time ago. Here's a suggestion (my father always said that advice is worth exactly what you pay for it, so feel free to ignore the suggestion. I ignore my suggestions stunningly well). Try this: pick one thing that you'd like to change, just one. And don't make it a big one.

Pick one small thing that you want to change and work on changing just that one. When you finally have that one changed—even if it takes years—then go on to the next. But don't go on until you have the first one changed.

What the hell, give it a try. You decide what you want to change and how to change it. In other words, take control of your own life for the long road ahead.

Packing for the Final Time

Not long ago, Mom and her doctors and I had "that talk" (the one every child dreads). Mom is ninety and recognizes that she can no longer live in her home—even with the help she has been getting. The time has arrived to find her a new place to live, a place with twenty-four-hour care.

It took me about a month, but we finally found a place she likes, that works for her, and that she can be comfortable in. With that, of course, comes the move. She has lived in a large home, has a lifetime of things, and even though the apartment she is moving to isn't small, it still isn't a house.

As she clears things out, people will be helping, going through everything she owns with her. Think about what is in your desk, your car, your bedroom and bathroom, and your office. Now think about someone going through all that stuff of yours. Is there anything you don't want seen? What will someone think when they see it?

The things we leave behind or must move one final time—by accident or design—speak stories about who we were. As we get older, we start to slowly move into that time where what we leave can matter more than what we have.

Do you have an office that you've been using for several years? Do you have books, recordings, and the minutiae of a professional life in that office? One day, you might turn off the lights and lock the door of that office on your way home and never return.

Is there a closet with boxes of things that haven't seen the light of day in years that you'd really like to go through? Should go through? Must go through?

The evidence we leave

Family and sometimes friends or legal representatives will go through the drawers, the filing cabinets, the bookshelves, and the closets. They will go through everything. Some things may be kept, some things may be shared, some donated, some tossed, some taken home and put in another closet for someone else to go through years or decades later.

It's how things happen. Some items kept, some thrown away, some donated to charitable organizations, and the rest are disposed of in estate sales or garage sales.

Perhaps, just perhaps, the things we leave really don't say much about us at all. I have quite a bit of "accidental" things in my home. Old gifts and more that describe the giver much more than describe me, but still, it's all there.

Stuff both valuable and worthless

1. Keys (those that fit something and those that no longer do—and haven't for years)

2. Wallet—what is in your wallet right now? An old love note? A faded picture? Credit card receipts? Phone numbers? Directions to a forgotten place? Pictures? Business cards?

3. Books—what books are you leaving? Are they trashy novels? Good novels? Biographies? Travel books? What did you read and what is the evidence of it? Or, perhaps the worst thing, aren't you leaving any books at all? How many do you have to give away? You may not even have any books to move. All your books may be on a tablet. Press "delete," and it's done.

4. Toiletries—what is in your bathroom cabinet, drawer, or shelf? A cologne or perfume? A deodorant? Does the toothpaste tube still have the imprint from your fingers? How about medicines? What medicines will have to be disposed of now that they're no longer needed?

5. Clothes—what clothes do you have hanging in your closet or folded in your dresser? Do you have anything decades out of date? Any old disco clothes? Any old double-knit? What's in there that, when someone sees it, will make them instantly think of you? Is anything there that smells slightly of your scent? Does the person removing the clothes gingerly touch them and remember the last time they were worn? Does it bring a tear? Will someone new be happy to receive it?

6. Car—are you going to sell it or donate it? Or will a family member be happy to get it?

7. Look around. See anything with your writing on it? Any notes? Shopping lists? Old cards you've saved? What has your handwrit-

ing on it, your signature? Our handwriting can say a great deal about us—what does yours say about you? Were you methodical? Were you always in a hurry? Were you just sloppy?

8. Food or drinks—what's in the house that you particularly liked to eat or drink? Is there something that, when anyone tastes it, they will immediately think of you?

9. Your special things—these can be anything: your golf clubs or basketball, your hobby things, your musical instrument, your things from childhood you still drag around with you (have any old trophies, yearbooks, models, or dolls?), your tools, and your briefcase. In other words, these are all the things that simply say "you" without ever saying a word.

10. Memories—what are the memories you leave with those who came in contact with you? Are they happy memories? Sad ones? When people think of you, do they do so with a smile or a frown? Hint—if they remember you with a frown, it may be time to rethink your life and how you live it. How sad that when someone hears you've died, they reply with, "Well, it's about time."

So, there are but a few of the many things we may leave behind after we depart this world. What else is there that retains a bit of you? It's possible that our worldly end can come so quickly, without any warning, that when it happens, we are unprepared. More than that, our friends and family are also unprepared.

Don't leave a mess, don't leave something that just brings sadness. Help people smile when they remember you, *because they will remember.* Wouldn't you rather they have good memories than bad ones? Walk softly and let the memories be sweet.

CHAPTER THREE

You Want Fries
with That Wine?

You can probably tell by the title that this section looks at food and drink. There has, I'm pretty sure, been more written about those two things than anything else on earth. And yes, we write about love, friendship, sex, war, sports, and all the other things people use to plow through life. Okay, fine. But think about all the cookbooks, all the restaurant and food reviews, the recipes that have been printed and handed down for generations, the menus that wax poetically about, well, fries, veggies, hunks o' meat, and other assorted things we use to sustain life.

My maternal grandmother had a piece written about her and her banana cream pie in a local Los Angeles area newspaper. I loved seeing that piece, written before I was in school. There she was, with a warm smile on her face and holding one of the pies that always graced her Christmas Dinner table. That's the best part of food and drink: connections to friends and family and warm memories.

By the way, the correct answer to the question, "Do you want fries with that wine?" is a simple "yes" (if no chocolate is available, of course).

A Warm Night, a Glass of Wine, and Things Can Happen

Of all the things in all the world, one of my least favorites is birthdays. To be more specific: my birthday. I just don't like them. And for all you people who say, "It beats the alternative." Well, how do you know? The alternative might be great.

Anyway, last week was my birthday—I had another one of the dreaded things. But, this one wasn't too bad. The week before, we had a celebration for all the April birthdays in my family (there are a few of us), so mine was watered down a bit. I could celebrate other people's birthdays rather than my own. And then, this week, on the actual day, things were pleasant.

My daughter (with some help, of course) made a cake, the gifts were simple and thoughtful, and the day was low-key and enjoyable. Later that evening, we went to dinner.

And that's when the trouble started

I decided to have a glass or two of wine with dinner. We were at Olive Garden (my birthday but kids' choice night) and somehow the conversation turned to ear piercing. My daughter had hers pierced a few weeks ago and, well, it got brought up. And that was when she said, "Daddy, why don't you have an ear pierced?"

And then my son piped up with, "Yeah, Dad!" And finally, to add more to the raucous noise, my wife added her two cents' worth. She reminded me that I've talked about it in the past. When we went to the San Diego County Fair, I would see the piercing booths and threaten to have it done. But I never did; the thought of having it done there didn't exactly sit well. Too many people, too dusty, too noisy, too... well, everything.

But now, we weren't at the fair, we were at a shopping center. After dinner, we wandered over to Claire's. Well, I wasn't worried—I wasn't worried at all. Of course, it might have been the wine...

And then I was inside the store. And then I was talking to a very friendly person who was showing me earrings. And then my *six-year-old* daughter was helping me decide on an earring. And then I was in the chair. And then I felt a pinch, and then it was over. Well, big woo.

That was astonishingly easy. And now I have an earring. Me. An earring. Me. Well.

My daughter absolutely loves to tell everyone that Daddy has a new earring. She says I can borrow one of hers. I decline—hygiene and all—and tell her why. She shrugs and says okay. But it's fine if I ever change my mind. I thank her.

I suppose getting an earring is better than getting a new Porsche. I suppose. Nah, who am I kidding here? An earring is cheaper than a new Porsche, so if you're going to do something crazy on a birthday, it perhaps makes more sense. But better? No way.

An earring?

I'd like to blame the earring on the two glasses of wine. But no, two glasses of wine wouldn't get a puppy goofy enough to put in an earring.

Is there a reason for me to wear an earring? No. Is there a reason for anyone to wear an earring? Of course not. But that's not the point. Women wear them, men wear them, kids wear them, pirates have always worn them (my daughter thinks it makes me look like a tough, mean pirate. It doesn't, but I'll take what I can get). There isn't a good reason to wear an earring except perhaps as a fashion thing, or simply for the hell of it. And that's my reason—simply for the hell of it (and because my daughter thinks it's fun). That's good enough for me.

I catch myself looking in mirrors occasionally when I walk by one. I'm not used to seeing it yet. But every time I see it, I like it more. Yep, I actually do like this thing.

The earring has never hurt (beyond the pinch when it went in) and is easy to take care of (for the first six weeks or so, I'm supposed to leave it in, twirl it a bit, and put antiseptic on it. Well, I can do that).

So far, the only real problem has been when I get out of the shower and towel off my hair. Because I don't feel the earring or anything, I tend to forget about it and the towel yanks it around a bit. Then I feel it. But other than that, it's been perfect. I hate to write that because I don't want to jinx myself or something and have my ear fall off, but it's a risk I'll just have to take. And I am learning to dry my hair much more gently.

So now I have an earring; my daughter is ecstatic, my son thinks I'm a teeny, tiny bit cooler (not cool, you understand, just a bit closer to cool), and I'm having fun. Not a bad birthday at all, as these things go.

Of course, we don't need earrings, but sometimes you just gotta do it for the look.

Coffee Elbow

Yes, it's true, I've come down with that most horrible of injuries, the infamous coffee elbow. Now, I'm sure everyone's heard of *tennis* elbow. That's a particular injury that tennis players get when, over the years, they have hurt their elbow from twisting it or over-playing.

I don't play tennis. Oh, yeah, I tried once when I was younger and foolish but, after spending a couple of very hot afternoons chasing a bouncing ball around a court, I promptly and intelligently gave up. Let's face it, there are much better ways to work up a sweat. Since retiring my tennis racquet, I never gave tennis elbow another thought.

Flash forward a few years. During these years, my elbows have worked perfectly, never failing to do exactly what I asked of them with no fuss whatsoever. So, what's the problem now? It's simply those few years.

I don't mind getting older, but why does it have to hurt?

Three weeks ago, I spent a day putting trim around our new kitchen floor (yes, I did a great job, thank you very much). I was on my stomach, using my arms in very unusual positions (mostly stretched out at weird angles), hammering away for hours. Well, the following morning, I awoke with a strong, dull pain every time I moved my arm. This is not a good thing for a writer, since writing requires arm movement (well, some arm movement anyway, to pick up the coffee cup). Luckily, the pain was in my left arm and I'm right-handed, *but still.*

So, I slept on it wrong, I figured. *No problem*, I thought, *it will go away in a few hours.* Well, a few hours and a few Advil later, the pain was mostly still there.

For the next four or five days, I pretty much ignored the problem, took the Advil, and proceeded with life. But, let's face it, when you start buying painkillers by the case instead of the bottle, you begin to think that perhaps someone should look at it. So, I went to the doctor to have an official elbow examination.

After looking the elbow over, the doctor turned to me and pronounced those words I'll never forget, "You've got mrphulpll-xxxzz."

"Huh?" I replied.

"Tennis elbow," he answered.

"Tennis elbow? How can I have tennis elbow? I don't play tennis."

"That's the popular term. The real name is the first one I told you, mrphulp-llxxxzz."

"But that doesn't change the fact that I still don't play tennis."

"You don't have to play tennis," the physician replied, his shoulders visibly sagging. "You can get it from too much unusual physical activity involving the elbows."

"Putting trim around a floor isn't unusual."

"Apparently, it is for you."

"Yeah, well, okay. So how long will it hurt?"

"Oh, two or three weeks…probably."

He told me a couple of things I could do and off I went, the proud owner of a tennis elbow. When I told people at work, they all laughed and said, "Right. We know how you got that injury. It was from years of lifting coffee can after coffee can. You don't have tennis elbow, you have coffee elbow." Okay, I do drink coffee and I do lift the glass or can with my left hand. But coffee elbow? Tennis elbow sounds so much more glamorous than coffee elbow.

Living with the pain and shame of coffee elbow

It's hard to tell people you have coffee elbow because, after all, they tend to laugh. So now I walk around with an elastic sport bandage on my arm and simply let them think it's to help my tennis elbow. The bandage does help the pain, and that's always a better thing than making so many trips to the drugstore for painkillers that the cashier knows you by your first name. But please, if you happen to see me somewhere, ask how the *tennis* elbow is doing. If you do, I'll buy you a coffee.

Give Me Food, I'm Not Hungry

Ah, our love affair with food. Everywhere you look, the portions in restaurants are getting bigger, much bigger. From Burger King to McDonald's to any steak house in town, the size of meals keeps growing, and so does our waistline.

Do we really need that much food? Do we need half-pound hamburgers, huge orders of fries, or shakes the size of oil barrels?

Probably nowhere on earth is a culture subjected to so many mixed messages. One commercial tells us to lose weight; another tells us where to get thousand-calorie soft drinks. Weight-loss clinics are springing up everywhere, while at the same time, we are told how great it is to order pounds and pounds of greasy, fried food.

Figuring it all out

How are we supposed to get it all straight? How are we supposed to be healthy when it seems all we really want is to just shove more and more fries down our throats? On television, we are inundated with ads that create a desire for more food, while at the same time we know how unhealthy it is.

There are numerous studies out there proving to us how unhealthy it is to overeat. We know this. And yet. There are scientists and physicians with absolute proof that too much fat in the diet leads to heart disease, high blood pressure, high cholesterol, and more. We know this. And yet. We continually see evidence all around us of the cost of being overweight. Insurance statistics, medical records, government evidence, and more prove that those who consume too much fat, salt, and sugar, and do not eat enough fruit and vegetables die younger, much younger, than those who eat a healthy diet. We know this. And yet.

But it tastes good!

There is an old saying that states, "If it tastes good, it's not good for you." Some of that is, indeed, true. Unfortunately, that taste is one of the reasons why we like to eat food that is slowly killing us.

There are other reasons, of course, for overeating. For some people, it may be habit. Some use food to relax, or to make themselves feel better psychologically, or they are just unaware of how much they are eating (the unconscious eater).

If you are in the business of selling food, you must make it taste good, be appealing, smell wonderful, be served in an inviting atmosphere, and create a need. The restaurant industry is great at this, especially fast-food restaurants. And that's one of the deadly combinations: restaurants that must sell food to stay in business, coupled with people who love or need to eat (and we all need to eat—it's just how much we need that creates the problem).

Please don't misunderstand me; I am not simply blaming the fast-food industry. They are, after all, just giving us what we demand. We need to learn to demand *less*.

We, as individuals and as a nation, need to want less food, be happy with less food, and love less food. And yes, I know that goes against some of our most basic instincts. But our health and our kids' health, even our national health, requires it. We need a national shout: *Want less!!*

And not only could we lose weight in the process, we might even save some money as well. Want to be healthier? Want to feel better? From now on, when you eat, order the small size. Get the small hamburger, the small French fries, the small soft drink. Save the money, save the calories, save your waistline.

Not just an American problem

Have you ever noticed that when you look at photos of city streets from Asia or Europe or the Mideast, you'll often see a McDonald's sign or the golden arches? You'll see signs from any number of US fast-food companies now. Look at photos from fifty years or more ago and you'll never see them. Hey, it tastes good, people want it, and we export and give it to them.

Western-style diets are fattening the planet. But it's more than that—it's also the reality of affluence. With more money to spend—more disposable income—people eat in restaurants more often, often eat foods higher in fats and sugar, and their weight goes up in proportion.

Japan never used to have problems with obesity. People primarily ate fish, rice, green vegetables, and ate very little sugar or processed foods.

That all changed after WWII. Just as the US started opening up more Japanese restaurants, so did Japan open up more American restaurants.

Add an increasing taste for Western food with ever-increasing income as Japan became hugely more affluent and a "perfect storm" was created that had obesity skyrocketing. Japanese got to taste French fries and then got to pack on pound after pound after pound. Lucky them.

So, where are you going to eat lunch today? What are you having for dinner? Are you going to eat French fries or rice? Are you going to eat beef or chicken? Are you going to eat a hamburger or broiled fish? Going meat or vegetarian? Or vegan?

What are you going to put around your waist? What are you going to make your legs and feet carry? What are you going to pack into your arteries and veins?

I know, I know, I know. I sound like everyone's mother. We know how to do the right thing, the healthy thing. We know what to do and we know how to do it. Even I do. And yet.

Goodbye Caffeine

The world loves caffeine. You may have read about my own affair with coffee a few pages ago. People drink caffeine-laden beverages everywhere you go, on a pretty much constant basis. Whether in coffee, tea, soft drinks, medicines, and more, we consume vast amounts of the stimulant.

We argue about the best kind of coffee beans and the best ways to brew it, we argue about which tea is the most flavorful or strongest, we argue about the flavors of various cola drinks. What we are discussing, of course, is the most flavorful way to get caffeine into our systems. These drinks—while some may taste good—are pretty much simply caffeine-delivery systems. But too much of a good thing (in this case, caffeine) just isn't all that good for you. Apparently.

Now, there are ways to throw away the caffeine crutch, and I'm here to help. You read correctly, I am here to help you live a healthier, happier, less addicted life by showing you ways to give up that evil drug, that scourge of the human race, that evildoer of our bodies, caffeine.

Ways to just say no to caffeine

1. Drink fruit juice.
2. Take ulcer medicine to help combat all the acid in your stomach from the fruit juice.
3. Drink milk (not that I actually like the taste of plain old milk, but if it can help one poor soul in the fight, go for it).
4. Take cholesterol-lowering medicine to combat the rise in your cholesterol from all the milk. (Unless you're drinking soymilk— my son loves chocolate soymilk—because there are no animal fats in soy. About saturated fats in the soymilk, I can't say. You're on your own there—read the damn carton.)
5. Take up running. Go for a nice long jog every time you feel like drinking something with caffeine in it. Sure, you won't have time to do much of anything else, but at least there will not be as much caffeine in your system. And no whining about needing the caffeine to help you run—just get over it and do it.

6. Scream at people a lot because you have become jittery from caffeine withdrawal. They probably deserved a good yelling-at anyway.
7. Run away after doing all that screaming to keep people from screaming back (see #5, above).
8. Exercise more—much more. This will not only help you keep your mind off the coffee or soft drinks, but you'll get in better shape.

Water can help

9. Take more showers. This will not actually help the caffeine withdrawal, but with all the running and exercising you are doing now, you will definitely need it (and those around you will certainly appreciate it—believe me, I know).
10. Spend time in a hot tub. This will help you relax, and relaxing is always a good thing. Okay, sure, you drank the caffeine because you were probably relaxed too much, but hey, relax about it.
11. Go on a vacation. It doesn't matter where you go or how much it costs; the important thing is getting away and relaxing in new surroundings.
12. Forget about how to pay for the vacation until you return. The vacation will help you relax (see #10, above) and not worrying about paying for it will also help you relax (see #10, above, again—why do I have to keep telling you this? Pay attention).
13. Yes, at some time, you will have to worry about paying the credit card companies about that vacation bill, but by then, you should be so relaxed that it won't matter as much.

Sugar, sugar, sugar, sugar

14. Drink lots of shakes. You can make these any flavor you want and (as long as you forget about chocolate or coffee flavor) they have no caffeine.
15. Keep on jogging and exercising more than ever—now you are adding #14 above!
16. Tell your friends what you are doing and what you are going through. They may help. Well, they probably won't help at all and will instead drink coffee right in front of you. If so, get some new

friends. As a matter of fact, get some new friends anyway—you can't have too many friends.

17. Get new-new friends to replace the new friends you just got because those new friends couldn't stand you nagging about caffeine all the time.

18. Ditch all the friends and become a hermit—sure, caves are hard to come by these days but keep looking, you'll find one eventually.

19. Come to the realization that being awake is far overrated—who needs it? Just go with the snooze...

20. Don't even think about hunting for caffeine tablets—just let it go.

And finally, simply read more. Reading helps get the mind focused, can be a calming influence, and is a way to forget about all the other stuff that takes up our time. See? Reading this wasn't a waste of time, after all—it's a way to energize your life and make it better.

Well, there you have it, twenty great ways to help you give up the horror of caffeine. I hope they help. But don't expect me to try that nonsense; personally, I'm headed for a caffeine-laden Diet Coke.

Kids and Food

I guess it's just been too many years since I've been a kid. I've forgotten all those delicious things children like to eat. You know, marvelous food like corn dogs, French fries with more ketchup than potatoes, cereal so sweet it makes your jaws ache. Ah, yes, the food of children.

Last night, the kids and I were on our own. My very significant other had an important meeting that lasted until almost 8 p.m., so we were on our own. Daughter just drank her bottle, cooed, and smeared applesauce in her hair. Son loved it—we had pretty much whatever we wanted and ate it in the family room watching TV. We called it picnic night. Even the one-year-old daughter had a ball seeing what else she could rub applesauce into besides her hair.

Son had a corn dog, French fries, corn, and a salad. Pudding and cookies were his dessert. Was this a healthy meal? Of course not. And he certainly doesn't eat like this on a regular basis. But last night, when it was just the three of us, he (we) indulged. But the point I'm making here is that he thought this was a great dinner.

Does green Jell-O count as a health food?

One afternoon, Son and I were discussing both good and bad foods. I happened to mention that most green foods were good. I, of course, was thinking about healthy vegetables. He, of course, was not. He pointed out that since green Jell-O was green, it must be really good for you. He almost had me believing it.

Children do not care in the least whether something is or is not good for them. They know what they like and that's all they like. But, too often, a child won't even eat something you know they like. And that can be frustrating

If it were up to Son, he would pretty much not eat at all. Eating is just not something he's interested in. Yes, he gets hungry: "Daddy, I'm way, way hungry!" But then, when food is suggested, he becomes less hungry. Especially at mealtime. He would rather do almost anything than eat. He'll carry on long conversations, will play with his food and the silverware, drink his milk, and talk some more. Heck, that's his favorite time to play with his sister—even when it annoys her (actually, especially when it annoys her).

Eventually, he will finally eat. And don't think that he has some pathological thing against food; he doesn't. There are times when he is "way, way hungry" and will eat anything in sight and then ask for more. But with him, as with many other kids, food is just not that big of a deal. He's lucky.

Food, the great evil we all need and love

Food is a horrible thing. Yes, it tastes good. Yes, it is good for us, and yes, it is a great social tool. But I'm not sure that we wouldn't be better off without it. Some of the world is starving and some of the world is overweight. Wars are fought over food; families kill each other over food. Think how much more peaceful the world would be if we didn't need food.

An interesting thing, of course, is that while we love food, we can also hate it. We love the taste, the texture, and the aromas. We hate the weight it can add to our bodies. We fight the temptation of food; we fight the weakness it brings out. We give in to that weakness with every fair, circus, and film. We cave in with every holiday, with every birthday cake. Food is the ultimate love/hate relationship.

So, what should we parents do? I guess just go ahead and beat our heads against that wall as we try to do the right things for our kids. We will have healthy meals, limit those between-meal snacks (especially the kind which are high in fats and sugars), and try the best we know how to see that our children eat healthy. And then we'll go out to Starbucks and grab a mocha latte on the way to 31 Flavors Ice Cream for a hot-fudge sundae.

Oh, not all of us do that, of course. Some stop at a bar for more "adult" calories taken in the way of liquid refreshment. Personally, I think the world would be a better place if those individuals got themselves a Slurpee instead, but there you go.

I had a friend a few years ago who, I'm pretty sure, never ate at all. His total caloric intake came pretty much exclusively from various forms of alcohol. I wouldn't be surprised if, by now, the guy was dead. If ever there was someone who needed to switch from beer to Slurpees, it was he.

But I digress; I seem to have wandered off the topic a bit, which is pretty much normal for me. But back to where we were, which was discussing kids and food, I wonder which one of those darling kids of mine spilled the pineapple on my keyboard.

The Most Vicious Question of All

Freedom, democracy, human rights are one thing, but all bets are off when it comes to the most vicious question of all, "What would you like to drink?"

Soft drinks such as Coke, Pepsi, 7-Up, Hires, Sprite, Mountain Dew, Dr. Pepper, and more, and each of their diet versions, plus hundreds of additional brands including those from nations around the world such as the Philippines, Japan, China, and more are locked in a worldwide war for the greatest prize of all: cold, hard cash.

And those are just a tiny few of the soft drink versions. Want to add beer to it? According to Tastessence, "It is impossible to have an exact number of brands of beer in the world. According to some estimates though, there are as many as 20,000." And that's just beer.

If we add wine, Quora notes that, "It is hard to measure, but it is plausibly between 100,000 and 200,000" different wine brands.

Life used to be simple a century or more ago. If you were thirsty, you drank water, coffee, tea, wine, hard spirits, or juice you squeezed from the fruit yourself. But around the turn of the century, a pharmacist in Atlanta, Georgia, while playing around with soda water and various things that would "perk one up," invented Coca-Cola. And the public loved it.

Needless to say, if the public is willing to spend vast amounts of money for a product, you can be sure that someone else will, in very short time, come out with another version. Pepsi and Royal Crown Colas were born. Soon after that, we began to see the root beers and fruit-flavored carbonated beverages.

The orange and lemon-lime drinks are delicious, as are the root beers. But as good as they are, they never came close to matching the popularity of cola. Why this is true, exactly, I'm not sure. Perhaps it's simply that there is something, a taste bud or some structure or other within our brains, that is programmed to like the cola taste.

Not everyone likes cola, of course. Some people can't tolerate the taste, while others simply prefer soft drinks of different flavors. But worldwide, in various ethnicities, age groups, socio-economic levels, and nationalities, the favored drink is usually a cola product (I don't have any evidence of this at hand; it's simply a guess based on what I've seen).

What is the point of this discussion? Today we'll bring the cola wars to a conclusion (no, we won't). We will declare a winner, point out the victor, decide what will be the cola triumphant (nope). Alert your friends and neighbors.

A truly fair test (more or less)

The problem with most taste tests is that they are conducted by the company, which wants their product to win. Even tests conducted by neutral third parties are still paid for by the soft drink company ordering them.

Let's face it: have you ever watched a commercial for Coke and seen Pepsi win the taste test? So, what we need here is a true third party. An honest third party who doesn't own stock in either company, has no relatives or friends working there, and doesn't own a television station that will probably go bankrupt when the losing soft drink pulls their advertising. That honest third party is (drum roll starts as the curtain rises and we see a lone figure on a black stage under a single spotlight, head modestly bowed) me.

Now, I know what you're thinking (no, I don't). You're wondering how someone whose usual soft drink is Diet Coke could possibly be fair to the others. Well, you'd be wrong to think that. I can be fair. I'm fair in everything. I don't drive a Ford product, but I certainly recognize that they make good cars. I use an iPhone but recognize that there are probably other good phones out there. So, see? I can be fair. And now, with that out of the way, we can get on with the Big, Awesome, Final, Absolute Last, Greatest Soft Drink Taste Test of All Time.

The moment of truth

I sat down with a six-pack each of Diet Pepsi and Diet Coke and proceeded to drink (not all twelve at the same time, of course. Good grief). In order to be fair, I took bites of potato chips, handfuls of M&M's, and munched on a large Subway sandwich between sips of the drinks.

Not wanting to make a hasty conclusion, I vowed to not declare a winner until at least three cans of each had been consumed. This was important because I didn't want some college student, doing an argumentative term paper, to write years after my death that I had been too quick to reach judgment. Fairness was certainly everything the sunny afternoon that Coke won the war (particularly if you add a smooth rum to it).

I know what you're asking right now: "What about the beer? You gonna do a taste test of beer?" Well, yeah.

And I did. There are (quite) a few that are drinkable, some good, a few very good. But honestly, it's all up to the discerning individual. Pacifico is good, as is Yellowtail and others. Many, many others. Mmmmm, ice-cold Pacifico or Yellowtail on a warm beach as the sun sets...my, my, my.

Now, should we move on to wine? Nah, me either. I'm tired of the whole conversation too. And we haven't even started to talk about Slurpees, Kool-Aid, root beer, or lemonade. For a quick break, I suggest we indulge in a tall, cold glass of sparkling water and call it a day. Ha, yeah, I'm kidding. Now, where did I put that bottle opener...

The Perfect Cake Recipe

I'm in the middle of a Grand Quest: looking for one of the most difficult things to find on earth. No, I am not looking for the cure for a disease or a car that gets 200 miles per gallon—although those would be really terrific things. I am not looking for that perfect vacation spot or even the best place to get perfectly broiled corn on the cob (although, if you find such a place, let me know).

No, what I am looking for is much more difficult to find than any of that other stuff. You see, I am looking for…*the perfect cake recipe!*

Do you have any idea just how difficult a challenge this is turning out to be? Didn't think so. Well, let me tell you, this is one daunting—*very* daunting—thing that I have decided to do.

Why have I decided to do this? Solely for you. When I find that perfect cake recipe, I'll share it, printed here, so everyone can indulge themselves in the wondrousness of a perfect cake.

All right! So that last sentence stretched the truth just a bit. Ain't no halo here.

The real reason

So, here is why I am really spending all of this time and precious energy on the Perfect Cake Recipe Search (from now on to be known simply as PCRS):

Because I am tired of lousy cakes! I want a good, no, a great cake. And I want this great cake to be big, have at least four layers, and be covered with only the finest frosting the world has ever seen. I want grown women and men to weep upon seeing it.

See now? That was easy.

Oh, wait a minute. There are a few other things this cake has to have. It should be chocolate: chocolate cake and chocolate icing. Or, it could be chocolate cake and marshmallow icing. Or chocolate cake with marshmallow filling and chocolate icing.

Wait! There is always white cake with chocolate icing. Lemon cake is also a good choice, lemon cake with lemon icing. Or, lemon cake with chocolate icing. See? I can be reasonable.

Never mind, no, I think I will stick to chocolate cake and chocolate icing. So, what do we have so far? Well, so far, our PCRS has narrowed down to a four-layer chocolate cake with chocolate icing.

Now, the cake must be fresh (but not just-out-of-the-oven fresh. That is too fresh, the cake must have a couple of hours to settle before you dare cut it) and must definitely be moist. Wait, first, let's come up with a better word than moist. I hate that word. So, anyway, a dry cake is terrible. Yes, nice and hydrated (not a perfect word, but I'm working on it), with four beautiful layers of cake and smooth, creamy, and luscious layers of rich, exotic chocolate icing between the layers of cake—is your mouth watering yet?

The great search

Now for the big question: Where am I going to find this cake? Sure, I could make it myself, but that is just not the same as buying a perfect cake that someone else has made for you. Not that I'm against making the cake myself; after all, I've made a few of them in my life. But to be perfect, someone else has to make it. That way, there's no labor involved, just the physical act of sitting down and enjoying—and that I can do with gusto.

So, do I get it at the bakery that is located inside one of the various grocery stores around town? Somehow it doesn't seem, well, quite the same. Do I shop for it at Costco? Now, Costco does have pretty good cakes, but a cake from a wholesale warehouse? Where's the art? Where's the magic?

Or should I look at neighborhood bakeries? I love neighborhood bakeries; the aromas of fresh-baked goods are almost intoxicating. I just don't know. Can someone please tell me where my perfect cake is waiting for me to rescue it, gather it in my arms, and take it home to be enjoyed by the family?

I guess that the only thing to do is start The Ultimate Chocolate Cake Search (which is different from the PCRS, which was discussed earlier). Yes, this search will involve travel, a whole lot of travel, as I go from bakery to bakery, buying cake after cake, in my search. True, I will have to do a lot of tasting of all these chocolate cakes, but I am willing to do that. No sacrifice is too great, not even the sacrifice of eating chocolate cake.

A sacrifice, you ask? Of course, it's a sacrifice—the calories, the fat, the risk of cardiovascular disease from eating seven thousand chocolate cakes. But I don't mind—nope. That's just the kind of guy I am. I promise to leave no chocolate cake ignored until I find the perfect one.

I'll scour the western United States. I might even be induced into traveling the entire country, if I have to—although that might be considered a bit much, especially by the rest of the family.

The perfect cake, the perfect cake recipe...it's all the same thing, really. Just one man's search for the finest dessert (in cake form, at least) the planet has to offer. Or I may say the hell with it and just make a key lime pie.

CHAPTER FOUR

Weird Times and Holidays

A great deal of thought went into the name of this section (okay, not really, but it could have). I mean, after all, aren't holidays and weird times pretty much synonymous? You'll have your own answer for that, of course, depending on what your holidays look like, but do they involve family? Do they involve food you don't always prepare? Do they involve someone imbibing spirits a bit more than usual (even secretly)? Do they involve gifts? Travel? Feuds? Strange uncles and aunts?

You can probably see where I was going with all that; just helping you remember what we all try desperately hard to forget until the next year comes steamrolling around. And then mixed with all that are the good parts. They exist too—yeah, it can be confusing.

I wonder why we forget so much about the holidays. Self-defense? Self-preservation? Maybe we just forget so much in order for us to be able to do everything again next season. Woo-hoo! More lime gelatin mold with preserved pears and mini marshmallows. Thanks, Aunt Gertrudis!

The next few pieces will help you remember even more.

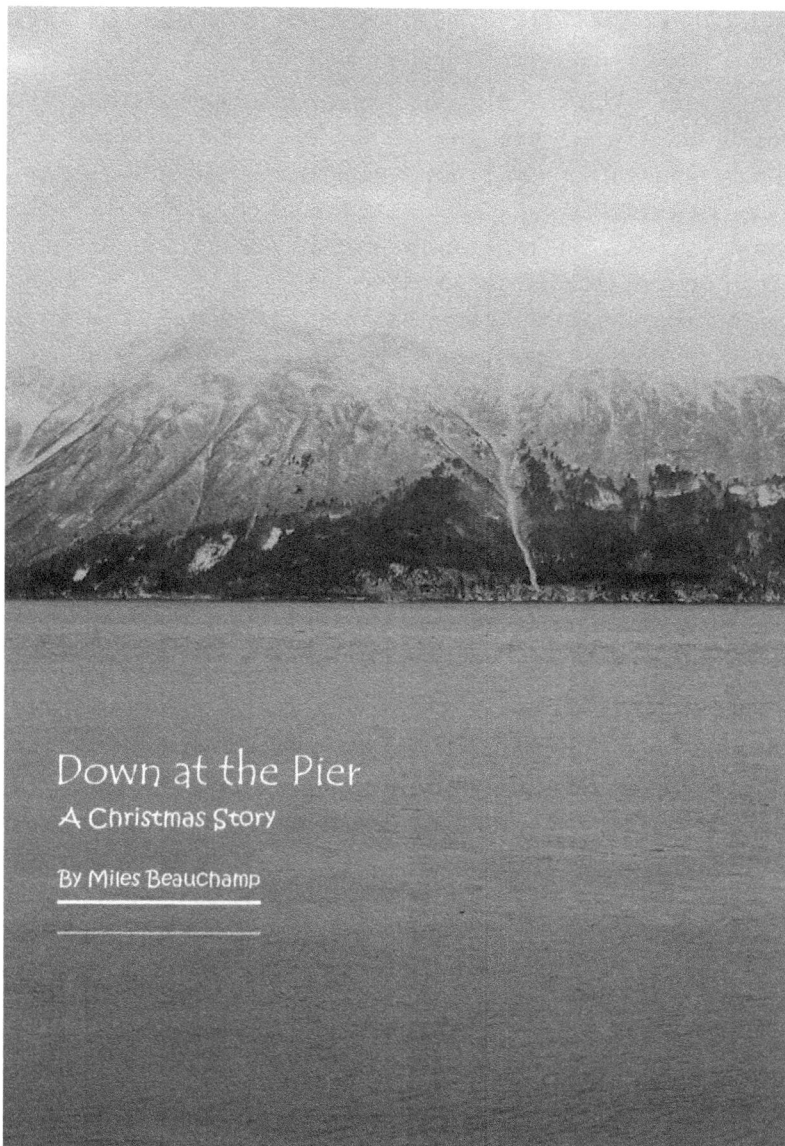

Down at the Pier
A Christmas Story

By Miles Beauchamp

Down at the Pier: A *Christmas* Story

Margie noticed him for the first time as September was drawing to a close, walking quietly past The Sea Shanty. Margie had worked at the Shanty—a small bar with a tourist name that served tourist food—for years. That's how it was at the end of the kitschy pier, rustic with sea salt and tourists. But now the summer crowds had left and only the year-rounders still came down to the pier.

Margie would probably never have noticed him except that she took a break at the same time he took his walk, that time after the day but before the night. At first, they didn't acknowledge each other, but then, as the evenings went on, they began to nod. Margie was the first to nod, and the man, after a bit of hesitation, nodded back.

Of course, Margie wondered who this man was. Then she started making up lives for him. In her head, he became a failed mercenary, a successful baseball player, an FBI agent, an Olympic distance runner, an Amazon snake catcher. But she realized the silliness of it all—the man was barely three feet tall and that just wouldn't work with the lives she had imagined. More than likely, he was a second-string jockey.

And on the two of them went, day after day, through September and October: a nod, a smile, a glance. But around the first part of November, the routine—this long semblance of a strange dance—changed. Margie left the restaurant at the usual time, leaned on the pier railing, put her usual Hershey's Kiss in her mouth, and reached to smooth out her sweater.

"Pardon me." The small man had, for the first time, approached her and said something.

"I'm sorry?" Margie asked, not sure if she had really heard him.

"Hate to bother you, but I was wondering if you had a match."

"Oh, a match. No, sorry, I don't," she answered, noticing the faint aroma of pipe tobacco around him.

"Thanks anyway. I thought I had a few left, but the box is empty." As he spoke, he twisted a box around in his hands—a small, heavy, wooden box.

Margie stared at the box in the man's hands and then quietly said, "I haven't seen a matchbox like that in years. My grandmother used to keep matches like that by the fireplace."

"I guess it is old fashioned…just like me."

"I didn't mean that. And you're not old fashioned, I guess. And what if you are old fashioned? What's wrong with that?" *Wonderful, another needy guy who craves validation for everything he does. I never should've come out here tonight*, she thought.

"No, I am a bit out of touch, I guess."

"I wouldn't know," Margie softly replied. *Go away; leave me alone to suck on my chocolate in peace, will ya please?* she thought. "Why do you say that?" she asked him while at the same time thinking, *don't answer, please don't answer.*

"Easy—I'm an old guy who's done nothing but make toys his whole life. And now no one wants the toys I know how to make."

"What toys do you make?"

"Just wooden toys. Puppets and things like that. Specialized toys, they call it now, and there's not a big enough market for it."

"I had a wooden puppet," Margie whispered, almost to herself.

"I know."

"You know? How could you know?"

"'Cause just about every kid used to have one. But not anymore."

"Yeah, probably not. Now, it's computer this and computer that."

And so, the two of them stood there, gazing out to sea for the next few minutes, both lost in their own thoughts.

"Well," Margie said, "I guess I gotta go back to work."

"Yes…So, want to have a drink sometime?" he asked while continuing to look out to sea.

Sorry, you're too fat, too old, and your nose is too damn red, she thought. "Okay," she replied.

"Good. Maybe next week?"

"Sure—after I get off work. At ten."

"All right, I'll see you next week—at ten." And with that, the two turned away—he to walk on as always, she back to work.

Margie left the Shanty at 10:30 p.m. that Tuesday night. She got off work at ten, but in all the years she had been there, 10:30 p.m. was the earliest she had ever managed. And that was tonight, and that was because she had a date, and that was because the small man had actually reappeared, and that was because…well, she didn't know why. But she was glad. Not glad in a giddy "I've got a date" kind of way, but in a "something to do besides go home alone" sort of way. Regardless, she almost smiled when she left the Shanty and the man walked up to her.

"You're on time."

"Still feel like having a drink?" the man asked.

"Sure. But what's your name?"

"I'm sorry. My name is Jarl Holger."

"Jarl Holger, that's unique. What kind of name is that?" Margie asked.

"Oh, sort of Scandinavian and Norwegian."

"Ah," Margie sighed. "Do you smoke a pipe?"

"No, but the man I used to work for did…does. Why do you ask?"

"Just thought I caught a slight aroma of pipe tobacco," she replied. The two of them had been walking down the pier as they talked, and very shortly, they reached the end and needed to decide where to go. "There's a good pub just a short way from here. They serve pretty good food there."

"Okay, sounds good," Jarl said in little more than a whisper.

The pub, though busier than the Shanty, was still more than half empty. The couple sat in a darkened corner and ordered hot buttered rum.

Margie decided to be the one to get into the heavier conversation. "So, where do you work?"

"You wouldn't believe me."

"Oh, sure I would." *Okay, so what line of nonsense is he going to try to give me now? Margie wondered. Can't one of these guys ever just be honest?*

"Fine," he quietly said. "I'm an elf."

"That's cool. What shopping center do you work at? Do you mind all those little kids climbing on you all day long?"

"I mean, a real elf—North Pole, Santa Claus, Christmas kind of elf."

"Well, good. Hey, listen, I better be going now."

"I knew you'd react like that."

"What did you expect? Tell someone you're one of Santa's elves… good grief."

"Remember I said I know you had a wooden puppet? Well, I made that puppet. Red clothes, black hair, tiny gold belt and slippers."

"How did you know that?"

"I told you, I'm an elf."

"Okay, just for the heck of it, let's pretend it's all true. You're an elf. Why aren't you at the North Pole?"

"I told you that too. I build wooden puppets—know how to build one or two hundred puppets an hour. But not many want those anymore."

"Why don't you make something else?"

"I like puppets. I like working with wood, painting their faces, attaching the strings in just the right length. I've been doing it forever. But I guess that's past. Now, I like to come here, look at the water. It's nice, the water…would solve so many things."

Margie looked at him, then closed her eyes. *Please no*, she thought to herself. *Please don't let this happen; I don't want to mess with some guy who thinks he's an elf and wants to end it all.*

But, for whatever reason, Margie took a long, second look at Jarl Holger. She saw his face by candlelight, looked into the eyes that had seen a thousand Christmases, saw the hands that had carved puppet after puppet, and somewhere, deep inside her, saw the smiles those puppets brought. And then she knew. "You really are one of Santa's elves," she whispered. "An elf can't…No, no, no. That just means you have to go back—even if you end up making just one puppet for one kid. That's Christmas, Jarl."

And Jarl sighed, a deep, tiny sigh. "I know."

Jarl's phone sounded—it was how Santa kept in touch—playing "Jingle Bell Rock."

"I've gotta go—it's getting busy at home. Thanks for the company." Jarl slid out of the booth and sauntered off, whistling the carol to himself. Margie didn't mind paying the check—and she left a large tip. It was, after all, Christmas.

The Anti-Thanksgiving

Thanksgiving is wonderful, I get it. I'm thankful for many people and things. However, there are things that it's perfectly okay to not be thankful about. In other words, we can spend a bit of time thinking about all the things we aren't thankful for. What am I not thankful for? Glad you asked.

Just a few things I'm not thankful for

1. Acid indigestion (particularly following too much Thanksgiving food)
2. Headaches after too much food, beverage, strange family members
3. Crowds
4. Drivers who cut you off
5. Drivers who won't let you in
6. Anyone driving a car on the day after Thanksgiving
7. Leftover turkey (or any turkey, for that matter)
8. Oyster dressing
9. Cranberries (cranberry sauce, yes; cranberries, no)
10. A cousin or two (no, I'm not mentioning names)
11. After-Thanksgiving sales (of course, I like saving money; what I hate are the crowds, the lack of parking spaces, the crowds, the store aisles piled high with so much stuff you can hardly walk, the crowds, and finally, all those crowds)
12. Television commercials advertising After-Thanksgiving Sales
13. Television commercials advertising Pre-Christmas Sales
14. The start of Christmas ads filled with cheery Christmas music, snow, sleighs pulled by reindeer, and a constant ho, ho, ho
15. The beginning of Christmas music being played anywhere and everywhere (don't misunderstand me, I love Christmas music, it's just that after a while, with it being everywhere, it can get on your nerves)

16. Christmas Specials at places that shouldn't have Christmas Specials. A Christmas Special at toy or department stores, fine, but please, spare me the Christmas Special at the car dealers, the golf courses, the cell phone store, the auto parts store, the beauty salons, the plumbing store, or the hardware store.

17. Weird recipes coming out to tell us all the things we can do with leftover turkey. Turkey meatloaf, fine. Turkey enchiladas, fine. Even turkey à la king, fine. But turkey omelet, not fine.

18. A Christmas sale on a case of engine oil is not a good thing

19. Fake snow, fake snow—and I'm not too fond of fake snow, either

20. Goose

21. Lines in front of the local Honey Baked Ham store as Christmas approaches. And couldn't anyone figure out how to smear some honey on a ham and bake it before Honey Baked came along? What's with people and their Honey Baked hams? That being said, yes, people love them, and even I have stood for over an hour in line to pick up one of them (actually, I wouldn't have done it on my own, but it got me out of the house for an hour as my wife was whizzing around getting everything ready for Thanksgiving Dinner with the in-laws). And this coming from a vegetarian. Go figure.

22. Christmas cheer (Here, I mean the fake kind of Christmas cheer. Real Christmas cheer is hard enough to deal with, but the fake Christmas cheer is a killer—as in, if you give me one more fake smile, I will probably have you killed.)

23. Christmas letters from family and friends when the only information they give is how bad things are going. I'm sorry you lost your job, the house burned down, you're getting a divorce, and the dog bit you, but this is Christmas; if you can't say anything good, then don't say anything besides Merry Christmas. Everyone is having a tough time right now, but these are the holidays.

24. Low-fat, sugar-free eggnog (or most any other holiday food).

Hey, it's a great time of year, so enjoy!

25. Toys! Toys! Toys! Toys! Toys! Toys! Toys! Toys! Toys! Toys!
Toys! Toys! Toys! Toys! Toys! Toys! Toys! Toys! Toys! Toys!
Toys! Toys! Toys! Toys! I'm getting sick of toys, ads for toys,
commercials for toys, kids begging Santa for toys, and the huge
crush of humans trying to get into a toy store before Christmas.
I feel this way because I have two wonderful kids who are even
now probably trying to find some Santa's lap to crawl up onto
and whisper what they want for Christmas. Well, one kid anyway—our daughter. Our son is past that age, although he says
he believes—he either wants to hedge his bets or just go along
with us for his sister's sake…and to keep us happy. Smart kid.

A Short Little Christmas List

Ah, 'tis Christmas. Another year just whizzed by and we almost didn't notice. How did a year go by so quickly? Well, it did, so suck it up.

This is, naturally, the time when many of you girls and boys around the planet (or solar system, for all I know) make lists to give to Santa Claus. But with all that writing, texting, instant messaging and emailing, there is a way to simplify it. I have designed a list that you can use to make sure Santa gets you everything your little heart desires. Feel free to clip it and use it anyway you like. Or, just take a photo of it and upload it to whatever page or site your antiquated parents still use.

Dear Santa, here is what I want for Christmas (and please don't be stingy):

_____ Cash

_____ Gift cards

_____ Games (we're not talking board games here, dude)

_____ Toys

_____ Smart Phone (we're not talking generic or, heaven forbid, clam shell)

_____ Bicycle

_____ Scooter

_____ Amazon gift card

_____ Plenty of "other" (this is not an excuse for you to slip in school supplies)

Okay, okay. Please also bring something for my parents and brother(s) and/or sister(s). Bring them whatever they want. Fine.

Now, back to where I was. Oh, yeah, my list. Please bring me:

_____ Online game credits

_____ Music downloads

_____ Movie downloads

_____ Membership to a skateboard park

_____ A skateboard

_____ Treasury bills (this will make Grandma happy 'cause she keeps talking about college and all)

_____ Online games and credits

_____ Actually, just a really big gift card so I can get the games myself because, Santa, you wouldn't understand

_____ A really, really, really big monitor to play all those games on (and extra game controllers)

_____ iPad

_____ Electric guitar

_____ Keyboard

_____ Piano (electric)

_____ New laptop computer

_____ Diva Diamonds

_____ iPod Touch

_____ Apple Watch (yes, the latest series)

_____ Snowboard

_____ Robo-Pong

_____ Video camera (professional)

_____ Scuba gear

_____ Boat (to go with the scuba gear)

_____ Concert tickets

_____ A Kindle

_____ An iMac

_____an Apple Mac Pro

_____a MacBook Air

Oh, did I mention that I wanted a new scooter? An electric Razor, Scrooser, Gigabyke Groove, or Works Rover (yes, I know those top out at over $7,000.00, but it's _Christmas_). Just don't give me one of those things I have to actually push. I'm surprised I have to tell you this, Santa. Really.

And as far as the video games go, don't bring me any dorky, childish ones or an old version. I want cool games, the kind that cool people play on cool systems. Cool. Oh, and the computer that's on the list? Power, Santa; it has to be fast and powerful. Don't be stingy (I say that with deepest love and respect for everything you do, of course). Gotta keep up that cool image, 'cause I'm cool. Love ya, Santa!

Whoops, almost forgot. Also bring world peace. And an end to hunger. And sickness.

Thank you, Santa!

Sincerely yours,

Insert name here

Well, kids, I sure hope that helps get Santa's attention and you get what you want this Christmas. If it doesn't, don't blame me. Just remember, you could have been a bit better, you know. After all, you did pick a few fights, you did tattle on someone, and you did spit on the sidewalk. How do I know all this? Been there, done that. Well, some of it.

We'll talk some more, but for now, just get to bed and don't bother your brother or sister. I mean it. Santa's watching.

P.S. Yes, there is a simpler way than copying this list; just Instagram it. Easier for you, easier for your parents to know EXACTLY what you want. You're welcome.

The Perfect Holiday Gift

You know you never liked fruitcakes, so why are you trying to give them away? Give cold, hard cash instead and make everyone happy.

Yes, cash, the perfect holiday gift. It comes in all sizes, never gets returned, the recipients are always grateful, and you never have to struggle with over-crowded shopping centers or paying huge delivery fees to make sure it arrives on time. Is that great or what?

Oh, sure, to some people it may seem a bit crass. But ask yourself, is it any crasser than battling through stores to find the last item of something on sale? Is it any worse than standing in the return lines? Is it any more crass than hinting day after day for a particular gift? Heck, is it any crasser than gift certificates to a gym for your spouse?

Of course not. Duh. And that's why, in the spirit of holiday gift giving, I'm once again printing a simple list you can use. Just cut out the list and circle the type of currency you want to give (or receive). Don't worry, once this idea catches on—and it will—the holidays will be so much easier. Okay, you probably won't find many "After the Holidays" sales, but still.

So, here you are, many of the world's major currencies, in alphabetical order (I'm nothing if not helpful). And yes, not all of the planet's currencies are listed; there are actually over 180 currencies in play (this can, of course, change at any moment). So, if you don't see the currency you need, look online where they're all listed or seek out a friendly bank near you.

The cold, the hard, the cash

Afghanistan Afghani
Algeria Dinar
American Samoa Dollar
Angola Kwanza
Argentine Peso
Aruba Guilder
Australian Dollar

Austrian Euro
Azores Euro
Bahamas Dollar
Bangladesh Taka
Barbados Dollar
Belgium Euro
Belarus Ruble
Bermuda Dollar
Brazil Reais
Bulgaria Leva
Cambodia Riel
Canada Dollar
Canary Islands Euro
Cayman Islands Dollar
Central African Rep Franc
Chile Peso
China Yuan Renminbi
Christmas Islands Aust Dollar
Cook Islands NZ Dollar
Coral Sea Islands A. Dollar
Costa Rica Colon
Cuba Peso
Cyprus Pound
Czech Koruny
Denmark Kroner
Eastern Caribbean Dollar
Egypt Pound
Eritrea Nakfa
Ethiopia Birr
Euro
Fiji Dollar
Finland Markkaa
France Euro

French Guiana Euro
French Polynesia Euro
German Deutsch Mark
Gold Ounce
Greece Euro
Guam Dollar
Guinea Franc
Hong Kong Dollar
Holland Euro
Hungary Forint
Iceland Kronur
India Rupee
Indonesia Rupiah
Ireland Euro
Israel New Shekel
Italy Euro
Jamaica Dollar
Japan Yen
Jordan Dinar
Laos Kip
Lebanon Pound
Luxembourg Euro
Macau Pataca
Madiera Islands Euro
Malawi Kwacha
Mali Franc
Malaysia Ringgit
Malta Lira
Mayotte Euro
Mexico Peso
Micronesia Dollar
Midway Dollar
Montenegro Euro

Myanmar Kyat
Netherlands Euro
Northern Mariana Dollar
Norway Kroner
Pakistan Rupee
Palau Dollar
Palladium Ounce
Panama Balboa
Papua New Guinea Kina
Philippine Peso
Platinum Ounce
Poland Zlotych
Portugal Escudo
Romania Lei
Russia Ruble
San Marino Euro
Saudi Arabia Riyal
Scotland Pound
Sierra Leone Leone
Silver Ounce
Singapore Dollar
Slovakia Koruny
Solomon Islands Dollar
South Africa Rand
South Korea Won
Spain Peseta
Sudan Dollar
Suriname Dollar
Sweden Kronor
Switzerland Franc
Taiwan New Dollar
Thailand Baht
Tonga Pa'anga

Trinidad and Tobago Dollar
Turkey Lira
Tuvalu Dollar
United Arab Emirates Dirham
United Kingdom Pound
United States Dollar
Vatican City Euro
Venezuela Bolivare
Vietnam Dong
Virgin Islands Dollar
Wake Island Dollar
Zambia Kwacha

Please note that the above list doesn't include them all—although, since the euro has come about, it has become much simpler. There are fewer currencies now than there used to be. Makes it easier for you, right?

I hope the list helps you give everyone on your list the perfect gift (or get you exactly what you want) this year, and if not, don't blame me. Maybe it's simply because you weren't as good as you thought you were.

Bad Holiday Gifts

We have all received them, the bad holiday gifts. You know the kind: heavy sweaters when you live in the tropics, bikinis when you live on frozen tundra, or a new gardening tool after you move into a condominium.

This piece is meant to help you from making the same mistake and doing the unthinkable—giving a bad holiday gift. Use it wisely and hope that everyone you give to truly enjoys the gifts you offer. And even more, hope that the people who are giving you gifts also read this.

Items that should never be given as holiday gifts

1. Motor oil
2. Real tools to children
3. A year's supply of anything
4. Notebook paper
5. Pencils
6. Used steering wheels
7. Used tires
8. Tires (unless attached to a Maserati—that's okay)
9. Chains for the tires
10. Patch kits for leaking tires
11. House paint (even if it is for your spouse who has been ignoring your other hints that the house needs painting)
12. Socks
13. Underwear
14. Hats
15. Bathing suits (sure, you've been saving it since last fall when you got a great deal on summer leftovers, but by now, the person has either outgrown it, put on too much weight to wear it, or hates the color and would not be seen dead wearing it at any beach on the planet)
16. First-aid products

17. Cheap wine
18. Cheap candy
19. Cheap flowers
20. Cheap jewelry
21. Cheap clothes
22. Last year's hot toy
23. Last year's hot shoes
24. Last year's hot music
25. Last year's hot sleepwear
26. Sleepwear
27. Cooking appliances
28. Appliances
29. Generic games
30. Generic software
31. Money orders for postage stamps
32. Postage stamps
33. Belts that would have fit you twenty pounds ago
34. Toys for teenagers
35. Okay, anything but cash for teenagers

So, there you go. A few items out of thousands, if not millions, of things you probably should not give for gifts. This list is not, of course, perfect. There are many things on the list that would be perfect for someone, depending upon whom that person is and what they do. After all, sometimes it's just a matter of luck. So, good luck.

How Long Did Those Resolutions Last?

Recently, I decided to look back and see just how well I managed to keep the resolutions that I made last year. Naturally, I had every intention of keeping them, but it appears that my ability to do so was iffy at best.

Easy New Year's resolutions that I hope I kept

1. Remember to turn off the lights (okay, this is a personal issue coming from a parent of kids who haven't yet realized that a light switch works both ways): **Yes**
2. Eat slightly healthy food (why get carried away, right?): **Yes**
3. Drink plenty of fluids—of one sort or another: **Yes**
4. Get better at my job: **Hell yeah!**
5. Be cool (yes, you can be cool past nineteen; it's not easy, but it's possible): **Um, probably not**
6. Yes, it is: **No, it's not**
7. Go somewhere: **I went to Wrightwood, so I'm sure that counts (oh, look it up)**
8. Do something (yes, I know this is vague, so it ought to be easy): **Yes, I did, indeed, do something**
9. Watch TV: **What's a morning without CNN?**
10. Watch more TV: **Sadly, yes**
11. Read the newspaper: **Yes, indeed**
12. Read more than one newspaper: **Always**
13. Be grouchy: **Oh, yes**
14. Be grouchy some more: **It's me, remember?**
15. Eat breakfast :**50/50**
16. Eat lunch: **Yep**
17. Eat dinner: **Yep**

18. Do not confuse any of the above meals with eating nachos in movie theatres (that just doesn't count—ever): **Um, well, I can't remember**

19. Kiss someone: **Oh, yes**

20. Kiss someone again: **Oh, yes again**

21. Hug someone: **Absolutely**

22. Be nice before noon (it shouldn't be that difficult if you try hard enough): **No, no, no**

23. Take a vacation: **No**

24. Pay for the vacation (yes, this is harder): **N/A**

25. Let someone else pay for the vacation (see time-share promotions): **N/A**

26. Take another breath: **I'm still here, so I must be doing okay with this one**

27. Smile at someone who doesn't expect it: **Who, me? Smile? I don't think so**

28. Frown at someone who doesn't expect it (unless they're big, have lots of tattoos, wear chains around their neck, and drive a Harley): **No problem here**

29. Make sure your health insurance is paid up (see number 28 above): **Always**

30. Pay the electric bill early: **Does on time count?**

31. Go somewhere that's not in a travel brochure: **Pretty much every trip I take**

32. Help someone find something: **I help my kids find something daily, so yes**

33. Stay in bed longer: **Nope**

34. Ignore the laundry: **Nope**

35. Ignore the kids: **Ignoring my son was easy—he ignores me, so no problem there. My daughter, on the other hand, would willingly climb on my head and twist my ears until I paid attention. So, this is 50/50**

36. Ignore your husband or wife, significant other, boyfriend, girlfriend, or me. Heck, just ignore someone—you'll feel better, and

after all, isn't that what it's all about? **Not a problem at all**

37. Ignore number 36 above: **No**

38. Demand peace worldwide: **Sure, but no one listens to me**

39. Work for peace worldwide: **Yes**

40. Strive for peace worldwide: **Yes**

41. Decide to do something you've never done before: **No**

42. Decide to actually have fun while doing number 41 above: **No, again**

43. Be nice to your boss: **Absolutely—I need my job**

44. Be nice to employees: **Yes**

45. Be nice to yourself: **Yes**

46. Just…be nice: **Well, I don't know if I'd go that far**

47. Decide to vote in the next election: **Always**

48. Be glad you're alive: **Yep**

49. Be glad someone else is alive: **Oh, yes, indeed**

50. Go back to school. There's probably no better time than right now to get more education, get a new education, or get retrained. Strive to keep yourself up to date and relevant for jobs and the job market: **I work at this daily**

51. Watch your electronic social identity: **I keep updating mine, so that counts**

52. See what's out there in this great big world and enjoy it: **Probably not this week—I'll work on it later**

So that's how I've done so far; how are you managing?

Water Shaded Words

The silence of writing
   is the sound of hope
Writing in a class
  an office
  at home
  in the car
  on a bench
  in a wrinkled bed
I carry the words with me
I sprinkle them around like holy water
    They're not
    I wish they were
Listening to the quiet of pen on paper or keys clicking
Listening to the ache of a mind struggling with listening
Will the words always be there?
Dear God, what if the words stop?
But words aren't everything
    There is dust following a Harley
    There is a boat cresting Pacific waves
A weekend in Tahoe
    requires no words beyond Mastercard
A morning driving across Wyoming
    offers more than I can ever write
Who needs words when there is the plea of an arched eyebrow?
Who needs words when there are
    late-night
    early morning
    passion-driven moments of lucidity?
Words can get in the way of an embrace
But today, we'll live with the words
Tomorrow, we'll live with the movement
And the door that connects them,
  the door that connects them,
I see reflected in a single bead of water running down your back

Chapter Five

The Asylum Called Home

The term "asylum" is not a negative one. Yes, it has certainly been used with negative implications associated with individuals dealing with various illnesses, but "asylum" means refuge, shelter, and sanctuary. That's what a home should be: your shelter, your refuge, your sanctuary. Okay, yes, sometimes homes do resemble the hospital in Ken Kesey's brilliant novel *One Flew Over the Cuckoo's Nest*. But that's not the point of a home; that's not the purpose of a home. And yet.

My home has, on occasion, resembled Kesey's descriptions and been a refuge at the same time. I suppose a good home is what you need it to be when you need it. I wonder how often that really occurs? It seems that it happened much more often when I was a child than now, but that may be because someone else was creating the home and not me. I've learned the hard way that it's not easy being the adult in the family…

Misery comes in many forms...especially in the form of "junk"

There I stood, surrounded by old, used junk, while strangers walked all over the newly mowed lawn looking for that one single bargain that would make getting up at six in the morning worthwhile.

There once was a time, not too long ago, when garage sales were few and far between and limited to your cousin's neighborhood and drive-in theater parking lots. Not anymore. Today, you can find garage sales anywhere and everywhere from Beverly Hills to Manhattan (gated communities run by snotty HOAs not included, no doubt). People realized that there was money in used furniture, appliances, clothes, toys, and whatever else they had taking up space in the garage. This didn't help the Salvation Army or other thrift stores, but money is money and people need all they can get. But still...

I have a love/hate relationship with garage sales. I don't mind going to them, especially if I'm shopping for rare and out-of-print books or music or other weird stuff you can occasionally find. You would be amazed at some of the things people sell for twenty-five cents, things like books printed in the 1850s. Go figure. But to actually be involved in a garage sale? With people pawing through *my* old stuff? I don't think so, thank you very much.

My involvement with Hell

Unfortunately, last week, a few assorted members of my family decided to get together and have a garage sale. The primary reason for this sale was so my nephew could sell a few of the hundreds of baseball cards he collects. He wanted to do this to buy more of them (and he did quite well, actually).

My sister sold a number of her dusty old Beanie Babies at a big enough profit to retire some of the National Debt, should she be so inclined. Apparently, certain Beanie Babies were rare and worth quite a lot at the time. Why either thing should be so, I can't begin to explain, but there you go.

Not wanting to be a drag on this sale of sales (okay, I really did, but my wife/mother/sister/nephew wouldn't let me), I happily and with a smile on my face volunteered to help. All right, all right, all right. No, I didn't volunteer; rather, I was dragged, kicking and screaming, into the thing. But nonetheless...

My physical involvement, as opposed to mental involvement, which consisted primarily of whining, initially consisted of borrowing my sister's minivan. Now, you need to understand something about her. She redefines the term "anal-retentively clean." *Really* redefines it, to a standard all her own. She has driven hotel housekeepers to leap from bridges simply discussing the wiping of a mirror.

Be careful of what you put in a car

I borrowed her overly large Toyota Sienna to move a few larger things that wouldn't fit in the car. Now, for a reason known only to the ages but certainly not to me, my nephew decided to sell an old non-low-flow toilet at this sale. A toilet which had been replaced. A toilet the plumber should have taken with him when he put in the new one but didn't. A toilet which should *never* have been put in the back of a spotless Toyota. Dear God, no.

Back to my nephew: He and I loaded this monstrosity into the van and took off for my parents' home, which, by default, had been chosen as the sale's location (they have the most traffic, which everyone hoped would generate more sales). Unfortunately, during the trip, the toilet fell over and broke. Don't ever get near an old toilet that breaks in the back of a Toyota Sienna. You would be amazed at the smell.

Nephew and I rolled the windows down, turned the air conditioner on full blast, and tried to keep our eyes from tearing. After a while, of course, we realized the absurdity of the entire episode and soon were driving down the road, heads out the windows, laughing so hard we were crying.

After we got the toilet out of the van, we became aware of the clean-up job that awaited us. We had to get this vehicle spotless enough to give back to my sister. Yes, we were worried. But with four gallons of Woolite Carpet Cleaner, a lot of deodorant, and the wearing out of three brushes scrubbing the carpet, we were able to return the van to my sister. I said thank you and goodbye rather quickly.

My nephew was the smart one: he stayed at his grandparents when I returned the van.

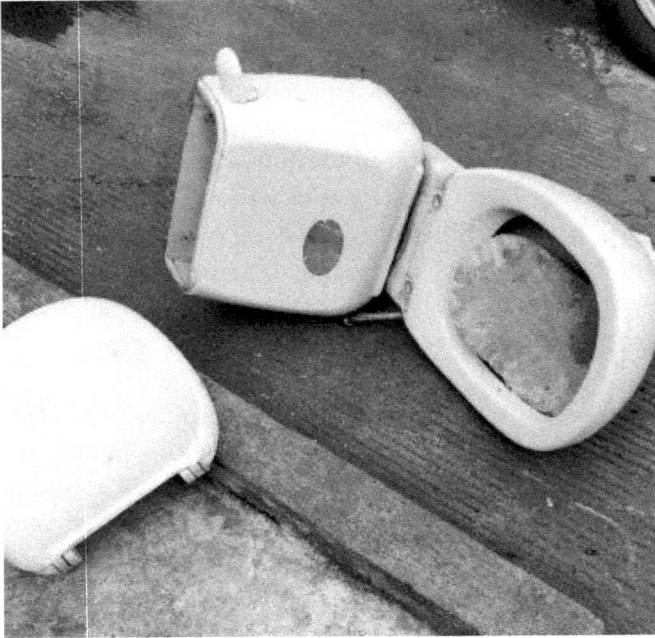

Some things just shouldn't be hauled inside a van.

Moving Day

Of all the things in all the world, moving is one of the things I dislike the most. Unfortunately, this is it, this is the week we move. I've been griping about this horrendous thing for a while now, but that won't do any good. Now it is simply a matter of just *doing* it. I hate it.

I cannot think of one person, with the probable exception of people who work in the moving industry, who like moving. Sure, there are some good things about it, like the fun and excitement of decorating a new home, seeing a whole new neighborhood, or simply the joy of starting a new chapter in one's life.

Well, yeah, yeah, yeah. Those things may be fine, but to do all of that, you must first *move*. And moving is pure misery.

We need more boxes!

In moving, one can never have enough boxes. I have made three trips to the company who is going to move us to buy more boxes. There are thirty of the miserable things sitting around my house right now, and it seems that this afternoon, I need to make another trip. We still do not have enough.

Personally, I don't think we ought to use boxes at all. We could just use the cars as two huge crates, throw everything in them, drive to the new house, and unload. Just make a few trips like that and, bingo, all done. But oh, no. My dear spouse has this problem about dishes getting broken, glasses shattering, and on and on. Go figure.

So now, on my way home, I stop and fill my car with boxes. And let us not forget the tape to seal them, or the Styrofoam popcorn to keep the contents from shattering.

I hate it, I hate it, I hate it

Yesterday, as I was in the garage packing and getting rid of stuff, I started sneezing. See, I have a problem with dust. I am highly allergic to the stuff, and yesterday, I was into the thick of it. It was like a mathematical equation: move something and sneeze half a dozen times. This went on all afternoon. I thought I was going to sneeze my brains out. After a while, however, I realized that would never happen; if I had any brains in the first place, I wouldn't have started this move.

At least, while packing the garage, I was able to get rid of a few things. I figured that anything I found that had been put in the garage when we first moved into the house, and had not been touched since, was good to throw away. Well, I, of course, was wrong. Naturally.

If I ran across anything of mine that I wanted to toss, fine. But if there were things that anyone in the family might have wanted to keep, it was hands off! How was I supposed to know what they wanted to hang on to? Besides, I found some pretty cool old stuff of mine that I might have a place for, too. But now the garage is just about finished; the kitchen cabinets have been emptied; the closets look awfully bare. The pictures and paintings have been taken down, tables have been cleared, and lamps have been placed in boxes. The rooms are starting to look bare.

Moving can be a very traumatic thing. The upheaval of family and things, not seeing familiar landmarks and learning new ones, and the stress of simply having to add new work to one's everyday chores can be very stressful. But it can also be enjoyable—just think of how much fun you can have getting rid of all those boxes and thousands of pieces of Styrofoam popcorn.

I wouldn't mind moving if I could use one of these.

Dishwasher Number Three

Ever hear a strange noise coming from your kitchen? And no, I don't mean teenagers raiding a refrigerator. I mean a legitimately weird noise. A sort of loud, whining grind that is most definitely not supposed to be in a kitchen. I heard one a few weeks ago and knew, from that noise, that I was going to be shopping soon. The appliance repair person confirmed it: I needed a new dishwasher. Not that he wouldn't have repaired the one I had—he most certainly would have—but he understood that even I'm not stupid enough to pay more for a repair than a purchase. Much more.

So, my daughter and I went looking for a new dishwasher. My son and I used to do this; now he just pulls out the "I have to be at work" card and he's free. But that's okay, I'll have the joy of showing another kid the thrill of appliance buying.

This will be the third dishwasher we've purchased and installed in the house since we moved in. Three. Three dishwashers. My pop would have had a stroke if he had ever had to put that many dishwashers in the same house. Then again, he was one of the original flippers, and we never stayed in a house long enough for a dishwasher to wear out.

Buying a dishwasher is easy, right? There are probably a hundred places in the area to get one, right? Just go to a store and have it delivered, right? In your dreams. And yes, that last sentence is dripping with sarcasm.

We went to appliance stores, we went to Lowe's, Best Buy, Home Depot, and who knows where else. We saw lots of dishwashers, but there was always a problem. The selection wasn't good, the prices were too high, the sales staff either didn't exist or didn't know anything about dishwashers. If I didn't want to talk with someone knowledgeable, I'd just buy it online. But that wasn't going to work this time. I needed that dishwasher soon…very soon. I didn't think Amazon Prime worked for dishwashers at the time.

What's up with that?

We were soon on the verge of buying one, even had the credit card pulled out, when I found out that it would be three to four days before it was delivered, and only then could we schedule the installation, which would be about two weeks later. Um, no.

We walked out of that nameless place a bit dejected. My daughter was tired (bored) with the whole thing, and I was just getting more impatient by the minute. As we drove into the parking lot at Home Depot, we saw a Long John Silver's and decided to have lunch. While munching on fish, chips, and hush puppies (I'm pretty sure that hush puppies are one of the original comfort foods, being made long before anyone ever thought of that term), I realized we were both tired and needed to get this quest over with.

On to Home Depot, where, of course, we bought a dishwasher. Selection? Price? I think exhaustion had more to do with it. But the selection was good, and someone actually talked to us once we tracked her down. In fifteen minutes, we had purchased a machine on sale, scheduled it for delivery and installation two days later, and were out the door. My daughter and I were ecstatic. She didn't show it, of course, being too cool for any silly display like that, but I knew.

In two days, it was delivered and installed, and life is so much better. What can I say? I'm spoiled; I've gotten used to germ-free dishes.

Appliances

The dishwasher naturally spurred me on to doing the ridiculous, like counting how many appliances we own. I don't really need to know that, of course. Knowing it won't change anything or make life easier. Naturally, that makes it a perfect thing for me to think about at 3 a.m

The total? Eight. Well, eight large ones plus, oh, I don't know, maybe twelve small kitchen appliances. Go figure. I've been buying appliances for quite a few years now, and it doesn't get any easier. Doesn't get any harder either, but you'd think that in the twenty-first century, it would somehow be simpler. Nope.

I hope it does get easier someday. I've run out of kids to go dishwasher shopping with. I'm pretty sure my daughter will run from the room if I ever say "appliance" around her. Besides, I'd hate to think that my daughter will be doing the same thing with her daughter that we did. Then again, we did have fun and, all things considered, Long John Silver's isn't a bad place to grab a quick lunch with your kid while looking for a dishwasher. I love me some hush puppies.

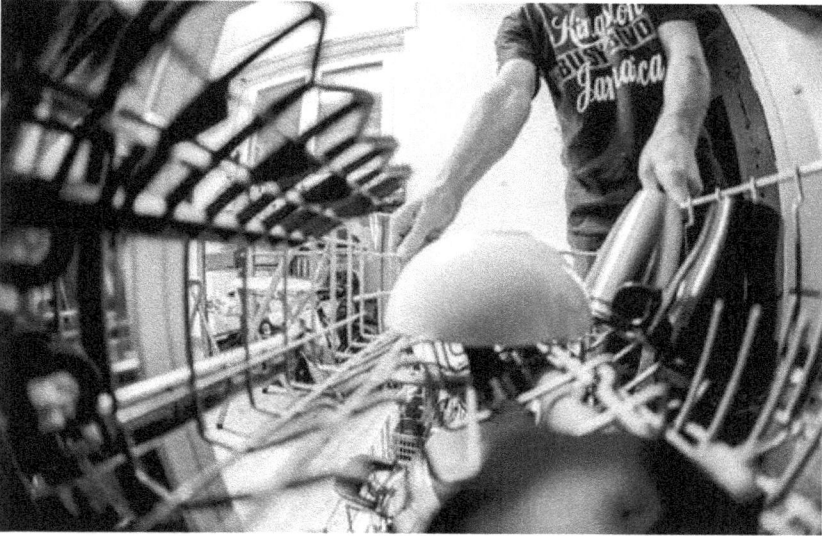

Okay World, Time Out

Up to this point, you've read about a few household problems. Now flash-forward a few more years, when the appliances seem to seek revenge...

You know how, most of the time, you just simply live your life and things slowly grind on? And then something happens. Recently, we needed to replace:

Oven

Refrigerator

Water heater

Are you kidding me? Are you freaking kidding me? An oven, refrigerator, and water heater? All in a couple of weeks? Why, yes—yes, indeed.

The oven

Let's start with the oven, a perfectly normal, built-in double oven. Worked great, and then one day, it didn't. I called an appliance repair place, they came out, did the usual diagnostics, and told me that it needed a new flinky-flabbule (at least, I think that's what he called it, but I could be wrong) module of some sort. I said okay, and innocently asked what the cost would be. I was told it would be close to $500. Let me see if I have this straight: put a $500 module into a twenty-year-old oven? Doesn't seem to make much sense, right? I started looking at new ovens, which, all things considered, shouldn't be that hard to do.

I was wrong.

Twenty years ago, ovens were smaller than they are now, and to buy a "normal" oven now, I'd need to rebuild the cabinet it goes in. No, thank you. So, I kept looking and found one that would fit. It looked okay, I bought it, and it was installed. Only then did I realize that, while the overall dimensions were okay, the *interior* dimensions were ridiculously small, and now I have an oven that looks normal on the outside but has much smaller than normal useable space.

But we're stuck with it for now.

The refrigerator

Then we needed a new refrigerator. The ice maker in our old one was leaking, the inside of the door had a crack, and it was nineteen years old (where did those years go??). It still worked okay, but the cost of the ice maker in a nineteen-year-old fridge, and an interior door panel that isn't made anymore, meant that getting a new one was the operative plan.

We searched, searched, and yeah, searched some more. Finally found one at Best Buy. Stainless steel, fingerprint-proof (HA!), and big enough to run a restaurant from—and it was on sale. Not inexpensive, you understand, just on sale.

Sale, right. My first two cars were a (very used) Renault and a (very used) Hillman Minx. The cost of the fridge was more than those two cars combined (the fridge does seem bigger than that old Renault, come to think of it), but I just have one vote in the family, and guess what? I lost.

The fridge was delivered and installed on a bright Monday morning. It fit. Not by much, but it did. And the interior was as large as it was supposed to be—it wasn't a scam like the oven (okay, I'm a little bit bitter over that oven).

Another fridge point: you can buy a refrigerator, but if you need hoses for it—and you do—you also need to buy those (and an install kit). Why doesn't the fridge come with hoses? Because then the cost would reflect reality. What manufacturer wants that when they need to sell refrigerators at the lowest price point possible?

Why not use the old hoses? Because they're twenty years old—haven't you been listening? And yes, I probably would have used the old ones but city codes, blah, blah, blah.

Preparation time

In getting ready for the fridge to be delivered, I go into the garage to turn off the water to the ice maker (and install a new filter at the same time, 'cause I'm nothing if not efficient) and find out the water heater is leaking. And, apparently, has been for a while. Oh joy, the day just got a whole lot more exciting.

The water heater

I start searching for water heaters. The vast majority are sold by Home Depot and Lowe's, and they won't even come out to measure without a credit card number. Problem is, I'm skittish about giving my numbers over the phone unless tied to a purchase (and don't much like it then, either). We spent hours not too long ago cleaning up an ID and credit card theft, and I really don't want to go through that again. Seriously, I do not *ever* want to do that again.

I blew off Home Depot and some other place I can't remember and started looking all over again for the elusive (who knew?) water heater.

Luckily, I knew a guy who knew a guy who came over (on a Sunday), looked at it, and said what we already knew. So, he and I jumped in his van and headed to, where else, Home Depot. We bought the water heater (plus install kit, hoses, and lines 'cause, just like the fridge, you have to) and a new stand (because it needed one), and he installed it all. And he installed it quickly, efficiently, and at less cost than Home Depot. And I didn't have to give him a credit card number to come by the house.

Sunday night

After a couple more trips to Home Depot and sending the kid to KFC because no way was any cooking going on during all of this, we managed to get everything accomplished. We had:

A normal-looking oven that's tiny inside (I hate that company)

A new refrigerator that cost more than my first two cars and is just about as big as the Renault (But, man, is this sucker gorgeous. My daughter fell in love with it. That's a bit weird, but who am I to say anything? She's taking cooking classes and may put this to really good use—at least, that's my hope.)

A water heater that holds water
A filter that filters without leaking
An old refrigerator to get rid of (Craigslist!)

Yes, I realize that, in the grand scheme of things, those problems were not exactly life-crushing ones. Annoying? Yes. Expensive? Yes. Time-consuming? Oh, heck yes. But some things in life, you just have to do.

Sometimes, ya just gotta take a break from appliances.

The Errors of Our Ways

Excuse me? Billions upon billions of mistakes are made every day? How can that possibly be? Those are fair questions, even if I did just make up the numbers.

But do the math. There are billions of people on earth of the age and with the capability of making decisions. All those people are going to make at least a few decisions each and every day (oh, just Google it). Of all those decisions, at least one will be a mistake.

Now, this doesn't mean that all these people are making huge, life-altering mistakes every day. But it does mean that a mistake of some kind will be made. Think about it, have you ever dialed a wrong number? Stepped incorrectly and fallen down? Made a wrong turn? Picked up the wrong thing when you were reaching for something? Made a mistake with your spouse, children, boss, family, and friends?

Ever got off at the wrong exit? Bought the wrong color or size of clothing? Thought it was a different date? Picked out the wrong socks? Bumped into a doorway or something else harder than your head? Ever eaten too much? Ever taken a wrong turn? Married the wrong person?

Well, you get the idea. We all make mistakes every day. And when you multiply that by the world's population, you get a staggering number of mistakes being made daily. This might not be so bad, of course, except what does it cost?

The cost of mistakes

How much does a mistake cost the planet? It depends, of course, on the size and kind of mistake. But mistakes involving money, with all the people who handle money every day, are obviously a huge number. Is it a billion dollars a day? Easily. A million hours of wasted time fixing those problems? Probably. How many jobs do the mistakes cost? How many people are made angry? How many customers are lost? How many lives are lost because of a "simple mistake"? And this is happening daily, around the world.

Buying from catalogs

More and more people buy from catalogs and online sites every day. Billions of dollars are spent now on mail order (electronic or snail) than ever before. And for all the ordering going on, it amazes me that there are not more mistakes than there are. Of everything I order, the mistakes are probably less than 2 percent.

On the other hand, can you imagine how many 2 percent of all the orders equals? Imagine 2 percent of every order from everywhere being wrong. That's a crazy-big number.

What should we do to stop the explosion of errors? Heck, I don't know. That's up to the individuals, businesses, institutions, and governments making them. All the rest of us can do is try to make fewer mistakes of our own and dodge the bullet when it comes at us in the form of an error. Over and over and over…

The Lost and Regifted

I began thinking about all the things in the back of our cabinets the other day when I started looking for something. See, had I thought about it, I would have done the smart, rational thing and simply asked my wife where it was. She knows where everything is—I don't know how she knows it, but she does. She says all women have this ability, and it comes from their *Uterine Tracking Device*. Men, not having a Uterine Tracking Device, will never know where anything is except those things located in the garage (the Uterine Tracking Device doesn't work in the garage, and men just seem to be able to find tools and car parts anyway).

But no, I was in a hurry and simply started opening cabinet doors and moving things around. This was a big mistake, a very big mistake. As I'm pawing through pots, pans, dishes, and things that I have no idea about, I start asking myself, "What all do we have in these cabinets?"

The list

Here is a partial list of the things that are generally stored in the backs of cabinets. Some of these are in my cabinets; some are in the backs of friends' and relatives' cabinets. The main thing is, some of these things are in all our cabinets.

The fondue set you received for a wedding gift

The second crockpot—the one you don't use because you like your other one better

The new wok

The old wok you use occasionally

The last frying pan from a set you received twenty-two years ago

The second fondue set you received as a wedding gift

The automatic lemonade maker

The ice-cream maker

The third fondue set you received as a wedding gift

The electric skillet

The snow-cone maker

The angel food cake pan

Two glass pots from a very large set of glass pots that were supposed to be unbreakable

Three rusted cookie sheets

An old woven chip and dip set

An old ceramic chip and dip set

Another old ceramic chip and dip set

A gummed-up muffin pan

A doughnut maker

An electric cookie press

A nutshell crusher

A popcorn maker

Weird "home and kitchen" gifts from last twenty-eight various and sundry celebrations

One thing to think about: if you don't use it, it's probably a good bet no one else will either, so why get it for them?

A nutcracker

Another nutcracker

A third nutcracker

A hot-air popcorn maker (thank God it's not another nutcracker!)

A small case of Sterno cans for the fondue sets

What? Another fondue set? Who makes these things, and does anyone ever use them besides someone on their third date making a dinner for a "special someone" they're trying to impress?

So, there you have just a partial list of some of the things lurking in the back of kitchen cabinets. What, right now, do you have in the back of your cabinets? And what things are you going to put back there today that you just received from someone?

Well, now is the time to start planning. Save those gifts you received and don't use. Why? Re-gift time, baby! Re-gift time is coming up, and with the economy in the shape it's in, well, this year will probably be the Year of the Re-Gift. Enjoy the fondue set.

Too Much Goin' On

My wife is a highly intelligent woman. The kids are bright and there's hope for them. But me? I'm afraid there's no hope for me at all. I'm not a stupid person—it just seems that way because of all the home-improvement things that I schedule too closely together. Our house has been an absolute unqualified disastrous mess for the past week, and it's not getting better any time soon.

We've lived in our house long enough that the interior needs some cosmetic work. The walls need paint, the floors need flooring, and… well, you get the idea. Plus, we wanted to lighten it up a bit, too much dark wood. It was time. But the simple fact of it being "that time" in no way means that it's actually going to get accomplished with any ease in the allotted period.

When you find yourself in this sort of situation, and you don't paint the house yourself, you need to find painters (*always* find painters—it will save your marriage and sanity). After you find a few painters, you must then get bids from them. You ultimately decide on a painter and work out the details: date and time to start, color and types of paints, what things we need to remove from the room vs. the things they will move.

Speaking of choosing a paint color, Glidden offers more than a thousand different colors. And that's just Glidden. Factor in colors from Home Depot, Sherwin-Williams, Benjamin Moore, Valspar, Behr, Pittsburgh Paints, Dutch Boy Paint, Dunn-Edwards, and—well, I could go on, but why, right? Suffice to say, there are a whole lotta paint choices. And you must choose one (or more). Hopefully, you and your spouse can agree on the colors quickly and easily (ha, ha, HA). I don't want to get into how many discussions my wife and I had about paint colors.

Paint day arrived

We did all the necessary things to prep for the painting, and on a bright, sunny Monday at 8 a.m., the painters arrived. We got along great from the start; they're professionals who treated my house like their own. I am so good with that. They started in and the changes looked remarkable from the start. What a difference paint makes.

My father was a painter before he went into the military in WWII and was one again for a few years when he mustered out. Back in those days, all painting was done by brush, and he told me stories of the fights the union made to keep it that way. He thought it was crazy—he loved rollers and, later, sprayers.

We're having the living room, dining room, and family rooms painted. The plan was for it to be finished by the end of the week because on Thursday, flooring is being delivered so it can become acclimated to the house (acclimate flooring? Heck, I'm not acclimated to the place yet). Early next week, that starts being installed.

Anyone who has ever owned property and had "projects" to do sees the insanity, right? Well, I did too but chose to ignore it because, well, the optimist in me reared his ugly head. I wish he would just shut up sometimes.

Any excuse to avoid work

Just above where the ceilings and walls are being painted, I'm working: my office is up there and I'm attempting to write a column, complete a new edition of *Disabled Literature*, work on chapters I'm contributing to a book with a fall deadline, and finish one more book due by the end of summer (mostly written—now working on the final 10 percent—the really difficult part. Yeah, yeah, I know, whine, whine).

The painters listen to good music, although most of it deadens anyway by the time it gets upstairs; all I get are fragments, which then have me wondering about the name of a song. Yes, I could use headphones to deaden the sound, but I don't; never really got used to them while I write. Besides, I like the music.

While all that's going on, I'm still taking my mother to her doctor's appointments and being with her at the hospital as needed; chauffeuring a daughter to and from school; remembering to let the dogs out and remembering to let them back in, blah, blah, blah. Of course, my wife helps, but she's teaching full time so she misses much of it (I wouldn't trade places—she teaches high school. No, thanks).

Our son helps and manages to hang out at home when I'm out running errands. And the beat goes on.

Of course, as with any project, there will probably be changes. In our case, those changes come daily, and more than one at a time. Luckily, our painter can swing with the changes we make without too many headaches. We see a needed change, ask him if it's possible and how much it'll cost. He says yes and gives us a good price, and the changes get made. But I think he's starting to avoid me.

Why Did I Ever Agree to New Bathroom Cabinets?

Let's face it, cabinets can get pretty funky looking after a few years. Let a dozen or so years slip by and, well, they simply need help. Too many scratches, too may fingerprints, too many spills wiped off…well, you get the idea.

We had a bathroom that needed help. The kind of help that only a power-sander, paint-stripper, new paint brushes, and paint can help. Oh, and new sink and shower faucets, new hardware, new blinds, and all the other things that are required for a job like this.

My son and I did it. Yep, we put on the old clothes, took the bathroom more-or-less apart, and started in. We painted walls, re-finished cabinets, exchanged faucets and towel racks, and screwed on new electric switch plates. Unfortunately, we're not stopping there. Next, we're tackling another bathroom because we're suckers for punishment.

The madness never stops

A few years ago, some of our doors needed help (replacement, to be more precise). In my entire life, I've never actually said those words before—at least, not in the same sentence—but I've grown up and I need doors. Well, I don't *need* doors, I need to *replace* doors. And the doors I need to replace are front doors. Excuse me, *entry doors*.

Replacing doors is not an easy thing to do. It should be easy, you'd think it would be easy, but no. It's not easy. At least, it's not easy when you're replacing a front door. Good grief—the choices are mind-boggling. Do I want wood or fiberglass? Stained or painted? What kind of hardware? What kind of windows if, indeed, I want windows in it? Do I want pre-hung or pre-finished?

I started out at Home Depot, but apparently, the three questions I had at the time went over their limit. We just never could connect. Then I went to Lowe's; very helpful people there, but they just didn't have something close enough to what I wanted—I wanted pre-finished, go figure. Next was Builders Emporium, and that was going pretty well—even got the opening measured—but getting someone to return a call was difficult, and I figured that if they couldn't do that, how well could they install a door? Now I'm headed to three "door" stores; my fingers are crossed. I think why I'm having a problem is that I'm making it too easy for them. I want to:

1. Pick out a door
2. Pick out the glass
3. Pick out the finish
4. Confirm the measurements
5. Order and pay
6. Let them install the thing

I've found out that it's just not that easy. They say it is, but they lie. They say they will call me back with prices, but they don't. They say that someone will be over to give me a reasonable bid to install. Not anywhere close to reasonable. I'm about to give up, and that's just to get a door. Believe me, it can get much worse.

Moving on

I'm willing to bet that you have a kitchen. And I'm willing to bet that, in this kitchen, you have cabinets. And I'm also willing to bet that in these cabinets, way in the back, there are things that haven't seen the light of day since you shoved them there when you moved in.

I started thinking about all the things in the back of our cabinets the other day when, without thinking, I started looking for something. See, had I thought about it, I would have done the smart, rational thing and simply put on shoes, gotten in the car, driven to a store, parked, found the item in the store, stood in line and paid, gotten back in the car, driven home, and finished. That would have been quicker than what I actually did.

I simply started opening cabinet doors and moving things around. This was a big mistake, a very big mistake. As I'm pawing through pots, pans, dishes, and things that I have no idea what they are, I start asking myself what we have in these cabinets.

Unload, put away, forget

When we moved into our house, we did the normal thing: we unpacked boxes and put everything away. We tried, as we were putting these things away, to place the stuff intelligently. You know, put the things you use the most at levels and in areas where you can access them easily. Coffee mugs and everyday glasses go low; wine glasses go higher. Well, actually, that's a bad example, but you get the idea. I want a wine glass within very easy reach.

That's how it all starts out. And then, over time, things get arranged again and rearranged until you have some sort of order worked out that only your family knows. No one else might recognize this order, but it works for you, so what the heck. And, gradually, the things you use the least get pushed farther and farther away. Finally, all that stuff is out of sight and reach and you never think about it again.

You never think about it again, that is, until some sort of fool's errand sends you searching through the cabinets for something when you should have asked your wife or husband for it in the first place. And then you come face to face with all the wonderful things you own and don't use—many of which you absolutely had to have because when you saw it on late-night TV, it looked so good and would save you so much time, energy, and money. Really want to save time, energy, and money? Go to bed.

And now you are staring at all those things and wondering just what on earth is back there, how long has it been there, does anyone in the family even know it's there, and what should we do with it now that it's come to light? Finally, you wonder if there is any way to prevent this from happening in the future.

The solution

Ha. There is no solution. Bathrooms wear out. Kitchens wear out. Doors wear out (okay, and people wear out, but let's not go there), and cabinets fill up. Find a wine glass and…deal with it.

CHAPTER SIX

An Absurd Existence

I suppose all existence is absurd when you think about it (something I caution against). One of the definitions of absurd is *illogical*, and could anything be more illogical than life? I mean, seriously, look around you. Poodles? That guy down the street? Your ex-husband, – wife, – boyfriend, – girlfriend, – partner, – pal, or the weird cat your neighbor used to keep?

How could anything be more illogical than the lives we lead? It doesn't matter who you are or what you do or how much you know. Bits and pieces (or maybe huge slabs) of your life are illogical. But that's beside the point anyway, because the pieces in this section have nothing to do with actually discussing anything illogical. Rather, they simply show by example out how absurd most of our existences happen to be.

Yes, I know that most of us certainly don't need examples of absurd existences. We live our own version of that existence. But it might be therapeutic to know that your absurdities aren't as bad as that person standing in front of you at 31 Flavors during a January blizzard.

A Billion Strands, a Billion Dollars

What is it with hair? We spend billions of dollars every year coloring, straightening, perming, weaving, cutting, lengthening, plugging, and on and on.

We have hair transplants, we buy pills to take, lotions to rub on, wigs and hairpieces to wear, and that isn't the tip of the iceberg, so to speak.

For whatever reason, a great deal of our identity is somewhat made up of our hair. Or, at least, our personal identity.

What's got me started on this today? I'm taking my daughter for a haircut. She wants a razor design underneath the hair, but Mom and I aren't really going for it. That's not to say I didn't let mine grow long in school or cut it in strange cuts, but this isn't about me; it's my daughter, and now I'm the parent. So there.

Cut, perm, or both?

There are at least nine billion different ways to cut hair. And that's just a conservative estimate. There may be a gazillion more, but after a while, counting becomes a bit tiring. Plus, I've never been good at math, and after a few dozen, who cares anyway?

With all those different ways to style hair, how does one choose the right one? As far as I can determine, there are just a few acceptable ways to pick the right "look." They are:

1. Browse through the hundreds of old and somewhat newer style magazines in the salon (although new is better than old, unless you want to end up looking like your best friend's father or mother—remember that person?). Like I said, keep the style magazine new.

2. Take in a picture of your favorite singer or television star. You won't end up looking like that, but self-deception always helps in fashion, grooming, and relationships (never mind that last one—I'm sure s/he really does love/like/tolerate you).

3. Offer a vague description to the stylist of how you want it to look as you stare at him/her in the mirror. It's likely neither of you

will end up happy with the style, but at least you didn't have to cut out pictures from magazines.

4. Let the stylist choose (they like this because they can be artistic, and they don't have to worry about creating your particular dream. On the other hand, they hate this because then the result is all on them).

5. Go with what you've always had. This is the easiest, the simplest, the most stress free. It can also be the least imaginative, most behind the times, dullest cut there is, but at least no thought was involved (and we all like that from time to time).

So, after you have the style chosen, there is still color (if you want to change it, highlight it, or cover the gray or purple). Not everyone does color their hair, of course, but most at least think about it at some point, and enough do to make it a billion-dollar industry.

Cutting and coloring may be fine, but what if you don't have enough?

If you think that you've been losing your hair, you have been. If you think that you're going bald, you are. All people lose hair as they age— no big deal. That is, unless you've been losing it prematurely (for most guys, prematurely means before eighty years old). And if you've been losing hair, or indeed have lost every last strand of it, you've been thinking about ways to get it back, or at least cover up the loss. Now it's time for the creams, the pills, the hairpieces, the wigs.

Yes, there are some medicines that can work, at least some of the time, for some people. Yes, it's expensive. But for hair? Many men will gladly pay the price.

But what if the drug won't work for you? There is still the tried and true toupee, the hairpiece, the wig. You can purchase some hairpieces for as low as twenty dollars (yes, of course, they look it), and the price can go to the thousands (and can actually look pretty good. We can still spot them, of course, but with the good ones, we don't laugh quite as loudly when you leave. It's nothing personal—we're just bored).

Some hairpieces can appear fairly lifelike. But it depends on the hair, the designer, the color, and how that color matches and blends with your own. Here's a clue, gentleman: if you are over forty (and especially over sixty) *add gray to the wig*. Natural hair on men after their fifties and even earlier generally has some gray in it. Natural hair is not always the same shade of one dark color.

Here are another couple of things about hair. If your eyebrows are dark brown, don't color your hair platinum blonde. If your hair is red, don't color it platinum blonde. Dark brown or red eyebrows underneath bright blonde hair can look absurd. So do blonde eyebrows underneath dark hair. Remember, match the hair to the eyebrows unless you're going for that particular look…and you're under thirty.

Men, if the color of the hair on your chest, arms, legs, and beard is gray, or partially gray, don't have solid black or brown hair. This screams insecurity. Ever see a guy at the beach and whatever hair he has on his body is gray and the hair on his head is solid black? Yes, the women on the beach are laughing.

If you are going to have hair transplants, find the best doctor on the planet. Nothing looks more absurd than poorly done hair transplants. Well-done transplants can, indeed, look fairly natural (note that the operative words there are "well done." The job needs to be *well done*—as in excellent, as in expensive and worth every penny, as in artistic, as in you want to kiss the mirror every time you walk by one). Got it? You want an excellent doctor, a brilliant doctor, a genius of a doctor. Remember, people see your head first. The idea is to never give them a reason to laugh. Never, never, never. Ever.

Finally, if you're tired of trying everything, and you just want to be done with it, go for the bald look. Many women have mentioned that they think it's sexy. But if you do go for that look, please remember to shave it every day. Razor burn from stubble on the top of the head is not cool.

A friend of mine finally did the bald look. He's happy with it. Yes, he does say that shaving takes a bit longer every day, but when comparing that to coloring, toupees, weird styles, and all the money he's spent over the past thirty years (he started going bald in his teens), he says he couldn't be happier. And apparently, some women think he looks sexier. If he had known that thirty years ago, he could have bought a Lamborghini with the money he would have saved.

Contrary to Popular Belief

Have you ever wondered where we learned all the weird things we know? I'm not talking about intellectual things or the knowledge one gets from school. I'm speaking of all the strange or bizarre stuff we hear. You know, that stuff from families and weird friends.

For instance, there is the number thirteen. It's supposed to be bad luck. What about walking under a ladder? That also brings bad luck. There are so many things in life that bring both good and bad luck that it's almost impossible to keep up with them all.

Well, forget about it. Those things you've heard are just so much nonsense. They're old, outdated, outmoded. We need some new bad luck signs, signs that have been created for life in the twenty-first century. And who better to give you those new bad luck signs than me? Read on and learn to watch out for all of the new things that can lead to the worst luck imaginable.

New bad luck signs:

1. A flat tire (what, you thought this would be good?)
2. Burned dinner
3. Green swimming pool water
4. Drooling dogs about to jump on your lap
5. Cats (any color)
6. A big green bug, headed for your windshield
7. Bees swarming outside your house
8. Bees swarming anywhere near you
9. Bats headed for your head
10. The sound of a rattlesnake as you enter your bathroom late at night
11. The sound of a rattlesnake anywhere near you
12. The screeching of car tires behind you as you jog
13. The sound of, "Honey, could you…" (fill in the blank yourself)
14. The words "trust me"

15. The sound of your doorbell when you saw a salesperson at the house next door a few minutes earlier

16. The fifteenth time you hear, "Daddy, I want..." while in the toy section

17. The sentence, "Could I interest you in..." (another fill-in-the-blank-yourself)

18. Anyone who says, "The repair will only cost..." (and still one more fill-in-the-blank-yourself)

19. The Health Department sign on the outside of a restaurant with a big letter B on it

20. It's three in the morning, you're on the freeway headed for Phoenix, and you glance at the instrument panel: the fuel gauge reads, "Empty"

21. A big puddle of oil on your garage floor

22. A big puddle of oil anywhere

23. A headache

24. A headache (Oh please, you thought a headache was good luck? I don't think so. Okay, maybe if you were going to work and a headache made you stop at the drugstore for Tylenol, and because of that, you missed a huge traffic accident that you would have got caught in. But other than something like that, a headache is definitely bad luck.)

25. Answering the phone and the person on the other end mispronounces your name. Ninety-nine percent of the time when that happens, it's a telephone solicitation thing. Someone wants to sell you something, wants you to donate something, someone wants something. This is never good luck...well, unless it's a police officer or firefighter selling tickets to their annual ball. That's a good thing.

26. A knock on the front door by a young man wearing a tie

27. Waking up in the morning after a horrible storm and the carpet is soaked

28. Realizing you're out of Kaopectate when you really, *really* need it

29. You notice that the air conditioner is blowing hot air—never a good sign

The list goes on practically forever, of course, but if I wrote that much, I'd probably get carpel tunnel syndrome, so why tempt luck, ya know?

What to Do When a Really, Really Big Disaster Hits (and you know it will if you live anywhere)

Most people who live in hurricane areas pretty much know what to do should a large hurricane occur. In Florida, they have been receiving essentially the same instructions since gators were found.

People who live in California have been getting the usual (I say "usual" because if you've been there anytime at all, you've had it drilled into your head) stuff about protecting themselves in the event of an earthquake.

Those hardy souls who live in the Midwest—primarily tornado alley—all know what to do when they see a tornado warning or hear the roar of a tornado barreling down on them.

In the north and northeast, there can be huge snow and ice storms—making everything too slick to walk or drive on or burying whole towns in multiple feet of snow.

In other words, pretty much wherever you live, there is a very good chance of a natural disaster occurring at some point or other. And today, all we're concerned with are natural disasters. The human-caused disasters would take more pages than I have the desire to write.

What do you do when disaster hits? You know the routine (depending on the type of disaster it is, of course): get away from windows, turn off the gas, stop cooking, etc., etc., etc. Well, big deal. That may appear, on first glance, to be good advice and all, but think about it for a minute. Will doing those things really save you? Okay, maybe. But hey, there are even better ways to protect you and your loved ones, plus those things you hold dear. I have listed a few of those better ways below.

Things to do when the ground begins to shake, the trees begin to bend, the mobile homes begin to fly, and the rain, snow, and ice come in sheets and floods

1. Run. What are you doing just standing around while the earth is moving?
2. Scream. The reason for this should be obvious enough, although it might be hard to be heard, depending on the noise of the disaster.

3. Cry—if the screaming does not help.

4. Kick yourself for not buying that hurricane/earthquake/tornado insurance, even if it was way too expensive and there was a good deal on a new Explorer.

5. Plan on getting serious about that move to Australia.

6. Yes, Australia. How many disasters do you actually hear about happening in Australia?

7. Make sure the neighbors are okay (you may still need to borrow their rowboat if the hurricane didn't destroy your driveway).

8. Try to remember where you left the kids.

9. Try to remember where your husband/wife might be, and is this the day they're bringing home groceries?

10. Or were you supposed to do the grocery shopping earlier and now, since you did not, will the family have to suffer through the disaster *and* hunger?

11. Run and close the doors; hopefully, the dog and/or cat will be locked outside (but not the kids—those, you want inside).

12. Tell your spouse you have no idea how the dog/cat got out, the disaster must have scared it (eventually, they might believe it, and that's all you care about).

13. Of course you will look for the dog/cat, just as soon as you get the Explorer out from under the garage roof (if the garage and Explorer are both okay, you will have to come up with another excuse—good luck).

14. Make sure the water is still running. If not, make absolutely certain that no one goes in the pool—you may need it for drinking, and you know how little kids are when swimming; they hate to leave the action to go to the bathroom.

15. Immediately check your stash of soft drinks.

16. Immediately check your stash of chips.

17. Immediately check your stash of movies (the internet might be out—think ahead. If the electricity is out, well, you're on your own. You might have to talk to each other. Good luck with that).

18. If the electricity is still on, power on the screens, grab your chips and drinks, and forget about the whole thing.

19. Ignore the dog or cat scratching at the door to get in, but in order to not seem as cruel as you really want to be, and probably

have every right to be in a disaster (never mind what the Red Cross says about being a good neighbor), give them any leftover guacamole, no matter how brown. It's not your fault if pets don't like it—at least you tried.

20. If you make it through, drag out that bottle of champagne left over from your wedding and have a drink. Make a toast to the fact that you survived another disaster. And then start making those plans for the move to Australia (number five above—remember?) because you never want this to happen again. Although, to be honest, you may have to wait awhile if property values have taken a nosedive.

Attention: The above column is only a joke—do not take it seriously. I do not want to be hearing from a large group of attorneys, should you actually do any of these things during a hurricane, tornado, earthquake, or any other disaster. For disaster information that is accurate, see the Red Cross, or any one of the myriad other city, county, and state agencies set up to deal with disasters. I take no responsibility for anything, and I do mean anything, which may happen to you or your loved ones for following any so-called advice appearing here. Besides, why would you believe anything I wrote, anyway? Sheesh.

10:02 a.m. to 10:07 a.m.: Five Minutes in the Life of an Email Account

Like all of us, I get an overabundant amount of emails. Some of it is work related, some of it is from friends, some of it is business and shopping notices, and some (most) of it is spam. My spam filter does a pretty god job with that stuff, but everything else usually gets through.

The other day, I was looking at my mailbox and was a bit overwhelmed by it all. And then I started copying and pasting. Below are five minutes from my inbox (with the pictures and most of the text removed).

Five minutes in the life of a mailbox

10:02 a.m.: Thanks for all the help. I sent it today. I got a message saying they were out of the office. I don't know what to do now it's out. I hope I get this!

10:02 a.m.: How about garlic French bread? Or suggest some other bread to go with soup.

10:02 a.m.: Please take a moment to complete a short survey about your recent experience at _____ Insurance Company. We expect that this survey will only take approximately 3 minutes to complete (they lie).

10:03 a.m.: A good thing you asked! I have 2 files on this disk. One is the foreword/table of contents/chapter 1, which goes up to page 47. The other file is ... unreadable.

10:03 a.m.: We have a little bit of a road trip this weekend playing our game. Game is at 9:30 am, and we are asking everyone to get there about 1 hour before game time to make sure everyone is available for warm-ups (and finds the place).

10:03 a.m.: The Centers for Disease Control have issued a medical alert about a highly contagious, potentially dangerous virus that is transmitted orally, by hand, and even electronically. This virus is called Weary Overload Recreational Killer (WORK).

10:03 a.m.: Can I get back to you? I have just come down with a cold and don't want to spread it around (especially to 2 kids).

10:03 a.m.: Your Expressway FasTrak® Account Statement is now ready to view online.

10:03 a.m.: To see more details and confirm this invitation, follow the link below.

10:03 a.m.: To receive your free STANDARD shipping discount on your order of $85** or more you must enter WWFREE in the Promotion Code box during checkout. This offer is only available on items shipped to a single address within the contiguous United States. Upgraded shipping options may be available at an additional cost and select items may incur Extra Shipping charges due to their weight or size. Most orders sent via Standard shipping will arrive within 3 – 5 business days.

10:04 a.m.: This meeting reminder was sent out a few weeks ago, but a few people were not sure they received it. Your calendar in Outlook has the usual meeting as 12 to 1:00pm meeting. This one meeting has an expanded time due to the learning assessment working session which we need to get done. More details are in the email below.

10:04 a.m.: Hi, I was wondering if you would be willing to donate around $5 for a gift for the coaches for the end of year party (no, I don't know what that will be yet). I wanted to order shirts for the coaches with COACH on the back. The long-sleeved T-shirt runs about $24 plus shipping.

10:05 a.m.: Your membership to AmericanGreetings.com is about to expire either because you have chosen not to automatically renew your membership, or your payment information is no longer valid.

10:05 a.m.: The good news is we've made it easy for you to continue your membership benefits! Just choose one of the following options based on your preference.

10:05 a.m.: Thanks to your generosity we have an abundance of Halloween candy left over from the Fall Festival! The PTA is selling this candy at a discount.

$1 for a standard size bag

$3 for a large bag

$5 for an XL bag

The candy can be found in the office workroom. Choose your size of bag and leave your money in the container.

10:06 a.m.: Hi everyone, here is the cost for the team party if we want to have it at Airtime.

$13 per player

$11 per sibling

$3.50 per adult

10:06 a.m.: Thank you for your recent purchases from Amazon. com. We invite you to submit reviews for the products you purchased or share an image that would benefit other customers. Your input will help customers choose the best products on Amazon.com. It's easy to submit a review—just click the Review this product button next to the product.

10:06 a.m.: Please note that all the items selected for backup (from your backup set) have already been backed up and the files have not changed since your last backup.

10:07 a.m.: Free Shipping offer good only on merchandise orders of $49 or more delivered within the 48 contiguous United States (excludes Alaska, Hawaii & Puerto Rico) by standard delivery to your home.

10:07 a.m.: Are you sure you want to permanently delete all the items and subfolders in the "Deleted Items" folder?

10:07 a.m.: YES

Tell me I don't have a life…

Tea, a laptop, and email. An explosion just waiting to happen.

Hit the Road! Leaving Your Significant Other, New Millennium Style

A few years (decades?) ago, Paul Simon released a song he wrote and sang called "50 Ways to Leave Your Lover." The song told how one could leave their lover, fifty different ways.

Now, jump to the current year. Does the song still hold? Oh, yeah. Are there new ways one can leave their significant other? Well, yes, there are some new ways to leave. And in my never-ending desire to assist, I have brought together some of those ways. I hope it helps…

New ways to leave: simply pick which one works best for you and then say it.

1. I have joined a new gym and you are not on the plan.
2. My Frequent Flyer Miles card does not have you on it.
3. I bought a new car; sorry, it is not family-size.
4. You didn't get an invitation to my birthday party? I wonder why…
5. Know the name of a good attorney? Want one?
6. Growing old is one thing, growing old with you is entirely another.
7. Yes, I am going on a Singles Cruise for my next vacation.
8. I need more closet space.
9. I need more kitchen space.
10. I need more living space.
11. I need more space.
12. Our retirement plans do not mesh.
13. I am a better person without you…oh, wait; I mean you are a better person without me. No, actually, I was right the first time.
14. My dog hates you.
15. My cat hates you.
16. My fish hate you.
17. I don't have a pet, but if I did, it would hate you.

18. My mother was right.

19. My mother was wrong.

20. You deserve better.

21. I deserve better.

22. We both deserve better.

23. No one deserves better, and I still hate you.

24. You like lousy music.

25. You burn through credit cards downloading the wrong music. How do I know it's wrong? My great-aunt dances around the kitchen listening to it, wearing only socks and a parka.

26. You like the wrong TV programs. For that matter, you like TV.

27. You refuse to watch *The Simpsons*.

28. You drink buttermilk and then want to kiss.

29. Your stock picks are lousy.

30. You do not work for a Fortune company.

31. You refuse to stop at Starbucks even though it's on the way.

32. You constantly stop at Starbucks.

33. You didn't want a new computer/cell phone/television.

34. You hate my friends

35. I hate your friends.

Best way to leave? Simply pack up and drive (or walk, hitchhike, run, skate, bike, surf, swim, fly...). But there were some good reasons for doing so. Simply pick which one works best for you and then say it or leave it on a note taped to the fridge. You could also just text it, but that might be considered slimy by some people. Then again, do you really care?

Not Exactly a Great Weekend

Went to Palm Springs not overly long ago to interview a writer, then had lunch with a few good friends and headed home. Had a bit of a drive ahead of me, but I was good with that—I like long drives.

I was headed to San Diego on Interstate 15 and I had just about gotten to Menifee, a little town between San Diego and Palm Springs, when my car decided it was tired of running. It simply quit at seventy miles an hour. I was in the fast lane. Won't that get your attention in a hurry!

I'm where?

I pulled to the side of the road, with Memorial Day traffic whizzing by me, and called AAA. I was about ninety miles away from San Diego, driving a Volvo (not many Volvo dealers thereabouts) on a Sunday afternoon—the day before a holiday.

AAA finally arrives and the driver of the tow truck informs me that he will tow me to the closest gas station. Now, even I can figure that this won't work. I called Volvo, who told me there was a dealership in San Bernardino. Called them, they would wait for me, and the tow-truck driver would go ahead and take me—for $107. Of course, I paid it.

I get the car to Volvo, but all the local car rental places have closed. The manager of the dealership would take me to a hotel—but then he decided to heck with it and stepped up and did the right thing. He gave me one of the dealer's demos and let me take off for San Diego—where I arrived, hungry, tired, and frustrated with the entire day. By now, you can imagine all the words I have been using.

By the way, did I mention that the dealer said he absolutely, positively needed the demo back Tuesday morning when they opened? No? Well, he did. So, come Tuesday morning, I was out the door at 5 a.m. And yes, there is a lot of traffic at that time anywhere near San Diego. A lot of traffic.

But I made it, I was at the dealer when it opened and signed the papers to let them do whatever it was that they needed to do to my car to get me on the way once again.

The dealer then took me to a car rental company so I could get a car;

at least that was covered by the warranty. So now it's at 10 a.m. and I've got a bit of time on my hands. What do I do? Ah, yes, the cousin.

I have a cousin who lives about twenty miles away from the dealer. I called, they invited me over, and I spent the day hanging out with them. Thank God for cousins.

After shooting the breeze with her and her husband, I arrived back at the dealer at 3 p.m., at which time my car was ready. They even washed it. I really like those people. Anyway, I retrieved my car—a few hundred dollars lighter (with a warranty!). Still, I am grateful for a good dealership, a good manager, and snack machines.

Shopping for a Wallet

So there I am, packing suitcases like mad to get ready for a trip. I get finished (mostly) and get ready to get the kids from school. As usual, I grab my keys, my glasses, and my wallet. That's when I noticed it: this wallet is falling apart. Really falling apart. So much so that it may not last another day. Great, one more thing to do. A miserable thing.

I not only hate shopping, I really hate shopping for wallets. It's hard to find one, they're displayed in far corners of the store, you can't find anyone to help you, and most of them are uncomfortable or downright ugly (the wallets, not the people helping you).

Nonetheless, I needed one, and so, I went shopping. Yes, of course, I can get one online. But wallets are personal, and I needed to make sure (of what, I'm not sure. Leave me alone). I actually find it easier to shop for a house or car than a wallet.

See, a wallet must do many things. It has to hold your driver's license, credit cards, insurance cards, business cards, club cards, gym cards (which you'll be sure to start going to one of these days), Auto Club card, ATM card, employee ID card, a photo of your kids from ten years ago, and finally, it has to hold all those little slips of paper you keep shoving in it.

Wallets tend to fill up rather quickly. And yet, you keep stuffing more in than taking out. Somehow, it all works out for a while, and then the wallet just seems to explode at the seams.

What? Again?

One day, you take out the wallet you have grown to know and love, and your spouse notices it. "Good grief! Don't you think it's about time you got a new wallet?" s/he asks.

"Don't be silly," you reply. "This one is still almost brand new!" Of course, you realize that it isn't, but you want it to be, and therefore your mind simply makes it so (the mind is very handy that way). You want it to be fine because you've shopped for wallets before and hate it.

But denial doesn't work for long, and eventually, you cave into reality and decide that, yes, you do need a new wallet. You start looking. But it's not an easy thing, finding a wallet. Wallets like the one you use now haven't been made for two decades. You keep looking.

You search for this wallet in all the usual places: kiosks. But no luck—you still can't find one. And now your money is starting to fall out, so you have to increase the search pattern. You climb on the Internet. You spend hours looking at various leather sights, some good, some not. But you aren't satisfied. You aren't having any luck.

One Saturday, yes, you finally start looking in, believe it or not, the big stores. You hit Target, Macy's, Kohl's, Bloomingdale's, Walmart, Saks, Neiman Marcus, Costco, Sam's Club, and even Long's and Rite-Aid drugstores. You see many good, even great, wallets, but you can't seem to find the one that is exactly right.

Then you realize why. You're trying to replace the old one, the one no longer made. Now that you've come to your senses, you can start the search once again, this time in earnest.

Today's the big day!

You wake up early in the morning, have a light breakfast, dress comfortably for speed and agility, and head to the garage. You check the car's oil, the battery, and the shocks. Everything seems fine.

You start the car and listen for any strange sounds. Nope, the engine sounds like the well-oiled machine that it is. You back out of the driveway with a list of stores to visit, directions to each one programmed in your phone. You've got it down, baby, and you're not coming back without that grandest of prizes: a new leather wallet.

You make the parking lot of the first store just as it's opening. No crowds yet, just the way you like it. You park, lock the car, and saunter into the store. Casually, you head to the men's leather goods section and begin looking.

After picking up and returning twenty or so wallets, you find one that might work. It's the right size, opens the right way, has the required number of slots for credit cards, a place with a window for the driver's license, everything you need. Then you look at the price. It's a bit more than you wanted to spend, but it is Gucci, and the leather is soft—very soft.

This is it; you've decided. This is the wallet. Well, it's the wallet provided it comes in black. A brown wallet is fine, but you've always had a black wallet, only a black wallet, your entire life. Why change now?

You start pawing your way through the display, sure that a black wallet is there. But it isn't. You look, and look, and look. No black wallet. You leave the store without looking back.

The next three hours are similar. You find another one that would work, but there is one little something wrong with it. You're about to give up when, at the last store, you find it. The black double-fold (none of that tri-fold stuff for you!) with exactly everything you need and want. And you buy it. It costs more than you ever thought you would spend. It costs more than a ticket to your first concert, but you don't mind because whatever you spend would be better than having to fill up the car's gas tank again. That costs more than your first car (at least to hear my father tell it).

Ah, wallets. So necessary, so messy. So handy, such a pain in the—well, you get the idea. But I suppose I'm lucky. However bad a wallet may be, it's infinitely better than a purse. Those things are like small suitcases.

Things That Go Bump in the Night

Remember when you were a kid and worried about every little sound late at night? Maybe you were right…All our lives, most of us have heard (or listened for) sounds in the night. Some we might have been afraid of, some perhaps not. But what were those sounds, really? Oh, sure, some might simply have been branches scraping against the house or noisy cars driving by. But what if…what if…they were more?

Sounds in the night

1. Wind
2. Rain
3. Snow
4. Sleet
5. Ice breaking off (okay, it doesn't much happen on southern beaches, but you never know)
6. The neighbor's dog
7. The neighbor's cat
8. The neighbor's snake (yeah, I once had a neighbor who kept a pet boa constrictor—I hated that house)
9. The neighbor's horse (those Texan neighbors)
10. The neighbor's chickens (and, even worse, the neighbor's rooster)
11. The party next door
12. The party next door
13. The party next door
14. The party next door (and, in this case, I wouldn't have minded the noise if they had just invited me, but that's another story)
15. The party down the street (if this can keep you awake, you know it's loud)
16. Axe murderers (somehow always worse than just the mundane killer with a gun)
17. Mass murderers

18. Zombies

19. Zombies

20. Zombies

21. Zombies

22. Zombies

23. Zombies (hey, when you're a kid and read something about zombies, you're convinced that they're everywhere...and they probably are)

24. Dracula

25. The wolfman (Unless it was the late Wolfman Jack, who was one of the greatest radio personalities who ever lived. I met him a few times; what a terrific guy. That howl of his could be heard on a clear-channel radio station coast to coast from Mexico all through the night. Come to think of it, yeah, Wolfman Jack might have been pretty scary too, in the wrong circumstances...)

26. Godzilla

27. Mothra

28. Any of the other dozens of monsters that Japanese filmmakers dreamed up (although they are also a bit humorous and *very* campy now)

29. Rabid dogs digging under the basement (weird friend—what can I say)

30. Dr. Frankenstein

31. Dr. Frankenstein's monster

32. Any physician who is probably going to give you a shot tomorrow when your mother takes you to see him or her because school is about to start, and you need those shots!

33. Teachers (Just what do those evil people do at night after they leave school? Probably run home and suck the blood of little kids and practice staying mean by kicking dogs.)

34. More zombies

35. Even more zombies (hey, there was this movie...)

36. Dentists (The heck with the "good for you" stuff your mom tried to sell you. It hurt, it didn't matter how good it was for you, and that's that.)

37. Wolves

38. Bears
39. Big snakes, small snakes, all snakes (Can't you just hear that slithering sound?)
40. Kidnappers
41. Brain stealers
42. Aliens from other worlds here to kidnap us and take us back to their world and use us as slaves (way too many comic books)
43. Mummies

The list goes on and on and on, but what the heck—if I don't quit now, even I'll get bored, and that's never a good thing. But what is it about the night? Is it bits of memory from our dim cave-dweller past? Is it just generic fear? Is it stuff we dream up to scare ourselves? Remember, we do like to be scared—just look at all the money-making horror films.

But, for now, there are forty-five horrific things that can, and indeed may, go bump in the night. How many have you heard? How many do you still hear? And just what is making noise under that bed of yours...

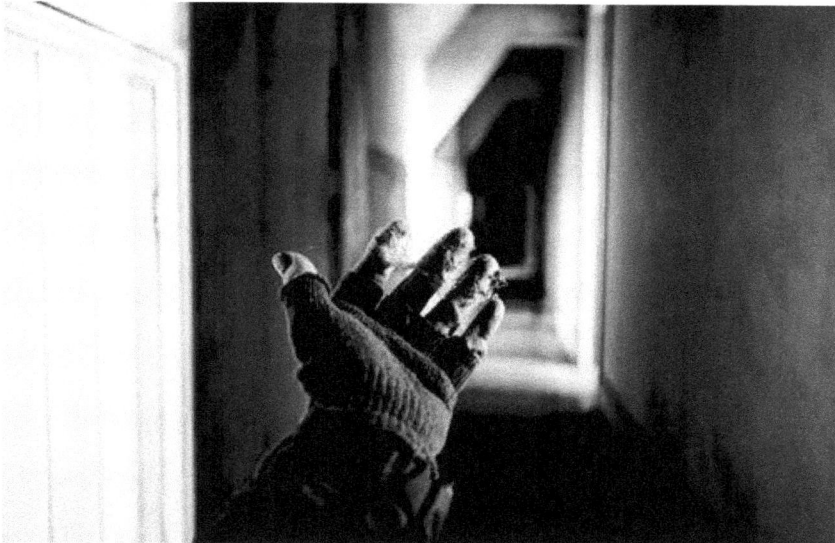

Time for Some Good News

Every once in a while, we hear the old refrain of someone being tired of hearing nothing but bad news. Well, I am going to change that, at least for right now. Today, in order to help us get in the right frame of mind, I am proud to present some really, really good news.

Good news from around the world

1. In California, a healthy baby was born to someone who did not use crack.
2. In Tokyo, a healthy baby was born to parents who were married.
3. In Calcutta, a baby was born to parents who never knew starvation.
4. In Hawaii, someone won a surfing competition.
5. Today, at the White House, someone smiled.
6. Right now, in the highest levels of government, someone cares about their job.
7. In New York, a lady received her money back on a defective item.
8. Thousands of planes will land worldwide without a problem.
9. Even as you are reading this, millions of women and men are getting home from work with no injuries.
10. Millions of kids had a great day at school.
11. Scientists discovered something.
12. Food was grown.
13. Thousands upon thousands of couples are being married.
14. Even more are leaving to go on vacation.
15. A couple who wanted to get pregnant did.
16. Any number of people got a great deal on a car.
17. Someone is being kissed for the first time and they are ecstatic.
18. Someone just got her or his first job.
19. 19.Someone is being kissed goodnight.
20. A chef is creating the finest dessert ever made.

21. An honest politician is going to work.

22. An honest attorney is going to work.

23. An honest doctor is donating time.

24. A teacher is looking forward to teaching—for the 5,000th day.

25. A writer is getting inspired.

26. A child helped with dinner without being asked.

27. A wife remembered that her spouse really is a pretty good person.

28. A husband remembered that his spouse really is a pretty good person.

29. Someone won some money in Las Vegas who really needed it.

30. Someone won the California Lottery who really needed it.

31. A nurse was inspired.

32. A minister was inspired.

33. A cop was inspired.

34. A firefighter was inspired.

35. A musician was inspired.

36. A painter was inspired.

37. A sculptor was inspired.

38. A mechanic was inspired.

39. A construction worker was inspired.

40. A chef was inspired.

41. A garment worker was inspired.

42. A baker was inspired.

Today millions of men and women, girls and boys are being inspired to do all kinds of things—some wonderful, some not. But here's the point: who are *you* inspiring today? Who are you working with today to make this the best year of their lives? Who are you helping?

It's all about attitude...

CHAPTER SEVEN

Time Off + Time Out

When you think about it, I suppose that time off and time out can mean pretty much the same thing. We generally use the term "time out" in some sort of event, whether it's sports or a family argument. We tend to use "time off" in work or some other area in life that is longer in time than an event. But basically, either one offers us an opportunity to step back, regroup, take a breath, and decide the next action.

People love to escape. We do it with TV, films, books, alcohol, drugs, and other assorted things for the short-term escape. When we need a longer one, we look at vacations. The serious among us look at vacation homes, timeshares, vacation clubs, and long cruises. The really serious (some might say, psychotic) buy yachts. For those individuals, there's no hope. Just shake your head and smile as you pass them in line at the bank. You can recognize them by their shallow breathing, bloodshot eyes, and slight aroma of teak.

These short essays look at vacations, R&R, and other similar means of escape. Yachts not included.

All Alone

Last week my wife took the kids and flew to Idaho for a graduation. Okay, let me rephrase that; it makes it all sound much easier than it actually was. Here, as Paul Harvey was noted for saying, "is the rest of the story."

One of our nephews was graduating from high school last week, and because of that, and it was summer, and everyone just felt like it, a number of family members decided to attend. There were aunts and uncles who live nearby, grandparents who don't live nearby but had (I mean, really wanted) to go anyway, and friends. You get the idea.

Michelle decided that she wanted to go and take the kids. This was fine with me because I had to work and wouldn't have to fly with a nine-year-old (who loves to travel) and a one-year-old (who doesn't). Oh sure, it would have been nice seeing the family and all, and going to the graduation, which are always important, but the calendar got in the way. Oh, darn.

The week before the trip, darling daughter wasn't feeling too hot, but she started doing okay. So, the kids were all set—now all Mom and Dad had to do was pack their suitcases. She started that more than a few days ahead of time—she's a very smart woman.

Traveling with kids

As anyone who has ever traveled with kids will tell you, over and over again, it's not exactly easy to travel with them. You have to pack for every eventuality, and pack more than one. Toddlers in diapers present even greater problems. You need clothes upon clothes upon clothes. You need sippy cups (and bottles, in case they get too upset or cranky and need some old-fashioned bottle comfort).

You need diapers and wipes and diapers and wipes and diapers and wipes. And that's just for the plane trip. You need their medicines, copies of their prescriptions, doctors' phone numbers, and medical insurance cards. Didn't think of that last one? Neither did we. Of course, Daughter got sick on the trip and Michelle needed to take her to urgent care. For this, she needed Daughter's insurance card that was in my wallet.

Luckily, we live in an era of modern communications. I took a photo of her card and sent a text with it to them in Idaho while still in my pajamas. Sometimes, technology really can be our friend.

Where was I? Oh, yes, packing. Don't forget the stroller and the baby seat for the car. By the time I got the three of them to the airport, it looked like I had luggage for an entire professional football team—cheerleaders included.

The flight

Michelle said the kids did okay on the flight there, although Daughter was getting a bit under the weather (see "urgent care" above). But they finally arrived and got settled in. And Daughter got sicker...and sicker. So, I was finally called (see "insurance card" above). She got some medicine and began to feel a bit better as the stay went on.

Everyone went to graduation (except Daughter, of course) and a good time was had by all. I guess.

All alone, all alone

While Michelle is in Idaho having a great time with family and sick baby, I'm suffering at home all by myself. Let me tell you, it's not easy being alone—there are decisions to make. You gotta decide what to eat, what to watch on TV, which lights to turn on and which lights to turn off. It's tough having to do all that.

For the first time in years, I chose the TV shows—me, just me. If I wanted ice cream and a beer for dinner while watching TV, I could do it. I didn't do it—but I could have if I had wanted to. If I wanted to watch nothing but the History Channel, I could do it. And I could do it looking like a bum. Shave on Saturday? Forget about it—there's no kid's soft face or wife's delicate cheeks to scratch.

In the whole entire house, the only things making noises were the dog and me. Okay, that's not exactly true. Have you ever noticed just how many things there are that make noises in homes? The microwave oven, the gas oven, the toaster oven, and even the toaster all make noise. They beep all the damn time.

One thing that doesn't make any noise is the phone. With my wife and kids out of town, the phone hardly ever rings. In fact, the few times when it did, the calls were for Michelle from people who didn't know she was out of town. Where are these people in the loop?

There is one downside to being all alone, and that is you are all alone. Loneliness does have a way of setting in. When that happens, you can always call or text or e-mail a friend, of course, but then that defeats the purpose of being alone. Nope, I loved being alone; I relished the thought of a house empty except for me (and the dog, which doesn't count because he's quiet and stays out of the way). Actually, I did like the dog being around. When you said something out loud, it made it seem like you were really saying it to someone (as opposed to going slowly insane, which would be a definite downside).

The party's over

Well, Michelle and the kids got home last Sunday. I met them at the airport, ready to attempt to pack their luggage back into the car. It was nice seeing them. I like being alone, but I love being with them. My son ran up and hugged me, my daughter grinned and said, "Da da." We had a big family hug right there in the airport.

Sure, it's nice being alone once in a while, but it's even nicer having the family back together.

Going on Vacation?

Have you started thinking about vacations yet? If you're like most people, you started thinking about this vacation as soon as you arrived home from the last one. Perhaps even sooner, if you were traveling with kids. But that's another story.

Or, just maybe, with the high cost of travel, you're thinking, "Why travel this year at all?" Well, the world is made up of snobs or people who desperately want to be one. The more you travel, the more snobbish you can become. And, after all, it's better to be a snob than want to be a snob. Just a thought.

So, where are you going? Planning a trip to Pacific Rim nations? Headed to the Philippines, Japan, or Tahiti? Or perhaps you've decided on a European vacation. Touring a Euro nation would be a good way to spend some time and money.

Maybe this is the year for a cruise, or a road trip up the east coast. That east coast road trip is always enjoyable, nothing like seeing Washington DC, New York, or Boston. It's always fun to give the kids a bit of history on a vacation. Not that they will necessarily appreciate it right away, but they certainly will later—especially when they take their kids on the same kind of trip.

Maybe this is the year for the Grand Canyon trip, the Colorado River trip, the camping in the mountains trip, the flight to the Grand Bahamas trip, the hiking trip through the Smokey Mountains, the rafting the Snake River trip. Or just go get an atlas and browse to your heart's content until you find something that grabs you and won't turn loose.

Deciding on where and how to go on a vacation can be an intimidating proposition. So, in order to remove at least some of the vacation-planning pain (you're on your own as far as the pain of paying for it is concerned), I've come up with the ultimate vacation-planner list. I hope it helps you have the vacation you and the family have always dreamed about.

If not, don't blame me—after all, there are numerous travel agencies to help out, the American Automobile Association (and other ones that help plan road trips), untold numbers of online sites to visit, and on and on and on. You get the idea—there is help for the planning challenged (like me).

So, use the Ultimate Vacation Planner, have family meetings, read things, and spend hours on the computer. You'll soon be a vacation planner extraordinaire.

The Ultimate Vacation Planner

1. Pick somewhere to go
2. Now pick somewhere you can afford
3. Try again

Okay, now that you have your destination, how are you going to travel? I have separated the vacation into four sections: flying, driving, rail, or cruising. Pick the one that matches your trip and go from there.

Flying

Unless you have a lot of patience, don't. Not that flying isn't great, because it is, but with security being the way it is, long lines are usually everywhere. On the other hand, it's much easier to fly across great expanses of distance than go by car. Also, flying can be expensive; however, if time is important, you've pretty much got to be in the air.

Driving

Road trips can always be magical, wondrous times to really get close to the family. Sometimes too close. What parent hasn't heard, "Are we there yet?" over and over and over again? Yet, seeing the country by car is unlike seeing it any other way. In a car, you can stop when the mood strikes, eat whenever you get hungry, see cities really close up, and probably travel in one of the least expensive ways (particularly if the family is large). Well, least expensive if you don't use much gas, make all your meals in the hotel room, and avoid most of the tourist spots.

Train trips

Trains are wonderful; you can see the countryside without actually doing the driving. Of course, you have to deal with trains and train terminals, but for now, that may be better than airports. Trains fall somewhere between flying and driving. They're faster than driving, slower than flying, you see more than from a plane, but often what you see is that space between a road and a track. There is a certain romance to train travel, though, and I've traveled that way on occasion and loved it.

Cruising

Cruising may be the ultimate lazy vacation. They do it all: they drive you, entertain you, feed you, watch out for you, and bring you back. Not bad. There are even medical people on board to help dislodge that piece of prime rib stuck in your throat because you just had to go to all the midnight buffets and eat too much, and your spouse told you not to eat that much but would you listen? See what happens when you don't listen? You get a piece of prime rib stuck in your throat. Slow down and chew more—the food will still be there.

Yes, you're on a boat with a bunch of people you don't know, probably wouldn't associate with back home, and would love to avoid if you could only figure out how. But for romance, probably nothing else beats a cruise; it all depends on what you want (although, if it's romance, a Disney cruise is probably not your best bet).

Okay, there you go, a planner to help you with this summer's vacation. I hope it helps and I hope you have a great vacation. Oh, and bring me back a souvenir (and I don't mean one of those glasses that held a tropical drink that you got on the ship—I want a real souvenir). Bon Voyage!

I know! Let's Vacation in Arizona in July!

Well, we finally went on vacation. We left San Diego and drove to Phoenix the first day. We wanted to spend a bit of time there so I could see some of the places my father hung out at when he was a child.

He, with his parents and three brothers, lived near the Capitol. We drove by the small house he grew up in and the capitol building where they played. This was during the Depression, eighty-five years ago. What a difference a few decades make.

His school is still there, although it has been closed and boarded up for years. It was a small elementary school, and we stopped and took some pictures of my son standing out in front, by the old flagpole. It was strange to imagine my dad at Son's age, also standing by that flagpole, two generations ago.

We didn't stay long in Phoenix; it was so hot that the car probably would have melted had we stayed more than overnight.

The Grand Canyon

When we left Phoenix, we drove to Williams, Arizona. This was the jumping-off place for our Grand Canyon excursion. We stayed at the Grand Canyon Hotel, which also has the depot for the Grand Canyon Railway.

The package we had included everything: the hotel, food, train excursion, Wild West show. So, we checked in, had dinner, kids went swimming, and we generally got ready for the following day.

After breakfast, we went to the show, which was fun, and then boarded the train. The ride to the Grand Canyon aboard the train lasts about two hours. We were given drinks and snacks, talked with the train workers, and enjoyed the desert scenery. Sitting in that car, looking out the window at the untouched rolling desert, seeing the black smoke come from the engine, you could almost imagine what it must have been like for those pioneers who traveled in trains across America. It was a wonderful couple of hours.

When we arrived, they gave us lunch, and then we headed to the buses for the tour of the canyon rim. Seeing that canyon in person is truly awe-inspiring.

There were people from all over the world on our tour, and everyone had cameras clicking away as they tried to get the size of the canyon in some kind of perspective. That wasn't always easy to do.

After the bus tour of the canyon, we boarded the train for the ride back to Williams. It was on this ride that desperados on horseback overtook the train and boarded. We were "robbed" by men in masks firing guns and demanding our money. After the sheriff chased them off the train, we got underway again for the final leg back to town.

Feeling queasy

During our two-hour ride back, one of the kids began to feel a bit on the bad side. After we got back to the hotel, she rested, started feeling even worse, and I went to the front desk and got directions to a clinic.

She hobbled to the car and I took her to a clinic. When we got there, it was empty of patients and the nurse took her right in. I loved that place. The doctor, who lived across the street, then came over. He examined her, gave her some medicine, and told her to get some rest. It was probably too much rich food, too much traveling, too much vacation, and he said she would feel better by morning. Luckily, she did.

The next day, we drove to Lake Havasu. We stayed at a nice place on the lake, ate British food at a pub near London Bridge, and generally behaved as tourists do when looking at the London Bridge in the middle of the Arizona desert. It was a bit weird, but we had fun. That is, we had fun when we could get cool. With temperatures at 110 and above, we pretty much went from air-conditioned place to pool to air-conditioned place.

Our trip was wonderful, and we all had a great time, especially the kids. Seeing things through their eyes is what is truly remarkable. But yes, we are all glad to be home. It is great to go and great to come back. And now, I can start planning on how to avoid next year's vacation…

Sure, it's beautiful; it's also big and hot.

It's Summer and Time to Get Wet, Toasted, and Full of Chlorine

Okay, gang, after a long, dark, cold winter where it hit—*gasp!*—sixty degrees here in Southern California, it's time to discuss swimming pools. No, I don't mean those in-ground, money-sucking, built-in pools that cost more than the house I was born in, nope—I'm talking about those above-ground pools that can be bought at Walmart, Target, online, and just about anywhere else that sells sporting and play stuff.

Type in "inflatable swim pools" and Google will return more than 1,100,000 hits. Now, that's just a bit too many to look at, if you know what I mean. So, you start with the first few pages, and by the time you've looked at a couple of dozen pools, you'll simply buy anything that will fit the space you have and is close to the amount you want to spend. Fair enough. One place I've been looking at has twelve of the round ones up to fifteen feet in diameter.

Not the little plastic pool you remember

Have you seen some of the "portable" swimming pools lately? There's one that holds 5000 gallons and costs almost $2300. There are square ones, rectangular ones, round ones, shallow ones, deep ones, and everything in between. Good grief, it's way too much to contemplate—after all, we are just talking about an inflatable kid's pools here, right?

These inflatable pools have filtration systems, chlorinators, skimmers, ladders, just about everything but a diving board and heater (the heater, you can get—just pay extra).

Do you want an inflatable pool, a hard-sided pool, or a semi-inflatable pool? Oh, sure, you can go all out and get a pool built in your back yard…if you want to spend more than 25,000 dollars or so, have a pool service take care of it, spend hundreds on power to heat it, etc., etc., etc.

Nope—as long as I have little kids who are happy with the inflatable, I'm good. Here's the thing, though. Remember when you were a kid? The inflatable pool then could be blown up by one parent without collapsing from lack of oxygen. If anything at all was needed, a bicycle pump did it. Your parents filled it and you jumped in—done in fifteen minutes and the afternoon was yours to play, splash, and get a sunburn.

Now, however, it's not quite that simple. The inflatable I bought for the kids came with its own electric pump to fill it with air, and it still took more than a few minutes to get it set.

Filtering a blow-up pool?

After the air comes the fun part—hooking up the filtration system. Yep—an electric filter that filters the water, adds chlorine, and keeps it clean. It's great for keeping the water a nice shade of blue and not green, but still…

Okay, so now hook hose A to nozzle B, and then hook hose C to nozzle D. Then extend hose A and hose C (careful to not cross them!) and connect A to hole A-1 in the pool and C to hole C-1 in the pool. Connect in that order. If you do not connect in that order, you will void the twenty-four-hour warranty, and all expenses (including but not limited to shipping, insurance, and lunch for the sales staff) will be your responsibility.

All right, maybe it's not quite that bad—but it's close. The set-up instructions ran to eight pages (the quick-set instructions only took three pages), and that didn't include warnings.

Naturally, I asked myself as I was setting the thing up why on earth I was doing it. Yes, I adore my kids; yes, I want them to be happy; yes, I want to please them (within reason); yes, I want to keep their mom happy (who suggested the thing in the first place)—but good grief! With all the inflation, all the hose connecting, all the filling with water, all the testing of the water, all the everything, well, it was not a one-hour job.

Speaking of filling it with water, you can't simply fill it with cold water. Let me correct myself: you CAN fill it with cold water, but then the kids won't go in and no one's happy, so why bother? What you must do is attach the hose to a faucet (adapter not included, of course) and empty the hot water heater into the pool. Then, and only then, can you fill it the rest of the way with plain old regular cold water.

It's party time!

After you fill it with all this various-temperature water, the kids finally want to go in. Naturally, they've been screaming and whining about getting in it since you started, but now the time has finally arrived. Only problem is, now they're riding their bikes and have no intention of getting in the pool.

What do you do? You open a beer, sit under a fan, and mumble quietly to yourself. But after the kids finally ride the bikes enough to get hot, they come scrambling to the pool. And that's when it all really, truly happens. That's when all your hard work gets rewarded with the smiles, laughter, and high-fives from the kids who are having the times of their little lives. Yeah, sure. Maybe it happens that way, or (more likely) they get in and start fighting over the inflatable toys you bought.

"I want the porpoise!"

"No, I want the porpoise!"

"You said I could have it."

"No, you said I could have it first for fifteen minutes, and THEN he could have it!"

Then you quietly walk in your home and tell your spouse it's her/his time to watch the kids...

Las Vegas in Summer

Ever notice how people who live in the desert always say that it isn't really hot there because it's just a dry heat? Well, I'm calling BS because hot is hot—dry or otherwise (just stick your head in an oven and tell me that the dry heat isn't really hot).

We were in Las Vegas recently—we went there to drop off our son so he could spend a week with his grandparents (yes, they say dry heat, and yes, they're wrong too). Luckily, Son doesn't mind the heat because he's young, very thin, and kids just seem to be able to take more heat than the rest of us normal people.

So how hot was Las Vegas this past week?

It's hot!!
It's hot!!
It's hot!!
It's hot!!
It's hot!!
It's hot!!
It's hot!!
It's hot!!
It's hot!!
It's hot!!
It's hot!!
It's hot!!
It's hot!!
It's hot!!
It's hot!!
It's hot!!

You might think that I'm exaggerating just a bit. Well, let's see. We were in the desert; the day temperature went to 115 degrees, and at night it got as low as 90 degrees. The sun beat down mercilessly, the breeze, when one did blow, was like what you feel coming from a convection oven, and the streets, buildings, houses, and everything else in the city radiated white-hot heat. Oh, yeah, I'm exaggerating.

So really, how hot was Las Vegas this past week?

It's hot!!
It's hot!!
It's hot!!
It's hot!!
It's hot!!
It's hot!!
It's hot!!
It's hot!!
It's hot!!
It's hot!!
It's hot!!
It's hot!!
It's hot!!
It's hot!!

Enough already!

It's just a little warmth, I kept saying to myself over and over and over again as I tried to slog my way through the heat waves to the car. Let me tell you how much fun that was—getting into a car that had been sitting in the sun all day!!

There was no relief—well, no relief except in casinos, of course. But we didn't go to any casinos; no casinos, no hotels, no shows. Nope, we went to see family and drop off a kid. This was not a "fun," in the usual sense of the word, kind of trip.

Now, I've probably griped about heat before—I'm not a fan of temperature above about seventy degrees. But that's just me. Obviously, a great number of individuals like heat—just look at how fast Vegas is growing. Or maybe they simply like growing cities (one of the fastest-growing cities in the US) and they see opportunities.

Yeah, yeah, yeah. Opportunities are fine and good, but you still have to live in an oven that's turned on.

And yes, it's:

Still hot!!
Still hot!!

Still hot!!
Still hot!!
Still hot!!
Still hot!!
Still hot!!
Still hot!!
Still hot!!
Still hot!!
Still hot!!
Still hot!!
Still hot!!
Still hot!!
Still hot!!
Still hot!!

But heat isn't everything. There's still a quality-of-life thing that's as important as anything else. So, let's see—what does Vegas have to make the quality of life good?

Diversified jobs
New housing
Entertainment
Recreation
Good schools
Lake Mead
Multicultural population
Good medical facilities
Central airport
On a transportation corridor
Large population

The list is much longer than this, of course. Let's face it: Las Vegas is simply growing for a multitude of good reasons. But what about that heat? Well, when you look at all the good reasons to live in Vegas, it makes complaining about heat seem a bit, well, childish. Right?

Actually, no. Imagine the electricity used to air-condition that city— especially the hotels themselves that bring in the vast majority of money and tax revenue. It's a never-ending circle; one needs the other, which needs the other, which needs the other, and on and on.

What does the future hold for Las Vegas? Where will Vegas get its water and power as the population keeps expanding? How long can it keep up this increase in population? Anyone want to roll some dice on it?

Staying Cool. No, Not That Kind of Cool. If You Have to Ask, You Aren't

July will be oozing in, if it hasn't already, and that means the heat of summer. Heat is a tough thing to control. You can put on enough clothes in winter to get warm, but you can't take off enough clothes in summer to get cool. Trying to, however, can certainly be fun.

Even though the heat of the year is coming on like calories in a bakery, there are ways to get and stay cool. I'm going to outline a number of those ways here. Feel free to use any or all of them as necessary to stay as cool as the person you hope you are.

Twenty-five ways to stay cool in the summertime

1. Buy an air conditioner for your house and use it. Yes, this is the easy one, and why did someone have to tell you this?

2. Use the air conditioner in your car, unless you don't have an air conditioner in your car, in which case, you now must ask yourself what on earth you were thinking when you bought a car without air conditioning.

3. Go buy a car with air conditioning if you see yourself in number two above—and then look up "no brainer."

4. Go to the beach. Sure, there are thousands upon thousands of people already there trying to get cool too—as well as surf, swim, picnic, tan, play volleyball, ogle people in thongs, fish, and all the other assorted things people do at beaches besides just getting cool—but it's a big beach.

5. Go to an enclosed mall. Yes, this is what shopping centers pray for—a hot day when hordes of people will descend upon the place in search of cool temperatures and bargains. So, go ahead and shop until your blisters bleed or you run out of money—whichever comes first.

6. Eat in restaurants more often. This will not only stimulate the economy and get you out of the kitchen, it will keep you in good graces with anyone who lives with you and cooks.

7. Take a trip to the mountains—in northern Canada. Go north and keep on going until you get cool.

8. Build a swimming pool in your backyard (the family *and* neighbors will love you for it).

9. Eat more ice cream (yes, this may have the undesired side effect of making you gain weight, which will make you hotter, but until that happens the ice cream will help you stay cool. It's a side effect—deal with it).

10. Go out to your front yard (yeah, a back yard is okay too), turn on a hose, and simply stand under it while letting the water run over you. WAIT!!! Do not stand under it right after turning it on. There is water in that hose that has been in the hot sun all day. Wait until the water cools off, or you're liable to get cooked. If you live in an area of drought, forget you ever saw this.

11. Start munching on ice cubes. You can do this all day long, and it has a great side effect of annoying people around you—and if you break a tooth, your dentist will benefit as well.

12. Get in the car (sure, gas is expensive, but you're hot, remember) and head straight to the nearest 7/This is a great place to get things to help a person cool off. First, of course, there is the ice-cold Slurpee (wonder if anyone has thought of a beer Slurpee?). After that, there are soft drinks, beer, and any number of other things to help you take the edge off summer heat.

13. Go ice-skating. Okay, you have to actually learn how to do it, so you don't break something, but after all the lessons, just think how cool you'll be while skating around on ice. And another thing, if you are going to have to take lessons for a sport, what better way than to take them on an air-conditioned ice rink?

14. Take an Alaskan cruise. It's got to be at least somewhat cooler sailing next to a few icebergs.

15. Fill a big bucket with ice, add water, and start dunking your head in it (do I need to remind you to hold your breath?).

16. Have an operation. Have you ever noticed how cold hospitals get?

17. Get a job flying, planes are cold.

18. While traveling, stay near a coast. Do not go into the interior of the country—especially don't go into the deserts (unless the desert is Las Vegas. In Vegas, there are enough things to do without ever having to leave the hotels and casinos. You can stay

winter-cool all summer long and never see the great outdoors).

19. Get a job in an ice factory. You can go to work in the middle of summer and need a parka.

20. Go to Lake Tahoe. The lake is clean, clear, and ice-cold, having been fed by melting snows (at least, this is what their literature says).

21. Take up water skiing (even better is to do it at Lake Tahoe).

22. Run through your neighbor's sprinklers (ask them first, so you don't surprise them and have them turn their Rottweiler loose).

23. Occasionally open your freezer door and stick your head in. You can't do this very often, because if you do, your ice cream will melt; plus, how would you be able to yell at the kids for doing it if they caught you?

24. Run your bathtub full of cool water and then add ice. Now get in. WARNING: This will be very cold, and you can't stay in long—besides, your skin will wrinkle, and who needs more of that? Warning: shrinkage may occur.

25. Find someone to follow you around wherever you go to fan you and spray you with water.

And there you have twenty-five ways to stay cool over the long, hot summer. I hope it helps. If not, I'll see you at the beach. I'll be the one with a beer, a book, and a smile.

One Fun Summer

Well, we did it—the family finally got off the North American continent. We went to Great Britain for a couple of weeks so I could pick up a degree (hey, graduation was at Canterbury Cathedral— how could I resist?).

We left San Diego a little after 1 p.m. on Delta Airlines, changed planes in Atlanta, and arrived at Gatwick Airport in London the following day. We flew Delta both ways and the flights were absolutely perfect. Delta got us there on time, with minimal fuss, and rather comfortably, when you consider there were three adults and two kids—one of whom is two years old and can have "her moments," if you know what I mean.

Our timing was perfect—we weren't back a week when the latest terrorist alerts occurred, and the airports became an impossible, jammed-up mess. Sure, it always took us a bit of time and hassle to get aboard, make connections, and wait for an agent, but all things considered, we had it pretty darned good.

Great Britain

We arrived at Gatwick, got our luggage (and there was a LOT of it), and got to Hertz. In the Hertz lobby, I took a good look at the five of us, the baby seat, the stroller, the luggage, the bags, and thought that there was no way on earth we were ever going to get in the small car I had reserved.

The agent said she could give me a Ford Mondeo station wagon at the same price—but it had a standard transmission. I said sure, even though it meant all the driving was now going to be up to me.

We got the car, loaded the car, and took off in the car for Faversham. Picture it: the very first time in my life I'm driving on the right, we're climbing on a freeway to go around London, I'm shifting with my left hand (never done that either, obviously), and I don't have a clue where to go.

Actually, I did have a clue—but I needed a whole lot more than that. The directions I was given to the house we rented had been written by someone who knew the area and wanted to give me the shortest route. Hey, we all know shortcuts—there is no easier way to get lost than following someone's shortcut. I had to stop four different times for directions as we made our way south, but everyone I asked was extraordinarily nice and helpful (even the guy in the small camera shop in the middle of a neighborhood God knows where, who I'm sure had never before had an American walk into his store and ask for directions).

But we finally made it to Faversham, found the street we needed with more help (let's face it, the road signs there, if you're not used to them, can be a bit hard to see—or even find), and drove up to the house. The owners of the house were waiting for us to give us the key and help get us acquainted with the place.

The couple who owned and rented the cottage to vacationers were very nice, and one of them even took my wife into town to get a few things to tide us over until we could go shopping the next day.

Finally, darkness came, we turned on the television, and we collapsed. But it was okay, because we were there, we had taken showers, we had opened a domestic British beer, and we had coffee for the morning. Life was good.

Driving

First, even with me doing all the driving, we drove for hundreds of miles and we didn't have an accident, didn't get a ticket, and didn't get yelled at by anyone. Not too bad, if I do say so myself. Now, my wife might see things a bit differently, but that's her problem. Yeah, I ran on to the shoulder of the road once or twice, and yes, I ran off the road once or twice because there wasn't always a shoulder on the one-lane road. And, sure, getting that damn Mondeo into reverse caused a few choice words to float through the air on occasion. But be that as it may, I got us there, we did what we wanted, and I got us home.

We drove from Faversham to Dover to Warwick and all around the place and saw more things than we ever could have any other way. For London, however, I didn't even want to think about driving. Everyone says it's a nightmare, and the last thing I needed was a huge, crowded city in which to drive. So, no, for the two times we went to London, we took a train and tours.

We came, we saw, we toured

The train from Faversham to London Victoria Station was about an hour of quiet, air-conditioned comfort. When we got to London the first time, we did a tour—one of those on/off tours. It was great, we saw the usual sights, got off at the Tower of London where we spent a few hours touring Beauchamp Tower and viewing the Crown Jewels, toured some more, got back on the train, and went home.

The second time in London, we took taxis, we walked, we stood in line after line at Buckingham Palace, and then we got back aboard and trained it on back to Faversham. The only time we actually did a tour was in London (just too much to see), and it was great. For everywhere else we went, we just slogged along, got lost and found our way again, tried to remember just where on earth we had left the car, and explored. It worked for us, and we got off the "beaten path" a whole lot more and saw more than we ever would have otherwise (at least of the things we wanted to see).

Sure, we saw castles, cathedrals, jousting knights, and all the usual things, but it was the rest of the time that was some of the best. Dinner at the Rose in Bloom Restaurant was perfect, as opposed to the Subway we had to eat at once, which was certainly not perfect. Speaking of food, some of it was so-so, some was excellent, and some was, well, not perfect (the not-perfect was usually supplied by American chains like Subway and McDonald's. And I'm sure they really were okay— we were just judging by what we taste at home versus what we tasted there, and it didn't match).

Finally, the day came to return to reality and leave England. We drove back to Hertz (made it!), checked in the car, found Delta, and settled in for the long flight home and attempting to get adjusted to the time.

Searching for a Speedboat

A few weeks ago, we decided to buy a speedboat. No, make that a runabout. See, insurance companies hate the term "speedboat." Guess what? This past Friday, I found a "runabout" (wink, wink). It's about twenty feet long, has an open bow, and is powered by a 140-horsepower inboard-outboard MerCruiser. This thing flies across the water. Not that I would ever go fast. No, never, not me.

The search for the boat was the most interesting part. I've seen probably hundreds of boats of various sizes. I've been to boat dealers, private individuals, marinas, you name it—if boats were for sale, I was there.

The wrong time to buy

As with most things in life, timing is everything. And if you want to buy a boat and get a good deal, the time to look is not in the middle of summer. So, naturally, here I was, in July, looking for a boat.

One of the first boats I saw was a terrific eighteen-footer. It had everything, was in great shape, and the family wanted it. I made an offer. Admittedly, it was an offer on the low side, but hey, that's half the fun, seeing how much money you can save buying something you absolutely do not need.

The salesman looked at me like I was out of any mind I might have ever had. He just shook his head and said slowly, "No, I don't think that will go. Maybe if you doubled the offer..."

I walked away. My father taught me well: never be afraid to walk away. So, I did. I knew that there were lots of boats and I would find one eventually. But I may have shed one or two tears.

Did you know that there are speedboats that sell for more than 50,000 dollars? It's true. I'm not sure who can afford one of them, but they're for sale. I didn't buy one of those monster machines. Okay, maybe I wanted to, but bank balances got in the way.

Searching, searching, searching

I kept looking, driving from one dealer to the next, from one marina to the next, from one house with a boat in the driveway to the next. Always, the boats were too expensive or not good enough. And don't forget, there are other things involved with buying a boat like this. You also buy a trailer. You buy a hitch for this trailer and have it installed on your car. Purchases for "stuff" for the boat are made. Things like life preservers, paddles, coolers, etc., etc., etc. The list is endless.

But you forget all that in the excitement of looking. And looking. And looking. But if you look long and hard enough, you'll usually find what you want. And last Friday, I did.

I saw an ad for what sounded like the perfect boat, so I went to see it. A private individual was selling it, and after meeting the man and his wife, I knew that this was the boat. The man and his wife were from Sweden. She kept running her hand along the boat and saying how she was going to miss it.

He just looked at her and shook his head. They hadn't used it but three times in the past year and were just too busy to keep it.

It was obvious that the people cared for the boat. He had records on it from when it was new, everything about the engine was in pristine condition, and he had answers for all my questions.

We came to an agreement on the price, and last Friday, I drove off with a boat in tow.

And no, we haven't had it in the water yet. There were a few things I wanted to have done to the boat before we took it out. And so, even as you read this, the boat is at a boatyard draining my wallet. But that's to be expected, for as someone once said, "A boat is a hole in the water in which you pour money."

Yeah, it's only a boat. But still…

CHAPTER EIGHT

Ramblings in the Key of Life

You know how there seems to be, in most families, that one peculiar relative who can just ramble on about anything and everything? Well, that's not what this section is about. Yes, the works are all over the place in terms of content, but that's not the sole point. Various and sundry things occur to us every day as we go through life, and that's some of what we peek at.

Sure, there may be a bit of nervous laughter as a memory surfaces from the depths in which you buried it, but then again, you may just be ecstatic that what is described didn't happen to you. Even if it probably did.

The best sort of ramblings are those with a purpose. That may be counterintuitive, I suppose, but I've found the ramblings that stand out are those that had a point. Even if that point was a snarky comment at the end of a road trip with no destination.

Personally, I love road trips; even those with no destination. Maybe those are the best: you start the car and head out, willing to let life wash over you in wherever way it happens. That takes a bit of courage and willingness to have fun, even if the rest stop is dirty *and* crowded.

A School without Students is a Desolate Island

Schools are built for people. Students go there to learn, while adults go there to teach, maintain, and administer. When you stop to think of all the people on a campus on any given day, it can be mind-boggling. There are teachers, assistant teachers, student teachers, coaches, nurses, secretaries, counselors, principals and assistant principals, cooks, cleaners, maintenance workers, security staff, volunteer parents, and others. Finally, there are the students who are, after all, the purpose of everyone else being there. And since schools are people-oriented, schools without people are strange, eerie places.

Earlier this past week, I visited a virtually empty campus. The only people there were a couple of grounds workers, and while there, I noticed how very strange everything seemed. It was too quiet, too serene, too peaceful. In other words, it was just *bizarre*. This place needed people, cried out for people, begged for people. Dry drinking fountains, basketball hoops hanging without movement, hallways echoing with the sounds from the steps of a single individual—me—classroom doors closed, and no lights shining from any window tend make a school fairly drip with loneliness.

A school office without secretaries and teachers bustling in and out, headed for the prep room, is just plain weird. Schools aren't supposed to echo, they're supposed to blast sound from every corner. A dry office coffeemaker is just too, well, odd. Remember the noise from your own school? What did the playgrounds, the hallways before and after classes, and the cafeteria sound like?

Schools are created for use. They are designed and built to handle crowded hallways with the shuffling of hundreds or thousands of feet; long lines of hungry students in cafeterias during lunch; playgrounds teeming with children and adolescents during breaks. Architects and planners sit behind computers and drawing boards trying to ensure that the largest number of individuals are moved, routed, and accommodated with the greatest possible ease and efficiency.

Without students, a school is just a warehouse for desks

People are a school's entire purpose for being. Without people around, a school is no more than a silent, cavernous shell echoing with ghosts— the ghosts of kids and staff long gone, of echoed laughter, quiet sniffles, whistles of warning, and the sound of backpacks thrown every direction imaginable. Empty schools are lonely places. In fact, an empty school may be one of the loneliest places on earth. Even the wind sounds different in an empty school. Open schools have breezes, empty schools have sighing winds.

There are, certainly, other lonely places. A desert or mountaintop can be lonely, as can being in the middle of the ocean. But these are natural places. While you may be riding in a small boat on top of the waves, underneath the ocean's surface, all manner of creatures are going about their lives. The desert and mountains abound with everything from cacti to pines, lizards to woodpeckers, tumbleweeds to flowers.

No, it's not the natural places which are lonely; it's the places we humans have built that seem to get the loneliest. We build in the possibility of our own loneliness while we create the great and marvelous things that help give us our humanity. We have created schools for a purpose singularly unique, the education of others beyond ourselves and our families. Animals teach their young to find food, build nests, and become hunters. So do we, but we not only do it for our own young, we do it for everyone's children. We teach the children of people we will never know, the children of people we might loathe if we met, the children of people who couldn't help us, wouldn't help us. And we like to do it, get pleasure in doing it, feel more humane for doing it, and most wouldn't think of doing anything else.

A school's critical purpose

We strive to teach people to be better, smarter, kinder human beings. This is the purpose we have given schools, the critical purpose, the only purpose. And during those breaks when students are playing and working, and employees are playing and planning, schools are just too silent. Even with all the maintenance, all of the cleaning, all of the upgrading, all of the "catching-up" schools are accomplishing during those quiet days or weeks, they still seem a melancholy place.

Think about your own school years—do you first remember the buildings or the people? Picture their faces, their voices, their laughter, their smiles, and their frowns. See the kids running in the halls, pushing each other on the swings, fighting over the mundane, and arguing over the trivial. That's what we remember, and that is what's important.

Schools without the sound of human laughter, human arguments, human learning, and human interaction are not places one should spend much time. Schools need people because schools *are* people. Visit one during the next open house and revel in the spirit, the energy, and the optimism. You'll be amazed at what an *alive* place it is.

A closed, desolate elementary school echoing of kids.

Beauty Can Be Everywhere

There are beautiful things around us everywhere we look. Imagine the beauty of a sunrise or sunset, snow freshly fallen in a forest, the power of the ocean swells.

There is the beauty of Hawaii, of a jungle after a tropical rain, of the Grand Canyon, or of city lights glistening in the dark of night.

A steaming cup of coffee or tea in the early hours of a cold morning is something beautiful to behold.

A freshly washed car is a thing of beauty—particularly if you were the one who washed it.

Can there be anything more beautiful than the smile of a baby?

Well, yes, there can be something more beautiful than any of those things. And that is the astounding view that you get when you open the dirty-clothes hamper and it is empty.

No dirty clothes to wash!
No dirty clothes to wash!

Monday morning, I groggily stumbled into the bathroom shedding clothes, getting ready to take a shower. I opened the hamper to toss in the clothes and saw one of the most amazing things I have ever seen. It was an empty, pristine dirty-clothes hamper, devoid of any dirty clothes whatsoever.

Yes, we did laundry the day before, you know, the final laundry before a new week starts. Like most everyone else who goes through a ritual of this kind, we emptied all four hampers (ours and the two belonging to our kids) and carried the stuff into the laundry room to be sorted, washed, and dried.

There did seem to be quite a bit of laundry, especially since we had just gone through this same procedure Wednesday. See, Wednesday is the first laundry day and then Sunday is the second laundry day. Why we have two laundry days, I'll never know, other than if we just had one laundry day, we would never get through it all.

So anyway, there it was, a perfectly clean and empty laundry basket, so beautiful to the eyes and mind.

As I stepped into the shower, I began to contemplate all the beautiful things around us—not the usual beautiful things, but objects that we don't normally think of as beautiful, like an empty laundry hamper. That led to thinking of other weirdly attractive things because, well, what else do you do in the shower while in the middle of shampoo and cream rinsing?

Twenty weirdly beautiful things

1. A spotless sink
2. Streak-free mirrors
3. A back seat with no toys
4. A dog during that short time between baths and getting dirty again
5. A child during that short time between baths and getting dirty again
6. A bathtub during that short time between baths and getting dirty again
7. A tie perfectly knotted
8. A freshly made omelet
9. An empty wastebasket
10. Brilliantly clean shoes
11. A perfectly tuned car
12. A clean—really clean—garage floor (does this every really happen to anyone?)
13. The cleanliness of a windshield after it rains, and the wipers are brand new
14. A computer that works as well as the ad promised
15. A photo that comes out the way you imagined it would
16. A perfect bowl of rice
17. A newly opened bottle of Baron Philippe de Rothschild wine
18. An icy-cold drink on a horrendously hot day
19. The smell of a baby (after the bath, for God's sake)
20. Money in a wallet you thought was empty

Okay, I'll grant you that on a list of beautiful things in the universe, the twenty above would probably not rank all that high. But on a day-to-day basis, those twenty are pretty damn beautiful.

That's the key: "On a day-to-day basis." We generally recognize rare beauty, or beauty that we see rarely. We are awed by the beauty hanging on gallery walls, or seen in park and civic statues, or heard from symphony orchestras.

But on a day-to-day basis, there are all sorts of other kinds of beauty. Beauty comes in all packages, wrapped in all sorts of guises, played from any number of instruments.

Too often, we have trouble recognizing beauty for what it really is when we see it every day. Heck, a snore can be a beautiful sound if we have been in a silent, lonely bed for too long.

Sometimes, we just have to remember to look.

British Sports Cars

There have been hundreds of different car makes and models manufactured over the years since Karl Benz patented his first gas-powered car in 1886. Some of the cars have been great (Bentley), some not so great (Yugo). But few cars evoke as much reverence and romance as the classic British sports car.

The very names roll off the tongue: *Jaguar, Morgan, MG, Austin-Healey, Triumph, Lotus, Sunbeam Alpine, TVR, Aston Martin.* What marquees, what style, what open road romance.

And what difficult cars to maintain!

But let's face it, one does not buy a British sports car in the hopes of carefree, trouble-free, turn-the-key-and-go motoring. No, that's just not what British sports cars are all about. It would be nice if that were the case, but it isn't.

A British sports car is all about running with the top down, gliding down the open road, and the gentle, melodic roar of the racing engine drowning out the day's noise. That's what a British sports car is all about.

The trouble is, most people also want their car to not overheat, to start every time, to be comfortable, and to know that the car will get them back from wherever they go.

Unfortunately, with a classic British sports car, there is no guarantee that it will always start, that it will be comfortable, or that, most importantly, it will get them home. Particularly those sports cars of the twentieth century.

But so, what! This is a true sports car

Do you like sports cars? Do you like the romance of wind in your hair, the feel of the wide-open spaces, and the growl of an engine? If so, you may ultimately own a British sports car.

I do.

Now, please don't think that I'm knocking the world's other sports cars. The Ferrari from Italy, The Nissan 370Z from Japan, the Corvette from the US, or the Mercedes AMG GT from Germany are all truly magnificent automobiles. They hug corners, they take your breath away with speed, they are gorgeous, and, yes, they will pretty much always get you home.

So, what is it about the British sports car that evokes such reverence among those true sports-car buffs? I don't have any idea, except that when behind the wheel, you enter a slightly different world. While the Mercedes or the Nissan are state of the art, the Jaguar or Aston Martin take a step or two back in time. You go back to when driving was a pleasure, something you looked forward to, something romantic.

The look

What is it about the whole British-motoring look? You know, the tweed jacket with leather patches on the elbow, the driving cap worn at a jaunty angle on the head, the corduroy trousers, and the comfortable leather shoes. Plus, for the real look, one probably needs a pipe lightly clenched between the teeth.

Well, personally, I don't own a tweed jacket or smoke a pipe. But I still relate to that look. I see myself as that character, whizzing through the shady lanes, top down, glancing at the gauge to see if there is enough petrol in the car to get to the next hamlet for a spot of tea—or a cold one, depending on the time of day.

But there is something besides the look to the whole thing, something almost mystical about British motoring.

I owned a Jaguar XKE. It was given to me by my father, who bought it new over fifty years ago. The car was in pristine condition—always having been garaged, meticulously cared for, and driven very little. It was his third or fourth Jaguar—he's owned one as long as I can remember. But they were always second or third cars—never a car that was actually driven anywhere except for pleasure. And oh, what pleasure they gave.

As my father got older, he knew that this would be his last Jaguar, his last sports car. And he decided to simply save it for me. A few years ago, he handed me the keys and the title, and now the XKE that was his was mine. I sat in the same seat, felt the same steering wheel in my hands, felt the same rush of the wind.

He went places in the Jaguar, only I drove us. But it was still just for pleasure, to lunch or the golf course. And yes, there really is nothing like the feel of a Jaguar, a British sports car.

Can a car be romantic? How can something made of steel, chrome, leather, and plastic be anything remotely romantic? But, yes, some cars are romantic; for instance, the Thunderbird from the late 1950s, or the Gull Wing Mercedes from the same era.

But the car that was voted the most beautiful of all time by automotive critics and writers is the Jaguar XKE. Do I agree with them? Without a doubt. And why is the XKE beautiful? I'm not sure—perhaps it's the sleek lines coupled with the sensuous curves. Maybe it's the perfect use of chrome and leather. Or just perhaps it's the leaping jaguar on the front of that long hood that does it. Like I said, I don't know. All I do know is that, whenever I drive it, someone at a stoplight always gives me a thumbs up or tells me what a gorgeous car it is. And I have to agree.

Thanks, Pop.

Changing Sounds

Heard anything interesting lately? That's an old line, certainly, but one that has a bit of significance; think about how many sounds there are in the world. In among all those millions of sounds are ones that appear—and disappear—daily. There are things you can hear today that your grandparents never dreamed of when they were kids. For example:

* Cell phone ring tones from a symphony orchestra
* The clarity of music streaming from a satellite
* The incessant dings, beeps, buzzers, tweets, and more of all the electronics that surround us
* Cars that speak
* Computer sounds: operating system sounds, mailbox sounds, saving, deleting, and recovery sounds...well, you see where I'm going with this one. I could write three columns on my computer and its various operating systems' sounds (or noises, depending on your point of view, I suppose).
* The sound of a baby's cry through a monitor...or a watch
* The sound of wind blowing on Mars
* Watching TV on a watch
* That unique ring...from the front door...of a dollhouse
* The sound of a news broadcast from a phone
* The sound of a hundred different kinds of music from a phone

Disappearing sounds

Just as important as new sounds is the fact that there are also many sounds that are disappearing or are disappearing as live sounds. We may have recordings of some of them, but the live sounds are flitting away:
Consider just a few of these disappearing sounds:

* The scratch and hiss of records being played on a record player
* The jingle of coins being fed into a payphone
* The unique sound of a portable Byrd respirator as it helps some-

one breathe
* The bells inside of an old black phone with a dial
* The sound of an engine in an electric car or motorcycle
* The unique and irreplaceable sounds from animals that disappear from earth as those animals become extinct

Wouldn't it be lonely to be the last of a species? You would probably keep searching for a mate, a familiar sound, a something, but nothing would ever vocalize back...

The wonderful sounds

So, what is the best sound, do you suppose? I imagine that it all depends on the listener and circumstances. One universal "good" sound seems to be the laughter of children. But there are many people out there who would disagree with that, and who think that the best sound is the sound of one hand clapping. Humph! Get off my lawn, you little thugs! They're wrong.

The pure, clear, uninhibited sound of a child laughing does seem to be a near-universally joyful sound. It cuts across cultures, races, languages, ethnicities, religions, place, and time. That laughter is infectious, can bring out smiles, can make us forget—if only for a moment—some of the darkest pain.

Here, in no particular order, are a few other really great sounds:

Popcorn popping
An ice-cold drink being poured over ice
Something frying in a skillet
Snow falling (listen carefully...)
A storm
Waves gently lapping up on shore
A baby sleeping
People screaming, laughing, talking at a fair
The school dismissal bell
An engine starting on a very cold, wintery morning
Someone saying, "I love you"
The simple sound of a breath when you see "that person"

Chasing a Ball in the Rain

What is it with golfers? From where I sit writing this, I can look out a window and see a golf course across the street. The course is full, and men and women in strange clothes are waiting to tee off. And rain is pouring down.

Now, I can understand enjoying a sport. I can understand being passionate about a sport (I guess). But to enjoy a sport enough to pay anywhere from $50 to $150 or more a game, play in the rain, and spend hundreds and even thousands of dollars for the equipment, well, that I just can't seem to understand.

Don't misunderstand me or think that I am someone casting stones who doesn't have a clue about the game. I've played golf and used to for years. My father taught me golf, and he and I would play together beginning when I was about twelve years old. I understand the game and can see the sport involved.

But, and here's the kicker, I'm not insane enough to spend thousands of dollars to join a country club, buy the latest clubs made out of space-age material, and own my own golf cart designed to look like a Rolls Royce. I will admit to a certain degree, perhaps even a large degree, of insanity, but I'm just not quite that crazy—at least, not yet.

Then again, perhaps I am that crazy and just don't spend that kind of money because I can't afford to spend that kind of money. Personally, I would rather think that I'm too sane to do it, but you never know.

It's just a club and a little ball

I have seen grown men get so angry playing golf that they scream obscenities, throw their clubs on the ground, stomp on them, and storm off the course. Naturally, his friends collect the clubs and drop them off at his house because they know he'll be back tomorrow or next week to play again. Is this person always a "he"? Oh, please.

Women never seem to get *that* angry at the game. They get passionate about it, they get angry at it, and they have been known to cry at difficult shots. They just don't seem to get insane over it in quite the same way. Perhaps they have more patience than men, perhaps the game doesn't mean that much in any sort of "macho" sense, or—and I suspect this is the case—they're simply smarter and refuse to let a little rubber ball ruin their day. Do please understand, I'm only speaking of amateurs here. Pros of both sexes are pretty much equally insane.

And the rain falls on

It's raining harder now, and a foursome has just stepped up to the tee. One man is wearing red pants, a blue shirt, and white golf shoes. Another man is dressed in green pants, a vomit-yellow polyester shirt, and green patent-leather golf shoes. The third man is dressed in orange-striped Bermuda shorts, an orange polyester shirt, and white golf shoes with brown socks. The final gentleman of this gruesome foursome is wearing black shoes, black pants, and a black shirt. His golf bag is black and so is his glove. I guess what we have here is the Darth Vader of the country club set.

I need some Pepto Bismol 'cause I'm gonna be sick.

Golf does share something with car racing, sky diving, rodeo riding, and other extreme sports. The participants all wear gloves. Now, golf gloves are great. Cute little gloves generally in white, brown, or black (other colors are available, however), with the end of the fingers cut off. But here's a question: If you need a glove to play the game, why don't club makers change the handles?

Golf club sets can run anywhere from a couple of hundred dollars to thousands of dollars. Theoretically, club makers invest time and money into making the best possible golf club handle imaginable. If that's the case, why wear a glove? Yeah, yeah, yeah, I know.

Golf courses

A great deal of money goes into the building of golf courses. Hundreds of acres must be purchased, and it must all be irrigated with increasingly scarce and expensive water. A golf course architect is hired to design lay the course, and the whole thing has to be constructed and seeded. After that, it takes an enormous amount of water to get the grass growing and to keep it that way. Equipment must be purchased to mow everything and workers hired to maintain the course. And that's just the course.

The clubhouse, restaurant, bar, pro shop, parking lots, cart tracks, and roads must be built, signs installed, and employees hired. The pro shop must be stocked, carts bought, equipment delivered, the clubhouse stocked, and pros engaged. And this is just to open the course, all this money spent before the first person has had a chance to hook or slice their first ball. So far, not one ball has had a chance to land in the rough (anything not green and smooth), sand traps, or water hazards (lakes both big and small and other assorted pools of murky water). No wonder it's so expensive to play.

Stop the insanity

Golf widows and widowers have never understood the power of the game on their spouses. They share this with spouses of individuals who are passionate about fishing, tennis, running, backgammon, skiing, scuba diving, sky diving, mountain climbing, dirt biking, and any of the other hundreds of ways we use to annoy ourselves.

I've never understood it either. Although there is this, there are times when it's simply fun to be out on that course. Your swings are going great, the ball is being hit straight and true, and the person you're playing with talks a mean streak of philosophy—or is at least good with political trivia. Actually, if the talks are good enough, you don't even mind an occasional bad shot. Well, at least not much.

Deeply Buried Feelings

Today, I did something that I have not done in years: I walked on an elementary school campus. My son and I were there because it was the start of his very first day of school. It brought a rush of nostalgia, fear, and very fond memories.

As I walked him to his classroom, feelings swept over me and I was not sure, at the time, exactly what those feelings were. But after having thought about it, I know those feelings were generated by the place, the time, the sights, and the smells.

What is it about schools? And I'm not talking about homework, grades, bullies, good teachers, bad teachers, dating, sports, classes, etc., etc. What I am talking about here is that part of school that gets to the very core of our beings. The part that we remember even seventy years later (just ask my dad), the part that creates feelings as much as memories. We spend a great deal of our life in school. Between elementary school, middle school, and high school, most of us clock in at least thirteen years. And that doesn't take into consideration any time we spend in trade schools or college.

Many, many things happen to us in school. We grow from young children to adults, we learn how to write, we study language, math, science, geography, geology, history, and on and on. But, first of all, in that very first year, we start on the track that allows for everything else.

Not only do we start learning from books and teachers, but just as importantly, we start learning from our peers. We learn how to interact with lots of other kids, how to deal with problems some of those kids create, and we learn *how* to learn.

Fear and laughter

As a child, you walk into the classroom for the first time, look around, and ask yourself, *Who are all these kids?*

You might even think, *I do not want to be here. I want to go home. I want to go home now!!*

But no, you have to stay. And then you start to settle in. You put your backpack away, store your lunch, and then get ready for the teacher to start. And most of this is the same year after year. You might have a bit of fear, but there is also the sound of laughter from kids, and that sound can be very inviting.

When I walked my son in, I was amazed at the walls (they were covered with the usual ABCs, pictures, sayings, and with whatever else teachers use to decorate their walls to make them look more inviting—and have been using for decades). There were the little chairs, the tables close to the floor, the bright overhead lights, the teacher's desk in the corner.

One wall was mostly windows, which could be opened; cabinets were along the bottom third of the other three walls, and sitting on those cabinets were projects of all kinds.

The classroom he is in could have been my classroom so many years ago (okay, except for the computers). I imagine that there is only so much you can do to decorate a room, but the feelings that were brought out in seeing it were enormously powerful.

The room even smelled the same (probably from clay, Play-Doh, finger paints, glue, library paste, lunch bags, and other assorted things in first-year elementary school rooms), and smelling that aroma also brought out feelings long forgotten.

Sounds, smells, sights. They have so much power to bring memories to the surface. And the other morning, as I was walking my son into his class and experiencing the feelings that the memories brought out, I was very glad of one thing: that it was nostalgia that I was feeling and not the trepidation of my first day of school.

Remember something like this?

Late-Night Thoughts

What were you thinking about late last night? You know the time, it's that gray area after we get in bed, turn out the lights, and start to drift off but before we go to sleep. People view the night in so many different ways. For some, the night holds nothing but terror. For others, it is their favorite time. A vast amount of songs, poems, stories, plays, and films take place at night or are about night. Or, indeed, are written at night. The night inspires creativity, terror, passion, love, and warmth.

We still have vestiges of the awe surrounding night. For eons, we viewed the night with fear, with superstition, with dread, with hope. There were no security lights, no alarms, and no police cars cruising the neighborhood. Yet hope also existed, because for all the fear that came with night, there was still hope that you would wake up—and do so healthy and strong.

How do you view the night? Personally, I rather enjoy the night. Long after the sun has gone down, after the birds have quit singing, the phones stopped ringing, and most of the cars are parked in their garages, I'm still awake. Whether writing, working online, reading, or, yes, even watching television, I'm still awake with the night.

One of the many good things about the time after midnight

My best thinking comes late at night. After the house is quiet and my son and daughter are tucked in bed, after the dog is quietly snoring at the side of my chair, after my wife has long since gone to bed, and after the crickets have called it a night and are giving their legs a rest, I'm still awake.

What am I doing still awake? I'm thinking. After all, there are so many great things to think about. And yes, there are also other things to think about, things like when to get a haircut, what color the next car should be, and whether pineapple belongs on a pizza (no—no, it does not). But beyond that, there are a few really wonderful things to ponder. For instance, the other night, I got to thinking about the first thing that led to the first higher-level thought. Okay, maybe that's not so wonderful, but I thought it was very profound at the time. And it was interesting.

Scientists who think about these kinds of things (and writers awake late at night) have often thought that fear was what led to speech and higher thought. For example, one might want, or in fact desperately need, to shout, "Run for your life, big snakes ahead!" If you can't put that kind of thought together, you can't say it.

Or perhaps the first thought was something along the lines of, "I'm hungry, and Fred (not his real name) over there has a moose leg with a lot of meat on it. If I take it away, I'll get the meat. But then he'll probably kill me. Maybe it's better to just politely ask for some." And from that, we might have the first rational thought.

My own thoughts on the first thought

Personally, I think that one of the first thoughts, if not the very first, was nothing more than figuring out how to tie a knot. I can hear you thinking, *A knot? Are you crazy? Why a knot?* Well, I'm glad you thought that because I, for once at least, have an answer.

To start with, let's explore some of the other various possibilities of that "first thought":

1. *Hunger*: Starfish get hungry too. Are they thinking? Not as far as anyone knows.

2. *Cold*: As in, "Hey, I'm cold." Now, this one is possible, because after this thought, one might look for a warm place. But rats do this too. Now, some people might argue that rats, in fact, do think—at least enough to work their way out of a maze. But hunger (see above) is enough of a motivator for that as well.

3. *Heat*: As in, "Whew!" But all animals seek shade, no higher thought required.

4. *Fear*: As in, "Help, a tiger is after me! A saber-toothed tiger!" Now, this one, like the gargantuan snakes we discussed earlier, is a definite possibility. Fear is one of the greatest motivators of all time. And I would probably vote for this one, were it not for the fact that other animals could get afraid and warn each other of impending problems as well. Like parakeets. Enough said.

So, that leads us back to the mundane. And what could be more mundane than tying a knot? Just look at what early humans would have used knots for:

* Tying clothes together to make them warmer
* Making pouches to carry water and food
* Making bows and arrows to hunt and defend themselves
* Aiding in delivery of the young and fixing wounds
* Tying up bad guys so they can't escape
* Tethering the family elephant
* Tying branches together for shelter

There you go, as silly and mundane as it sounds, perhaps nothing more serious, intellectual, or intellect-developing than tying a knot was responsible for putting humans on the path to higher thought.

More than a few billion people worldwide of various faiths may dispute this, of course, but it was something to think about one quiet night.

Old Clunkers, Lovingly Remembered

Karen Carpenter, back in the early seventies, sang a song which had the line, "Rainy days and Mondays always get me down." It always struck me as rather sad, that line, because neither rainy days nor Mondays ever particularly bothered me. I like rainy days (although Mondays are iffy).

Now, I suppose that had I been raised in a place that rained a great deal, I would feel differently. Then again, maybe not. I lived in South Florida during my middle and high school years and it rained there a lot. During the rainy season, from about the beginning of June until mid-September, Florida could be swimming in the rain (excuse the pun). The days were hot and muggy, and then, most every afternoon, came the downpours.

The car windows would steam up with condensation, the roads would get deep with water, and, if you weren't careful, you could drown the engine and find yourself stuck in a busy corner. This would especially happen if you tended to drive old clunkers as I did during most of my high school years.

The Renault

Looking back over my life so far, I have noticed that I tend to remember things based on the car I had at the time. The very first car that I called my own was a 1964 Renault with rather large patches of rust. The car was cream colored with a red vinyl interior. It was a horrible car, but it was mine! Friends and I would load it up with radios, blankets, food, and Cokes and head for the beach. Unfortunately, it leaked water around the windshield and had a push-button transmission that sometimes worked. The poor Renault didn't last very long at all.

The Hillman

My next car was a Hillman. These odd cars were made in England, and my father found this particular one from an old gentleman who lived down the street. It was a four-speed, with gear shifter on the steering column. You moved the shifter in the opposite way you learned. Why?

England, of course. One of the rear doors had to be wired shut, and water made the car break down constantly. You would think that an automobile manufacturer in a country as wet as Great Britain would see to it that the engine compartment would stay dry. But not Hillman; any puddle at all and the engine conked out. This car lasted about as long as the Renault, which is to say, not long at all. But I liked it, and my friends and I drove it everywhere. I don't remember who I sold the Hillman to, but I hope that, by now, they have forgiven me.

As a teenager, I always wondered why my father would suggest old cars for me, his favorite (okay, only) son. Now, of course, I know why. I was a car destroyer. If there was a sand dune to drive over, a swamp to drive through, a street to slide down in the rain, I would be there. I've always had a love affair with cars, but I didn't want to shine them, I wanted to play with them.

The Pontiac Catalina

I was into my third car before I reached eighteen. This was a four-door Pontiac Catalina: a red monstrosity that, at one time, had air conditioning that worked and an automatic transmission that didn't leak. By the time I got my hands on it, however, the tranny leaked like a sieve, and the air hadn't worked in years. One good thing this car did have was one hell of an engine. This multi-hundred cubic inch V8 engine would roar and take off down the road like a race car from your wildest dreams.

The Pontiac didn't last long, either. It sucked down the gas, the transmission needed too much work, and the end came soon.

The Volkswagen Bug

By now, I was ready to graduate from high school and would need a more reliable car. So, Pop and I went looking and found a sky-blue VW Bug. This car was almost new, in great condition, and would be, or so we thought, perfect.

In that Volkswagen, I had four accidents, put in a new engine, and replaced the front end more times than I care to count. That car was repainted so often that, well, let's just say that the body shop never had to order that color. They kept it on hand for me.

It took four cars to get me through high school. I'm not proud of that fact, but there you go.

Picking Memories

Ah, the soft beauty of summer. Those months of warm weather, days at the beach, rocking in a hammock, walks on the shore of a nearby lake, evening dances, and ice cream cones. It was a time of love, convertible tops, drives with friends up the coast for a fire in a ring on the sand and s'mores. It was a time of lemonade, homemade ice cream, Slurpees, and dancing till midnight on the beach at Daytona.

Summer was Key West in the morning, Waikiki at sunset, rowing the Colorado River, and hiking the Blue Ridge Mountains. Summer was a day in Julian, sleeping under the stars in a quiet forest in the San Bernardino Mountains and roasting corn in a pit. Summer was mimosas and shaved ice, bathing suits, hiking boots, sunscreen, and backpacks. Summer was a backyard barbecue, a picnic, a spontaneous get together with old friends.

But summer is more than dreamy visions. During this summer of Over-the-Line weekends, trips across the Golden Gate, and looking for space at Ocean Beach, 6,480 plants and animals went extinct, according to Science Daily. While 15 million moms and dads, sisters and brothers visited Disney World, 1.4 billion moms and dads, sisters and brothers had no access to safe drinking water. Close to 300,000 would die from malaria and 750,000 would die from water-related deaths. For some, summer will be the high point of their lives; for others, it will only be a warm, fuzzy glow when recalled sixty years later. For many, it will be the last summer they experience. For others, it will be a summer of captivity, degradation, and hunger.

Summer is a time of growth—for wild animals and for crops. But global warming and severe shortages of water in many areas are making that growth ever-more tenuous. Rain forests shrink from our need for bare land; slash-and-burn land clearing gives open land but takes away oxygen, possible medicines, and the habitat of so many creatures.

Summer slowly wanders away. School has started, and so drifts off another summer like so much smoke on a breezy day. But while our social clocks may say an end to summer, our physical clock—the one that has governed us for millennia—doesn't say that at all. Our internal seasonal clock says, "Okay, change is afoot, but summer is not over yet for me. No way, not a chance."

Perhaps we should pay closer attention to our inner self that is screaming for attention. Perhaps we should go out and flip some proverbial coins. Do just one more thing. Personally, I want to do one more thing during this end of summer that doesn't require scanning a credit card or entering a code word. Sure, money is important, but time is so much more; your hands are more important; your mind is more important; your words are more important. Your presence is so much more important.

Here's a thought: after the beach, after Disneyland, Sea World, and the zoo, after whatever vacation you managed, why not spend whatever time is left involving yourself in someone else's life? This doesn't mean you have to barge into your neighbor's house and tell them how to live *their* life. No, no, no. I'm talking about involvement in a good way. It means that you look at your near neighborhood and far neighborhood and decide to do something. Simply decide to do something. In your near neighborhood, you could look around and see if an elderly person is struggling with a lawnmower. If so, mow their grass. Is a family member wondering how to get somewhere? Drive them. Someone out of a job? Buy a week's groceries for them.

In most people's near-neighborhoods, the things that are most needed are companionship (is someone living alone? Do they get many visitors? Why don't you visit?) or chores done around a home. Do someone's chores. Find something in your neighborhood you can do and just do it. Clean out a gutter, take someone a pie (or better yet, dinner). I had a friend who used to send pizzas to people he didn't really know in his neighborhood. All he knew was, they were struggling. So, a couple of times a month, he had pizzas delivered to them. They never knew who did it, and he never discussed it. All he ever said about it was, "They were hungry." And that was his way of helping.

As for your far neighborhood, well, that stretches as far out as you want it to or can push it. This may take a bit more research on your part. But, whatever you do, there are so many things that don't require donations or money of any kind. You can donate time, energy, and talent. You can help Amnesty International with a check or with circulating petitions. You can help Red Cross/Red Crescent with money or with doing any of the hundreds of jobs they need help with. Hospitals need help, and so do libraries.

The point is, your summer doesn't have to end on a low note, but a high one. Your summer can end not in discontent but rather end leaving you so contented you're like Grandpa after eating Sunday dinner. You groan, you stretch, you massage your belly, you look around, and you smile.

We have within us the ability to create our own summer smiles and help create smiles for someone else. We have the ability to turn a summer of discontent into one of contentment; into one of contented bliss that has nothing to do with cruise-line midnight buffets, inclusive packages at Disney World, choosing seats on Delta Airlines, or frantically trying to see whatever it is you can see in the short time you have.

Find your contentment wherever you are and with whatever you're doing. And remember that it's only from discontent that anything ever gets accomplished. When we're contented, we're not very motivated to do anything. It was discontent that drove Thomas Edison, Mother Theresa, and Martin Luther King. Revel in your discontent, be glad for it, and then do something with it. Summer ends and fall and winter are approaching. When you look back on this summer, what will you remember? The good (there was some) or the bad (and yep, there was some). You can't pick your memories, but you can choose how you respond to them and what you ultimately do with them. What will you do with yours?

Quality Assurance Inspectors

Ever go to a store or online site of one sort or another, buy something, and then when you get it home and unpack it, a tiny piece of paper falls out? You know that piece of paper; it usually says something like "Inspected by," followed by either a name or number. It doesn't seem to happen as much as it used to—maybe the inspectors are going anonymous now.

My question is this: Just who are these people? Now, I realize that sounds simplistic, but think about it. Have you ever met someone who said that his or her job was "dishes inspector"? Under their name on their business card, does it read, "Inspector 47"?

This all came about because, at work today, I opened a new file cabinet and a small piece of paper fell out. The paper read: "QUALITY ASSURANCE NOTICE." Underneath that was, "The quality of this product was inspected with care by," and under that was a line with the name of a man typed in. Finally, there was this: "Please include this notice with any correspondence concerning this product."

Is a job at risk?

So, let us say that you noticed a problem with your new file cabinet (there wasn't with mine, it was fine). You bought it, took it to wherever you needed it, removed it from the box, and got ready to put files into this quality file cabinet.

Suddenly, as you opened a drawer, you realized that the tracks that hold the files were missing. The cabinet looked good, the drawers all opened quietly, but there was no way to hang your hanging folders. So, what do you do?

Of course, you start looking around for something that gives information on how to contact the company. You find that on the back of the cabinet, something that says it was made with (pick your term) pride, excellence, the customer in mind, etc., etc. There is a phone number there, and you decide to use it.

Who do you call? Sure, you call the manufacturer, but then what? Do you complain to the innocent person who answers the phone? Do you ask for a supervisor? A manager? The president of the company who, by gosh, should be there taking calls like these?

Nope, you decide to ask to speak to the inspector, the person who, with his or her own hands and eyes, inspected your filing cabinet.

Now, tell me. Does this person really exist? Is she or he really there? Does this person stand on the assembly line, day after day, and inspect? There have to be inspectors, right? These inspectors have names, right? So, there is a very good chance that the person who inspected your cabinet is there right now, still inspecting away.

Here is what I want to know. If something gets by an inspector, does that inspector get in trouble? Is this person's job at risk? Does the company count how many problem calls they receive? Of course. And then they know who let those problems slip by. Have you ever met someone who was fired as a quality assurance inspector? Nope, me either.

What makes a good inspector?

Are there special things that make an inspector good at the job? Could a robot do an inspector's job? Maybe, maybe not. But right now, while some things are inspected by computer or robot, many others simply cannot be.

But have you ever noticed that all these "Inspected by" notices are not really in the right places? Sure, pants or shirts or even TVs are good things to have inspected, but the things that I want inspected are, I think, much more important. For instance, who is inspecting the ice cream at 31 Flavors? I've never had a bad ice cream there—that inspector must be doing a good job. Now, this is a job I could really sink my teeth into (sorry, but I couldn't resist).

Who is inspecting paper clips and toothbrushes? Who is looking after the socks, or even more important, who is inspecting underwear?

Here's something else: Who is inspecting all the bags of charcoal that get sold over the warm summer months? What would happen if someone got a bad bag of charcoal and took it to the family picnic? Would it burn too fast or not at all? Have you even once thought about this? And yet, there we blindly go on sunny weekends, buying bag after bag of the stuff, ever-confident that our burgers, steaks, and fish will cook up just fine.

Who inspects sugar? More than that, who inspects artificial sweet-ener? Sure, it might look pure and all, but how could you be sure of how it tasted if you didn't test the occasional batch of it? And wouldn't *that* get old after a while?

I know an inspector we really need: a film and TV show inspector. Not one inspecting for nudity or violence, but someone inspecting for quality. Actually, never mind. If we had a film and TV quality inspector, there wouldn't be very much at all to watch.

Here is a final thought on the subject (I promise): Who inspects the "Inspected by" notice included with the product? And where was that notice?

Road Rage on the Information Superhighway

...and other brief thoughts...

The other day, I was working at the computer, trying to find information about a specific place in England. After spending what seemed like hours pounding out all sorts of arcane and confusing net addresses on a keyboard, I had to give up. The web is no place for a rational person, not that I've ever actually considered myself rational, but you know what I mean.

In the media of late, there have been far too many stories of something called "road rage." This affliction used to be called mad-as-hell-at-that-idiot-driver-from-Miami-up-ahead syndrome, but road rage sounds so much cooler. Now, of course, everyone in media has picked it up, and pretty soon, we'll see "Road Ragers the Movie" on Comedy Central. That is, if Netflix doesn't get there first and create a new TV series based on it (Queer Eye for the Straight Road Rager?)

Rage from being stuck in traffic, as bad as it may be, is one thing, but there is something much worse. Much, much worse. It's called Info Rage. Spending too much time, and then becoming frustrated, on the information superhighway, brings about this horrible anger. And a truly horrible rage it is—I've seen grown men reduced to tears; I've seen grown women fling desktop computers to the ground.

I believe we need to set up a department at the Centers for Disease Control in Atlanta to see what can be done to aid those walking around with this blind anger. For the small cost of just a few billion dollars, we ought to be able to come up with something resembling a cure. I volunteer to head the organization. Well, not volunteer, of course, but my salary wouldn't be all *that* high, seeing what psychologists get to help people live with the rage and all.

In fact, I'm pretty sure there is a cure for Info Rage. The problem is, the cure is not cheap, and people don't seem to want to spend the money on something that's good for them. But that's another story. The cure is simply this: turn off the computer (yes, this part may take a family intervention, but with enough patience, it can be done).

After the computer is off, jump in the car and head for the nearest airport and get on a plane (after going through the required four-hour security checkpoints, of course). The destination doesn't really matter, but a place that's balmy and warm would be good.

While you're there, be sure to swim, eat well, and stay far away from any electronic device (well, and sharks too. Just sayin'). This includes computers, tablets, cell phones, etc. Please note that this *does not* include cardiac pacemakers.

A couple of thoughts having nothing whatsoever to do with information or superhighways

Not to change the subject or anything, but I've developed a fantastic new way to lose weight. No special diets are involved, and you don't need to buy any particular food or dietary supplement. No, it doesn't involve stapling any part of the body. I bring this up now because you don't want to head to a tropical paradise looking 137 pounds overweight.

Since you're probably breathless with anticipation about this new diet, I won't keep you in suspense any longer. This fantastic new product is Miles's Exercise-While-You-Eat Program. You just strap weights on your wrists anytime you eat. You'll burn calories every time you move your arm taking bites. You add more weight to the wrist depending on just how much you want to lose on a one-to-one basis.

Want to lose one pound? Strap on a one-pound weight. Want to lose one hundred pounds? Simply strap to your wrists one hundred pounds (okay, not really strap, but through an operation, permanently fuse a chain to your wrist bones and attach those to the weights. That way, there's no cheating). Also, you can add extra weight to help speed your weight loss. The more weight on the wrist, the faster you lose. Nothing could be simpler. Look for a $145 book on this revolutionary new diet, coming soon.

Or, if you don't have time to read, you could come to my seminars. I'll be holding seminars in cities throughout the country in a location near you. Cost is minimal—certainly less than the cost of 300 prime rib dinners (with wine). Plus, if you bring a friend and that friend signs up, you get yours for half price! And if that friend brings a friend and that friend brings a friend, well, in no time at all, yours could be free!

And then you could start your own program of miracle weight-loss seminars and get rich in just days! And if those people signed up… wait, it's sounding too much like multi-level marketing. Never mind (call me later—we'll talk).

Just imagine if all the people who come up with various multi-level marketing and other scams actually spent that time doing something worthwhile. Those people, the ones you ultimately see being carted off to jail, are very smart people (not smart enough to keep out of jail, but no one's perfect). After all, they have to come up with the plan, design it, sell it, and stay ahead of the legal profession. What if all that intelligence was put to good use? We could have pollution-free cars, calorie-free food, clothes that never got dirty or wrinkled, and sauerkraut that actually tasted good. Okay, that last thing would never happen—could never happen—but we could have some pretty good things, anyway.

Here's the plan: for every good invention that a prisoner comes up with, their prison time is reduced by 1 percent. There are thousands of prisoners. Give them a *good* incentive to try and do something for the good of humanity and reward it with something the prisoner values. Let's just see what happens.

The horror of another seminar.

Still/Still/Still Asking

This is still one of my favorite questions to ask people: Do you wonder about things? I ask this because I do. I wonder about lots of things, and people tell me that I have always been that way. My parents say that I asked questions non-stop. It would often drive them crazy, but they always took time to answer me. I suppose that might be why I still ask lots of questions—growing up with always having the freedom to ask.

Now that I have kids of my own (good grief!), I am starting to get some of these questions asked of me. Well, at least by Son, who is eight. Daughter, who is ten months old, is not asking a whole lot of questions just yet. Although she does look at me with a great deal of wonder now and then.

It seems that, lately, there have been an increasing number of questions running through this brain of mine (or at least the thing that I use that passes for a brain). Some of these I've asked before, and some are new—the repeats are here because, so far, they haven't been answered. I don't know why they haven't been answered, but there you go. However, I am still asking.

Just some really simple, and not so simple, questions

1. Why does the phone ring or someone knock on the door just when you get in the shower?

2. Why, when you think you're being smart and turn off the phone before getting into the shower, does no one call?

3. Why does the thought of changing the oil in your car never surface until you are in a hurry to get somewhere? If I have all the time in the world, I never think of it, and when I'm in a hurry, I always do. Go figure.

4. Why aren't sanitation workers paid more? They do an amazing job in a difficult environment.

5. Why does a kid always have to go to the restroom in the most crowded place there is, at the worst possible time? Since having children of my own, this has really been brought home. I'll ask

my son three times if he has to go, and he will say no three times. Then, just when we get in bumper-to-bumper traffic, he'll announce—with some urgency—that he has to go, *"right now and I can't wait!"*

6. Why is the trade-in value of your car less than your kid's bicycle? Why are kids' bicycles so expensive?

7. Why do they only make pumpkin-flavored ice cream once a year? Come on, it's good stuff and deserves to be on the shelf longer than the time between Halloween and Thanksgiving.

8. Why do all the good things to eat have to be bad for you? And is anyone working on this? We'll spend billions on bombs but very little on finding replacements for fat-laden, sugar-enriched foods. It's time we work on our priorities.

9. Why do you have to wait in restaurants when empty booths and tables are in plain sight? And then, when you're seated, it takes forever to get served. And this is one of the very reasons that fast-food restaurants have become so popular. Well, that and price.

10. Why do English majors have to study algebra? I understand why math majors have to study English—you still have to read and write—but very few English majors are involved with higher mathematics (I'm pretty sure contracts must be signed).

11. When will NASA get on with serious planetary exploration? The Mars Rovers were great—now put some astronauts on Mars. Exploration is good for the human race.

12. Why is it not possible to eat just one potato chip? Believe me, I've tried (okay, I haven't tried all that hard).

13. Why does the phone *never* ring when you need it to ring?

14. Why do we insist on putting so much trash in a plastic bag that the bottom rips out? Are we that optimistic or just too lazy to get another bag?

15. Why do we insist on eating when we're not hungry?

16. When was the last time you went on a diet? Yesterday? Yeah, me too. It lasted until today.

17. How did I get hooked on sour cream and onion?

18. How did I get hooked on Coke?

19. How did I get hooked on chocolate?

20. Never mind, I know the answer to number 5

21. Why do we insist on doing stupid things?
22. I once read something about "left-handed" sugar. It is exactly like regular sugar, with one molecule changed. Because of that single change, the body will not absorb the sugar. It tastes exactly like regular sugar, but with no calories whatsoever. Where is this stuff? I want it. I want it today, right now, this very second.

I grant you that these are not earth-shattering questions, but I was thinking about them—probably to avoid doing any real work. Feel free to add any of your own to the list...

The Great Party Test

Have you ever gone to a party and then the next day someone asks you how it was? Me too. Then you need to stop and think about it, try to remember specific incidents, before coming up with the answer.

Well, worry no more. I've come up with a fool-proof way to let you know each and every time whether or not a party was good. It's called the "Great Party Test," and if the party you attend passes it, you had a great time, whether you liked it or not.

The Great Party Test

1. Did the police ever have to be called? The fewer police, the better the party (unless they're invited guests, in which case, this doesn't apply).
2. Were paramedics there for any reason other than to use your house to get into the backyard of the house next door?
3. Was the weather good? If not, did you have a plan for that? Why not? Haven't you learned by now?
4. Did you run out of anything? And I do mean *anything*. Be sure to check the paper supply with as much diligence as you do the beer supply.
5. Has the entertainment been set? At one time, not too many years ago, entertainment would have consisted of a musician or games. Not anymore. Now, even for a child's party, you need to take entertainment very seriously. For kids, there are pony rides, clowns, magicians, air jumps, and on and on and on. For adults, there are musicians, magicians, bands, and a whole lot more. And, apparently, you need this entertainment to be as good as possible. I guess someone thinks that a child's mind might be ruined by too few ponies or something…
6. Cost. Did the party cost more than your first house? If so, the party was good; if not, well, your friends may speak to you again someday. Your spouse or kid? Probably not.
7. Were more people invited than can ever fit in your home?
8. Did the vast majority of them RSVP and say they were coming?

9. Are you thinking of how quickly you could close escrow on a new, larger home?

10. Were the logistics you used in military training easier than those connected with the party?

11. Did you forget at least two people that absolutely, positively had to be invited, and now you have to drive the invitation over to their house with some lame explanation of how the invitation must have gotten lost in the mail?

12. Did you have to rent chairs, bar equipment, sound equipment?

13. Did you have to store things in your neighbor's garage?

14. Did you then need to invite your neighbor? The one you hate?

15. Have you taken an oath to never, never, never do this again? Did your spouse just laugh and remind you of the next child's birthday in five weeks? Did you go and look in a mirror for more gray hair?

My parties never look like this. If yours do, please invite me to one!

The Things You Leave

Think about what is in your desk, your car, your bedroom and bathroom, and your office. Now think about someone going through all that stuff of yours. Is there anything you don't want seen? What will someone think when they see it?

Then things we leave behind—by accident or design—speak stories about who we were. As we get older, we start to slowly move into that time where the things we leave behind can matter more than the things we have.

Do you have an office that you've been using for a number of years? Do you have books, records, and minutiae of a professional life in that office? One day, you might turn off the lights and lock the door of that office on your way home and never return.

Is there a closet, or a number of closets, with boxes of things that haven't seen the light of day in years that you'd really like to go through? Should go through? Must go through?

The evidence we leave

People, family and sometimes friends or legal representatives, will go through the drawers, the filing cabinets, the bookshelves, and the closets. They will go through everything. Some things may be kept, some things may be shared, some donated, some tossed, some taken home and put in another closet for someone else to go through years or decades later.

It's how things happen. Some items kept, some thrown away, some donated to charitable organizations, and the rest are disposed of in estate sales or garage sales.

So, for this little "play the evidence" game, imagine that you never walked into your office or home again—what would be found? What would be found in your wallet? Your bedside table? Your car? Your desk? I'm not sure, but I think that the things we leave behind, the things we leave because we had no warning or choice in the matter, will probably speak volumes about us.

The things we leave behind

1. Keys (those that fit something and those that no longer do—and haven't for years)

2. Wallet—What is in your wallet right now? An old love note? A faded picture? Credit card receipts? Phone numbers? Directions to a forgotten place? Pictures? Business cards?

3. Books—What books are you leaving? Are they trashy novels? Good novels? Biographies? Travel books? What did you read and what is the evidence of it? Or, perhaps the worst thing, aren't you leaving any books at all?

4. Toiletries—What is in your bathroom cabinet, drawer, or shelf? A particular cologne or perfume? A deodorant? Does the toothpaste tube still have the imprint from your fingers? How about medicines? What medicines will have to be tossed now that they're no longer needed?

5. Clothes—What clothes do you have hanging in your closet or folded in your dresser? Do you have anything decades out of date? Any old disco clothes? Any old double-knit? What's in there that, when someone sees, it will make them instantly think of you? Is anything there that smells slightly of your scent? Does the person removing the clothes gingerly touch them and remember the last time they were worn? Does it bring a tear?

6. Car—What does your car have in it right now? What is in the trunk or the glove compartment? What will the things say about where you drove last? What do the gas receipts reveal? Will the car immediately be sold or kept? Who will drive it?

7. Look around. See anything with your writing on it? Any notes? Shopping lists? Old cards you've saved? What has your handwriting on it, your signature? Our handwriting can say a great deal about us—what does yours say about you? Were you methodical? Were you always in a hurry? Were you just sloppy?

8. Food or drinks—What's in the house that you particularly liked to eat or drink? Is there something that, when anyone tastes it, they will immediately think of you?

9. Your special things—These can be anything: your golf clubs or basketball, your hobby things, your musical instrument, your CDs, your things from childhood you still drag around with you (have any old trophies, yearbooks, models, or dolls?), your tools, and your briefcase. In other words, these are all the things that simply say "you" without ever saying a word.

10. Memories—What are the memories you leave with those who came in contact with you? Are they happy memories? Sad ones? When people think of you, do they do so with a smile or a frown? Hint: if they remember you with a frown, it may be time to rethink your life and how you live it. I can't imagine anything worse than a life so lived that, when it was over, only bad memories were left.

So, there are but a few of the many things we may leave behind after we depart this world. What else is there that retains a bit of you? It's possible that our worldly end can come so quickly, without any warning, that when it actually happens, we are unprepared. More than that, our friends and family are also unprepared.

If there is one thing you can take away from this column, it should probably be this: don't leave a mess, don't leave something that just brings sadness. Help people smile when they remember you, because they will remember. Wouldn't you rather they have good memories than bad ones? Walk softly and let the imprint be good.

The Well of Inspiration

There have been millions of words written about that marvelous and most human of things called inspiration. Most of those words have come from better writers than me. But I started thinking about it the other day when someone asked me what the source was for my newspaper columns. In other words, where did my inspiration come from?

The Oxford English Dictionary calls inspiration a "sudden brilliant idea," and this is a definition I rather like because it makes such good sense. Apparently, inspiration needs to be an idea that is both brilliant and sudden. The sudden idea of driving one's car off the road is not inspired unless it is done at the last minute to avoid a huge truck. That makes it brilliant. And the two things together equal inspiration.

The root cause of inspiration

What caused humans to develop this ability to be inspired? There is something within us that allows us to be able to look at the stars and stand in awe; to be able to create lasting music that stirs us to the depth of our being; to be able to put pen to paper and create intellectual and emotional magic; to be able to look at a mathematical equation and see an answer never before dreamed.

Humans have philosophy and religion and art. We have science, medicine, engineering, and the ability to comprehend the past and the future. Do we have these things because we can be inspired, or can we be inspired because we have these things? A tricky question to be sure, but a valid one.

What inspires you?

Each of us has those unique things that inspire us. What inspires you? Here are the things that seem to inspire many of us, at least according to a random (and unscientific) poll I took:

Music
Coffee or other, stronger, liquids

Sunset
Sunrise
Rainy or stormy days
Love
Hate
Beauty
Children
Poverty
Success
Religion
Fear
Pain avoidance
Desire

The list could go on, of course, but I'm sure you can start to see a pattern. There is a similarity here, a simple one. The pattern is this: we are inspired by things beyond us, within us, from us, by us, and by many things out of our control entirely. We are humans, we are inspired, and in turn, we inspire.

From where do we receive inspiration? Some people say from ourselves, some others say from God, still others say from nature. Then there are those who simply say it is something wonderful known as the human conscious, or a well from which we dip wonder.

The final word has not yet been written on the magical source of human inspiration. I'm just glad—grateful, actually—that it exists.

DREAM IT
WISH IT
DO IT
Live LOVE Laugh
GER POR
SDP 318
YOU ARE SO WORTH IT
LITTLE THINGS
COUNT YOUR BLESSINGS
MY KIDS HAVE PAWS
EVERYDAY
HAPPY WIFE HAPPY LIFE
DREAMS DON'T WORK UNLESS YOU DO
HAPPY PLACE
love
WINE BECAUSE

Weird Dreams

Had any weird dreams lately? I had one the other night that had coach Pinot Noir serving as head football trainer for Ellen DeGeneres. No, I don't know why.

When I woke up, I lay there in bed for a few minutes quietly wondering to myself just why on earth I had been dreaming that dream. But dreams can be like that. Often, there may be very specific things that they can tell us (just ask any Freudian psychiatrist), but sometimes, no matter just how much you try to tear the dream apart, it finally comes back to *you just had a weird dream.*

All this got me thinking about what other weird dreams may be out there. So, I started asking people what strange dreams they've had. It's an interesting list.

Bizarre dreams

One person I asked told me all about his dream of sailing around the world in a small sailboat by himself, and there was never any wind in the sails. Another man offered this as his weirdest dream: he was trudging across the Sahara Desert. He walked over sand dune after sand dune after sand dune. The harsh, dry wind was blowing, the temperature was 125 degrees, he had no water, and buzzards were circling overhead.

My son used to dream of Santa Claus, which made sense at the time, and sometimes his dreams got a bit confused. Such as the dream when Santa Claus met up with the Easter Bunny and the two of them went trick-or-treating for Halloween. It took him a long time to explain it, and me even longer to understand. He's in his twenties now and I don't dare ask him about his dreams. There are some things a parent should not know.

Another one of his interesting dreams was this one: he said that the family was on a boat and we were sailing around the bay, when a submarine surfaced next to us. Then some sailors came out of the sub and waved to him. He said we all waved back, and then the sailors went back in the sub and it dove beneath the waves.

Dreaming of food

A friend of mine, when I mentioned that I was writing about dreams, shared some of his strange ones. Apparently, he dreams of food a great deal. I'm not sure why food plays such a large part of his dreamtime, but it does.

Anyway, in one of his dreams, he was at a state banquet. It was a very formal affair, with waiters in tuxedos, and an orchestra playing. He kept trying to get a dance with someone who also wanted to dance with him. But every time they approached each other to dance, there was a small earthquake, and everyone fled the room, taking their dinner with them.

Another friend said that her strangest dream was one in which she got married to a man she didn't know, and the minister performing the ceremony was her real husband. She wondered if the dream meant that she was subconsciously unhappy with her marriage. But then she wasn't sure about that because her husband was there performing the ceremony. Unless what it all meant was that she was unhappy, wanted to get out of her marriage and into another, better one, but wanted that to be what her husband wanted as well. It was a very confusing conversation, to say the least.

Anyway, we dream, we think about dreaming, and we dream again the next night. It seems that humanity has been wondering about their dreams since recorded history began. Dreams are fascinating things, scary or happy or anything in between.

Where Did All the Laughter Go, and When Did It Leave?

I've got a question and it's a serious one, even though the topic is humor. So, here it is: At what age did you quit laughing? Now, if you're like most people to whom I ask that question, you said something like, "What are you talking about? I still laugh!"

But, you know what? You probably don't. Now, please understand that I'm not talking about "adult laughter," that kind where we chuckle, we snicker a bit, or we cover our mouths when we have to laugh at something. Nope, I'm talking about the kind of laughter that wells up deep within us, comes barreling out, and we can't hold it in. The kind where you cut loose with a laugh that is loud, raucous, and won't stop. The kind of laughter we had as kids. The kind of laughter we had when we weren't shy about laughing, we didn't need to be grownup, we weren't afraid to laugh.

Remember that laughter? That wonderful laughter? What happened to it? When did you stop that kind of laugher?

Most of us stop that kind of laughing in our teen years. It's then that we start to try to look cool, be cool. And, for some reason, we never think it's very cool at all to laugh very much. Well, you know something? We were wrong.

A cool time of year

This time of year is always wonderful. It's graduation time—a time filled with laughter. The faces look so smart and learned. The eyes sparkle and the step has a pronounced bounce. These women and men *have graduated!*

From where did your child graduate? Was it from pre-school to kindergarten, or from elementary to middle school? Or, perhaps, your child went from middle to high school. Could it be that, this week, your son or daughter finally graduated from high school? Or, just possibly, your child is now graduating from a vocational school or college.

From wherever your child is graduating, it is definitely a *big deal!*

"Look at me, Mom! Look at me, Dad! Look at me, world! I graduated!"

One more success in life

I like graduations; they are wonderful success stories. There are, after all, many things that can hinder education. Just a few of the obstacles that can get in the way of a complete education include poverty, health, lack of motivation, peer pressure, drugs, violence, pregnancy, and lack of a role model. Yet, millions of people around the world are graduating this year. Millions of adults who raised these kids are seeing their own hard work pay off.

The world of the graduate *will never again be the same.* Some of the people with whom great and wonderful friendships were forged will never be seen again. Some people will change careers, while others will start new ones. Some people are continuing with education, while others are finally finishing.

Some individuals came to the school as children and left as adolescents. Others came as adolescents and are leaving as adults. All are leaving a bit wiser, a bit more mature (even if it is a fifty-five-year-old college graduate or a five-year-old nursery school graduate), and will never look at themselves in quite the way they did before they walked on stage to get that diploma.

We all made a difference

Sometimes, we hear about the impact a teacher had on a student. Well, you know what? I have never met a teacher whose life was not changed by their students, either.

Here is something you might think about. At some point in the distant future, you'll think wistfully about a teacher. Perhaps that instructor smiled at you during a depressing morning; maybe she truly made algebra not just understandable but so much fun that you made computer science your career. It might be that he taught you what good writing actually looks like, or he helped you further your own understanding of the cosmos. Maybe she just took the time to hear you.

This is the interesting part: that teacher you may think about years from now will have also thought about you. You have had an impact on your school and on your instructors that lasts lifetimes. Now the world is yours; treat it well.

CHAPTER NINE

Rants and Blusters and Things That Go Bump in the Night

Okay, fine. Yes, sometimes I do go off on a rant. But I mean, come on, have you seen what passes for men's fashion?

Anyway, it's difficult to go through life without a few rants, some blusters, and running straight into things that go bump in the night. Although, in all fairness, it's usually me that's going bump in the night. Want a perfectly reasonable and vile rant of your own? Stub your toe on a bed leg in the middle of the night. That'll get your juices flowing.

One night, I woke up with stomach cramps—the kind that say, "Haul ass, you need a bathroom"—and as I was hauling ass, I stubbed a little toe on a bed leg. I was not a happy camper at that point. Hop on one foot, grab the other one, and pray I make the bathroom. Oh, yeah, there were rants that night.

At least my spouse was compassionate, right? "Hey, can you be a little quieter? I'm trying to sleep!"

"Well, I'm trying to not bleed and poop on the floor!"

"Thank you, now do it quieter."

Oh, yeah, that was a great night.

Enough Already with the Beeps, Buzzes, Chirps, Bells, Chimes, Tones, Rings, and Musical Washing Machines

The past couple of weeks have been topsy-turvy and I'm ready to take a swim with the sharks. I've had it. Enough is enough—and *was* enough years ago. And it's getting worse. A lot worse. And I'm getting crankier. Now, please don't misunderstand me, I'm not on a rampage about noise because it might cause hearing problems, or health problems, or anything else. I'm ticked off about noises that are just abysmally, horrifically, dreadfully annoying.

I'm also not writing about sounds that exist to allow the visually impaired to live easier, less frustrating lives. There were many things my father owned—including his clock radio and his watch that spoke—which permitted him a much higher quality of life. I'm just writing about the sounds that are used because we can, because a company thinks it can charge more for a product that is seen to do more when it actually doesn't.

Let's be clear about another thing. I'm not speaking of volume; I listen to loud music. I'm not speaking of musical styles; plenty of people might find fault with my taste in music. My rant here is strictly limited to noise. What kind of noise? Well, in my car, there are probably a dozen distinct sounds. Push a radio button, there is a beep; push a climate button, there is a chirp; turn on lights or press another of a dozen buttons, and you'll hear all sorts of strange little tones.

Why would pushing a radio station pre-set button require a beep? We can figure out something was pushed because the station changes. The same thing holds true for any of the other things that make noise. Those sounds are there because something is happening, but we already know they're happening because something, yes, happens.

And that's just one of the cars—the others chirp and beep as well, but none of them make the same sound for the same thing. A climate change might chirp in one car but beep in the other. It's not only noisy, but even worse, its inconsistent noise.

Is it just the cars making all this noise? Of course not. In my kitchen, the oven makes two different sounds, the microwave beeps, the toaster chimes, and the toaster oven dings. The dishwasher pings, the phone chirps, and the under-cabinet TV peeps. And, remember, that's just the kitchen.

Every TV in the house has some quirky noise associated with it. The security keypad makes strange little sounds that can't ever be turned off. I called the company to check on this one because when I turn on or off the alarm, it chirps, which has been known to wake up a child; this would be all right if not for the fact that it's my child. If she's asleep, I really want her to stay asleep. Company said sorry, but there was no way to disconnect the keypad sounds. If I ever find a security company with a silent pad, I'm going to disconnect my current service.

So far, we've discussed cars, appliances, security pads, and TVs. Anything else? Oh, of course. There are telephone keypads, computers, printers, alarm clocks (not the alarm—the buttons to set the alarm), vacuum cleaners, toys beyond count, toys beyond count, and yes, toys beyond all possible count. Perhaps it's time to rethink unnecessary sounds. People deal with enough noise in their lives; why should we have to put up with even more of it from a microwave oven?

We shouldn't have to. Period.

But wait!

It gets even better! A few weeks ago, we got a new washing machine. The old one was going to cost more to repair than it was worth (it seems like everything is like that), so I went online and searched for a washing machine.

Google "new washing machines for sale" and see what happens. You get approximately 118,000,000 results. Excuse me? Nearly two hundred million hits for new washing machines? Who can even start to go through all those?

Not me. I went to the top few, found a couple of machines to compare, and we bought it at Home Depot. It was delivered and set up, and the family is happy once again. Okay, not really, but we're cleaner.

But, wait—again!

This new washing machine plays songs. I'm not sure what the songs or tunes are but, baby, it plays them. It has the usual beeps, dings, chirps, bells, moans, groans, heavy breathing, and musical notes. Oh, yes, it has the usual sounds that everything has. But even more, this thing plays songs. When a load is complete, you get a nice little jingle. How soothing. It's much more soothing, in fact, than the microwave's chirps.

So, let's see. In the past few weeks, I've been involved in the purchase of:

A Jeep
A washing machine
A really freaking big sectional
A coffee table that has a top that raises
A reading table
Fixtures for three bathrooms
Paint for three bathrooms
Supplies for the paint and fixtures for the three bathrooms

Trust Me, I'm Really, Really, Really Not Complaining, Really. However, Now That We're on the Subject...

Okay, I lied. I am complaining. But I have to—we all have to. And you know what I'm talking about: if we don't complain, *it will just get worse.* We must complain about the kinds of things that make you mumble to yourself, "What on earth was someone thinking?"

Examples? You want a few examples? No problem.

Proof that we live in a very bizarre world:

Example 1: Cell phone cases, face plates, or shells come in vast numbers of colors and designs. Do we really need cell phones in fuchsia with Barbie logos all over them? Is the baby-blue or purple or yellow phone going to make you look, or sound, any better? Yes, some individuals probably do need an Otter Box or a Ballistic Tactical Case, but most of the rest of the planet probably do not.

Example 2: Speaking of cell phone covers, let's drop the cover and just talk phone plans: there are too many. According to WhistleOut, there are 196,093 cell phone plan combinations in the US. Who could possibly look at even a fraction of them? No one. So, we blindly choose something that might work for us and then complain about it until we switch it for another one a few years later.

Example 3: A user guide for one of my previous phones was 136 pages long. That many pages for a phone? A phone? Are they out of their minds? I'm a guy; we don't read user guides. What were they thinking? Were they thinking? For those individuals who may be in a hurry, there's a quick-reference guide that is only eighteen pages long.

The guide for my current phone has no "pages" because it's an electronic file. I haven't checked yet, but that file is probably larger than the one containing my medical records.

Example 4: Bright-yellow cars. It's just too "lemon-like."

Example 5: Computer mice in multitudes of colors (some with whiskers). Oh, yeah, that'll make you more productive.

Example 6: Houses painted in colors not made for houses. You've seen these houses; we all drive by them. I saw another one the other day. Picture it: a blue house. No, I don't mean a light-blue house with contrasting trim. And no, I don't mean a house trimmed in blue. I'm talking about an entire house painted the same shade of medium-dark blue. The entire house, window trim, doors, garage door, all of it the same. I still can't understand why the neighbors didn't commit various sorts of crimes against that house.

Example 7: Fax machines in cars. "How did your husband die?"

"Oh, he was trying to fax in an order to a restaurant as he drove over to pick up the food. He hit another car driven by someone on their cell phone ordering concert tickets."

No one really uses these much anymore, unless it's in the back of a limo. And even that is probably more show than function. Heck, you can fax with a phone. Yippee.

Example 8: Chatting on cell phones while driving (yes, it's illegal, yes, traffic enforcement has cracked down, yes, people do it, making it unsafe for everyone). The weird thing is, the kind of conversation between people in cars are often similar to those who talk to each other all the time anyway. "Hi there. I just wanted to say what a great time I had at lunch."

"Oh, me too."

"So, did you see what he/she was wearing?"

"Can you believe that she/he would wear that to work?"

"Not since she/he got caught by his/her wife/husband."

"I know!"

"So, what are you doing this weekend?"

"Nothing, what about you?"

"Nothing."

"Too bad."

"Yeah. Oh well, see you later."

"Yeah, see you later."

You get the idea, I'm sure. And you've probably seen it or heard it as well. In fact, you may be one of those people. Nah, not you.

Example 9: Junk mail. Simply that, junk mail, whether paper or electronic. I'm sure there's a special place in Hell for people who send out mass flyers and email ads.

Okay, that's it for now. There are millions of things, but they won't all fit in one book. But doesn't it feel good to complain occasionally? It's not something we do a lot (okay, I sometimes do), but every now and then, it can make the load we all carry seem just a little bit lighter. At least, I hope so.

It's a Garage! They're Not Supposed to Be Clean

How clean is your garage? That's assuming you have a garage, of course. If you're lucky—or smart—you don't have one, and in that case, you can simply read this and make fun of your family and friends who do have one of the hated things.

Here's another question: how clean is a garage supposed to be? Sure, we see photos of spotless, near-empty garages in *Architectural Digest*, but just how close to reality is that for most of us?

The average garage for the average family (whatever your definition of average may be) probably has at least some of these items:

- Gardening tools
- Old paint (a few cans still good but most dried up long ago)
- Rope
- Snow toys left over from a weekend in the snow twelve years ago
- Tools (how many depends on how handy the user pictures him or herself); many go unused
- Rags
- Jumper cables (you never know)
- Oil
- A few old car parts
- A bicycle or two
- Cases of water, soda, and/or beer

There's more

Beyond those things, a good number of garages have:

- Skis
- Skateboards
- Barbecue equipment
- Hibachis

- More tools
- More paint
- Something flammable
- Dusty boxes of tax, income, and expense records
- Boxes of other papers too important to throw away but forgotten about years ago anyway
- New(er) beach umbrella
- Old(er) beach umbrella
- Sand toys
- Equipment from basketball, softball, baseball, tennis, soccer, golf, bowling, or any other sport someone, at some time, in the family indulged in

And even more

And finally, I imagine that at least a few garages have:

- A partially dismantled car
- A partially dismantled off-road vehicle
- A partially dismantled boat
- A jet ski or two or three (any one of which may also be dismantled)
- A hang glider
- An old trophy or two from childhood
- Items tossed out when you redecorated but liked too much to throw away (even though you admitted that it might just be time to let the disco ball go)

Now for my big mess

My suppository—sorry, I meant *repository*—of the rarely used, often unneeded, and generally forgotten items include:
Some of the above *plus*

- Dog leashes
- Old fish aquarium
- Old fish aquarium equipment including heater, pump, gravel, plastic plants, stones, miniature skin diver to aerate the tank, and

more—so much more

- Old plastic kids' pool
- Toys for the old plastic kids' pool
- Equipment for the new plastic kids' pool (for kids who, by the way, outgrew the thing ten years ago)
- Twenty feet of floor-to-ceiling shelving to hold even more stuff, such as the thirty-year-old reel-to-reel tape recorder someone gave me that needs to be repaired, so when I get it repaired I can use it to listen to old tapes of me when I was on radio (on the very remote chance I still even have the things)
- Boxes of old (as opposed to at least somewhat newer) books, although I have tossed some of those away. After all, why keep a history book that stops in the middle of the Nixon administration?
- Three tons of dust (this is just an estimate)

Finally, in most garages there might, *might*, be room for a car or two. But have you noticed how often people let a car that cost them tens of thousands of dollars set out in the sun and rain while they protect the stuff worth fifty cents at a garage sale? It doesn't make sense, of course, but hey, we're people—we don't have to make sense.

Stop looking and start cleaning

Back to the point of all this: I've been thinking about cleaning the garage, but you can't just rush into it. Certain steps and methods are required.

The means to a clean

- See a need (1-2 months)
- Recognize the need (2-3 weeks)
- Accept that the need must be satisfied (10 days)
- Begin planning stages (1 month)
- Start plans (1 month)
- Arrange necessary tools and/or equipment—including but not limited to garbage bags (1 week)
- Get motivated (2-3 days)
- Get motivated (2-3 days)

- Really get motivated (4 days)
- Start work (uh-oh, rain—see Weather Channel)
- Start work (whoops, soccer game—check schedule)
- Start work

You can see that, should I start immediately, there's no way to finish before the first of next year—even using best-case-scenario numbers (and we know that never happens). So, like I said, I'm going to putter (it's a thing dads do) just as soon as I head to the garage and find a soda and/or beer. It's not too early to start, is it?

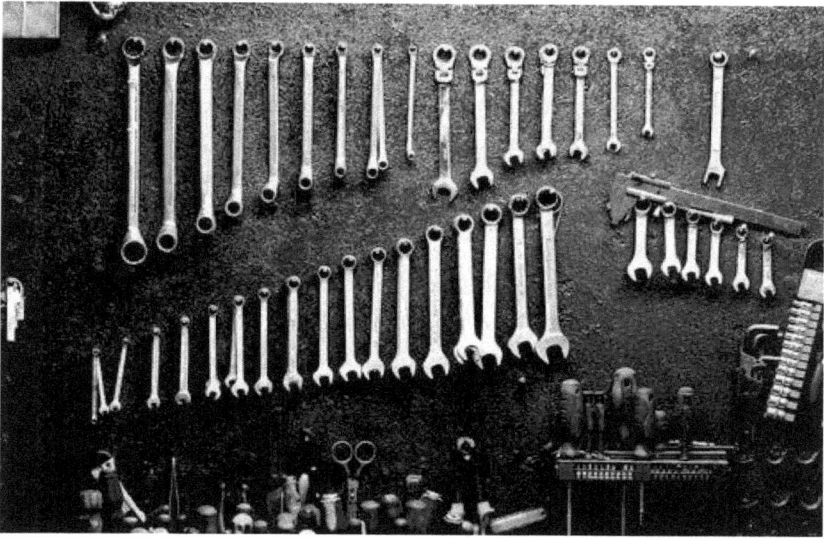

The garage décor we all know and love (hate).

It's Just Not That Impressive

Now that I have reached an age when I am no longer impressed by something simply because it's new, I have noticed something. I've noticed that there are a great many things in this world of ours that I am tired of. Oh, sure, we all get tired of things from time to time (like nosy, noisy neighbors), but there are also times when we can get fundamentally tired, horrendously tired, excruciatingly tired of various things.

For instance, I'm tired of over-priced clothes. The other day, I saw a jacket that cost $3,000. Excuse me? Three grand for an off-the-rack cotton jacket? I don't think so.

I'm tired of pompous people. I don't care how good you are at what you do—whether it's medicine, hair styling, writing, selling insurance, or anything else, you don't need to be a pompous ass about it. It may be good that you are proud of your accomplishments, but don't become insufferable.

I'm tired of skinny people. Yes, skinny people are healthier than the un-skinny, yes, they will live longer, healthier, happier lives. Too bad, I'm tired of them and their smug little skinny attitudes.

I'm tired of people who don't even have the time to smile—you know who you are. Smiling doesn't take any time out of the day, and it will make you more attractive, easier to be around, and much more likeable. Besides that, you're ugly when you frown—so knock it off.

I'm tired of people who think they need attack/hunting dogs in the city. They never keep them chained and fenced well enough, and eventually, the dog gets out and hurts or kills someone. They never understand why little Fido did that, even though "little" Fido weighed eighty pounds, was attack trained, and had the temperament of a pregnant rattlesnake with morning sickness.

I'm tired of men (yes, it's generally men who do this) making things overly complicated. Have you seen some of the music systems out there? Particularly in cars?

I'm tired of calories.

I'm tired of fat.

I'm tired of cholesterol.

Stay with me here—I'm just getting started

I'm tired of people who are rude to customers. If your job is to work around people, then be polite when you're around them.

I'm tired of coffee that costs more than a meal.

I'm tired of meals that cost more than a hotel room.

I'm tired of hotel rooms that cost more than dental surgery.

I'm tired of dental surgery than can cost more than many cars.

I'm tired of used cars that cost more than my parents' first house. Can you believe that? I'm driving around in a car that's worth more than the first house they ever owned.

I'm tired of television scripts that are just more of the same old thing. You watch one show and realize a short way into it that it's just a remake of a still older show that itself was a take-off on a show that aired two years before that one. It's a smorgasbord of scripts—one piece from column A (sexy detective) and one from column B (in trouble), and you've got another episode.

I'm tired of fourteen-year-old girls and boys being the arbiters of cool. I'm tired of cool.

I'm tired of having too few choices in so many of the important things (breakfast cereal—in which we do have enough choices—is not one of the important things). We don't have enough choices in energy, or fuel providers. We don't have enough choices in environmentally sound autos. We don't even have enough choices in tires.

I'm tired of icemakers that break down long before they should.

I'm tired of worrying about health insurance. I'm really tired of worrying that my children will have health insurance when they're adults.

I'm tired of worrying about Social Security. Fix it and quit stealing from it. Raise taxes or do with less—it's what we do at home and what we'll have to do with government programs as well.

I'm tired of medical expenses that put care beyond the reach of so many citizens.

I'm tired of utility bills that are so high that the elderly can't use their air conditioners (those who have them) and risk their health every summer.

I'm tired of the artificiality of fashion. In style—out of style—never in style—will never be in style, etc., etc., etc. It's fake fashion hand in hand with fake economics to sell clothes or whatever else. And after a while, of course, ideas run scarce, and the old ideas get trotted out again. Minis are in, minis are out. Want to save money on clothes? Never throw anything away—sooner or later, it will come back in style or you'll be so "retro," you'll be beyond cool, and either thing is okay.

I'm tired of celebrity. You know, celebrity justice, celebrity endorsements, celebrity appearances for a fee, celebrity faces everywhere, and on and on. We've become a celebrity-driven culture and it's sad.

I'm tired of conspicuous consumption.

I'm tired of cancer.

I'm tired of heart disease.

I'm tired of cardiovascular disease.

I'm tired of arthritis.

I'm tired of AIDS.

I'm tired of sadness.

I'm tired of being tired of so many things.

And on it goes, all of us trying to live, trying to stay alive and healthy, trying to prosper, trying to raise our kids to be productive, trying to leave the world a bit better place. At least, I hope we are.

Knowing Less Every Day

Can you take tools and material and actually build something? And I don't mean a balsa-wood model plane. I mean, can you build a tool shed, a real fence, even a nice, useable workbench? Even more, what, of all the things you own, whether your home, car, things at work, or anywhere else, do you know how to repair? Simply put, of the things you use, what can you fix? What can you build?

I'm thinking about this now because I need to build a shed on the side of the house to store some of the many bikes, scooters, and other things currently crowding the garage. After all, how smart would it be to put stuff worth a few hundred dollars in the garage and then make the cars, worth considerably more, sit outside? The only problem with this is, it takes time, energy, and effort to build something, and I would rather just buy it or have someone else build it. But I've been thinking that this would be a good project for my son and me to do together. He could learn, and I could save some money. Unfortunately, the main thing he may learn is how proficient I am at profanity when I hit my thumb with the hammer.

Build something? Hell, I don't even much like repairing things. And if you're like most of us on the planet, we use many more things than we can repair ourselves. For example, I use a computer and a printer that I do not know how to repair. Actually, that's true with most of my things. Do you know how to repair your car and the electronic brains on board? Can you work on an oven with digital readouts and computer-controlled time and temperature programs?

As I sit here in my office, I am amazed by how many things are computer-controlled or have computer memory chips to enable them to do what they are supposed to do. Here are just a few examples.

Things with brains in my office aside from me (and I'm not too sure about me):

Computer
Printer
Office-size refrigerator

Telephone
Ambient-sounds generator
Cell phone
Air purifier
Television

Things at home with brains besides the family (the dog is the exception here—he's never had a brain):

Refrigerator
Dishwasher
Oven
Television
Two music systems
Disc players
Eight telephones
Fax machine (why do we have this thing?)
Three computers
Two printers
Washing machine
Clothes dryer
Weight scale

I'm sure that I've forgotten a few things on that list, but isn't it amazing how, when we stop and think about it, there are so many things we own that we probably can't fix?

Now, sure, there are many things I can work on, but these days, if it has electricity in it, I'm pretty much out of my league. Take the oven, for example. In the past, whatever could go wrong with an oven could generally be fixed fairly easily. Even if it was out of warranty, you could call Bob's Fix-it Shop and Bob or his assistant would come over and fix it for less than fifty dollars. But now, with many ovens being computer controlled, you have to call in the factory-trained experts.

And what do the experts do? Generally, just replace a part. This nation doesn't repair things like it used to. It can't. So, we have the computer replaced, program it, and go on our merry way. And call it progress.

I suppose it is progress. After all, now we can program our ovens, microwaves, and bread makers to start working during the day (after we shove in a few ingredients before we leave for work), and when we get home, we have a nice, warm dinner waiting for us.

Unfortunately, there is still that clean-up part. And yes, the dish-washer is wonderful and energy efficient and all, but someone still must stack the dishes in the thing after the family eats. But here's a question: Did the family eat together? Does yours? Or does your family get together simply to stack the dirty dishes in the dishwasher and call it quality time? Too many families do that now—quality time is the seven minutes spent walking in the house after soccer practice.

Speaking of soccer practice, I would imagine that there are more people who know soccer well enough to coach it than can repair a toaster oven.

But maybe I'm wrong about all this; maybe it's good that we can't do everything. That way, more people have jobs; more people can support their families; more people can have time for other things in life, like the occasional weekend away.

Speaking of weekends away, I think it's time I took one. The only problem with that is that the family would want to come with me. Oh, I don't have anything against that; it's just that I'll have to hear the kids tell me the best way to pack the car. And I wouldn't even mind that so much, except how are they suddenly experts in packing cars? They can't even pack a laundry hamper. Just saying.

Of course, you can pack it; you just need time, energy, and insanity.

Life's (Almost) Deadly Sins

There are all sorts of "sins." There are sins of omission, the Seven Deadly Sins, sins against humanity, and the list goes on probably forever. This list isn't anywhere as serious as those—this is a simple list of things that make life more difficult (with a few of my own comments and observations thrown in because I can and it's fun).

My list has things that make life harder than it needs to be and yet never go away. So why do we do them? Sometimes we don't know what they are until we do them for the first time, sometimes we seem to be unable to learn until after we've done them a dozen times, and sometimes they simply catch us because we were looking in another direction.

Life's (Almost) Deadly Sins

Rudeness—in the grand overall picture of life, this one may not be as big as grand theft. But rudeness makes life more miserable than it needs to be, so why do it? Do we need to be so selfish that we're rude too?

Blowing a sneeze across the room

Coughing at someone (or coughing into your hand and then extending that hand to shake someone else's hand)

Giving the "finger" while driving (unless it's in Florida or New York, where it's probably necessary)

Arguing PC vs. Apple (it's boring, it's old, who cares, get over it)

Picking your nose while driving (Hey! That's glass all around you and we can see you. It's gross, so knock it off, unless you're in Texas—there, it's probably mandatory.)

Noise in movie theatres: the popcorn is crunchy—chew with your mouth closed. Oh, and shut up.

When you pull into the gas station to get gas and there's no one ahead of you at the pump island, pull to the forward pump. Don't make the rest of us have to drive around you because you can't be a tiny bit considerate. Get over yourself.

Speaking of getting over yourself, get over yourself.

Don't kick sand; it's not that hard to learn how to walk at the beach.

When you're eating in a fast-food restaurant, throw away your trash when you're finished. The rest of us really do not want to have to toss your used ketchup packets away because you're too lazy to do it. If you want full service, go somewhere else—it's not difficult to figure out.

Do you really need a pint of imitation butter product on your small popcorn at the theater? Quit pumping and go sit down.

If you are using a public toilet, flush it, just flush the freaking toilet already.

It's not all about you.

In fact, it's rarely, *if ever*, about you (or me either).

Littering. If people would simply throw away their trash in trash cans, we wouldn't need draconian laws like these: Massachusetts: Fine of not more than $5,500 for the first offense and not to exceed $15,000 for each subsequent offense. Oregon: Class A misdemeanor. Fine not exceeding $6,250 or imprisonment not exceeding one year or both. **Source:** *National Conference of State Legislatures.* (I have to say that Oregon was probably the cleanest place I've ever been, but do we really need laws like this to make us do something so simple, easy, and good for us? Yeah, I guess so—how bloody sad.)

Saying, "No problem," when someone says, "Thank you." We don't care whether it was a problem or not—if it's your job to do something and someone says, "Thank you," just reply, "You're welcome."

Here's a sin for you: Not replacing an empty toilet paper roll. We don't care how you put it on, if the paper hangs down in front or in back, just don't leave it empty. And then we promise not to leave it empty for you.

Question: Is life really so boring and dull for you that you need to express yourself on bathroom walls? If so, put the pen down and go do something. Join a club, take a class, go somewhere, jog, anything, just get a life. Writing on bathroom walls will not make you immortal, famous, or funny. It just proves you really are the person you wish you weren't.

Drinking does not make you smarter. It's not a sin to drink, just to make the rest of us listen to you ramble about what needs to be done and how you would fix it. If you can make something better, go do it. If you can't, then go home and watch TV.

Here's my last almost-deadly sin: wasting your life. This is your shot, your chance. Don't waste it. Go help someone, go back to school and start a new career, apologize for your mistakes and then move on.

You can change your life and make it better. Plus, you can make the lives of those around you so much better too.

There you have my incomplete list of life's (almost) deadly sins. I'm not sure what started this topic; it was probably when someone said, "No problem," and I took off from there. There are thousands more, of course, but to list them would be committing another sin: being more boring and crankier than even I have any right to be.

Shopping for a New Computer? I'd Rather Kiss a Rattlesnake on the Mouth

Lately, I've been shopping for a new computer. Again. While this is not one of the most difficult things to do in life, it is one of the more miserable.

First is simply deciding which brand to go with. There are a great number of brands and types of machines out there, and simply coming to terms with which one is best can be mind-numbing.

Do you want Acer? Lenovo? Apple? Dell? HP? And on and on.

So, what do you do? You take the information you already have—the machine you've been using—and start asking friends and co-workers. You visit web sites, you read the literature, you look at ads, and you see what other people are using.

And you start to get confused.

But you look, and you look, and you look. Finally, you decide on two different machines. You compare them side-by-side. You scratch your head and take Tylenol. And some more Tylenol.

The serious shopping starts

I started out looking in stores, thinking—silly me—that I could simply go in, find what I wanted, and buy it. I knew better, of course, but I'm a dreamer…Naturally, I needed (wanted) the computer configured in very specific ways.

With everything I do, I have to have terabytes worth of memory, huge hard drives, and…well, that list could go on, but we're already bored, aren't we? I never did find what I needed in the stores, as good as the machines that I saw were.

Next stop: online (as usual—just like the last few I've purchased). After looking at site after site after site, I narrowed it down to one… and something else. But good grief! Each site had any number of computers that could be configured any number of ways. Added all up, I probably had choices that numbered in the hundreds, if not more.

And you get more confused…and take more Tylenol.

But after days (okay, two weeks, but why bother counting; it doesn't change the facts), I finally narrowed it down to two specific machines.

Now, the real fun starts: that side-by-side comparison I mentioned a lifetime ago.

But it's not easy to do a side-by-side comparison. Sure, you think that it will be—after all, what could be easier than comparing two machines? But each computer has its own quirks, its own configurations, its own pricing and bundle pricing. And Special Pricing, and Today's Special! Pricing and This Week's Special! Pricing and THE VERY LAST TIME YOU WILL EVER SEE A PRICE THIS GOOD ON THE FACE OF THE EARTH NO MATTER WHERE OR HOW OFTEN YOU LOOK SO QUIT LOOKING AND JUST BUY ME!!!!!!! Pricing.

Oh, but don't forget, there is one thing about the weekly specials— the companies don't tell you the day they change. If you wait one day too long, whammo! The special has changed and you're back to square one. Or even further, because not only has the machine you've decided is the one you really need no longer on sale, it's not being offered at all any longer.

And you go to take more Tylenol, except you see that you've run out. So, you jump in the car and head to (fill in wherever it is you get your Tylenol: CVS, Rite Aid, Walgreens, Albertson's, or, for those with a real doozy of a computer-buying-spree headache, Costco).

Now, here's a sad thing. When you get in the store to buy the Tylenol, you start looking around, wondering if they sell computers. Sure, you know that Rite Aid doesn't sell them, but you never know…

And if it's Costco you went to, well, you know they sell computers. You ask yourself, "Why didn't I look here?" But you know why. Sure, there are some good prices on a few good machines, but none anywhere near how you need one configured.

Never mind, back to the Tylenol-by-the-bucket aisle. Of course, while in Costco, you spot a few hundred other things you really, really need. Things like a two-gallon bottle of ketchup, a gallon jar of pickles, four tires (you only need two, but you went ahead and got all four because you're going to be there having them put on anyway and they were pretty cheap), fifty-five rolls of paper towels, 148 rolls of TP, six cases of Diet Coke because you do, after all, drink a great deal of it, two cases of Pacifico because you do, after all, drink a great deal of it (just not as much as you'd like), three best-sellers, a bag of socks, two chickens (as you stand there hoping you have room in the freezer, you wonder why the vegetarian in the family is buying chicken), and an inflatable wading pool for the kids.

So, two hours, four tires, two huge slices of pizza, a gross of, now, Extra-Strength Tylenol and all sorts of stuff later (and you're glad you brought the Explorer, and even then, you still had to tie some of the stuff on the roof rack, which turned out to be a great option, after all), you leave Costco and head back home because, hey, you still have to buy a computer.

Once home, you give the computers once last look and decide on Apple. The big, expensive, hyper-fast Apple because you're still hungover with buyer fatigue from Costco. You configured it exactly the way you wanted it, the person you messaged with was helpful, and you won't have to sell the house to afford it (although you may have to rent out a room to make the payments).

Not a bad day, after all. And, hopefully, by the next time you have to go through the process again, your kids will be old enough to do it for you.

So, How Ya Gonna Vote?

Yes, ladies and gentlemen, the time is quickly approaching when we'll all need to make those crucial voting decisions (at least for those of us who have both registered to vote and then actually go do it). Unfortunately, far too few people actually take the time to vote. And that's sad.

Voting is one of the most crucial things a citizen can do to protect themselves. Protection from what? Well, that all depends, I suppose, on what your own personal political demons are. The Republicans need to vote to keep out the Democrats, and the Democrats need to vote to keep out the Republicans. It seems that voting is often more about keeping something *from* happening than helping something *to* happen.

Voting beyond the party line

Voting responsibly takes a bit of doing. One needs to study the issues, talk to the candidates (or, if nothing else, at least read their pamphlets and websites), see who is recommending whom, fight their way through all of the television and radio commercials, turn on PBS once in a while, and generally "study up on things."

The only problem is, that's too much work for a lot of us. The only issues we want to know about are those which interest us, which may impact our wallet, or which may put someone else behind bars for doing something we don't approve of.

What do we do? We look at the ads in papers, watch the commercials on TV and listen to them on radio, and make up our minds by thirty-second spots of slogans.

Decision by sound bite

It appears that "decision by sound bite" is not too far off the mark right now. Whoever has the best ad agency spending the most money generally walks away with the election. I'm not saying this is a bad thing, I'm just pointing it out. Not that you needed it pointed out, because we already know all of that. We just don't choose to do much about it.

Oh sure, occasionally we, as a group, do something good in the voting booth. We vote for school bonds even if we don't have kids in school, or we vote for a library (not the branches, of course, but for a big, municipal, ego-booster of a library. But at least that's something).

Decision by sound bite. Who has the best jingle? Who has the most celebrities speaking for them? Who has the most money? Who is *really* sponsoring the new propositions? Who wants laws, zones, special assessment areas, or regulations changed? What in the heck is going on? And do you really care? And don't nod, or say yes, if you're not going to vote. What you *say* isn't as important as what you *do*. And in this case, the "doing" involves going to a polling station and voting.

So, how ya gonna vote?

We all need to take a little bit of the ever-dwindling amount of time we have and really do some reading and watching and listening. We should understand what can occur if we *don't* vote.

Finally, we ought to remember that if we don't vote, we really shouldn't complain because we could have done something about it but chose not to.

The Best Time of Year for Making Money

There are, of course, holidays throughout the year. But nothing comes closer in money-making time than winter. The United States will celebrate Thanksgiving, and then, along with large parts of the rest of the world, will celebrate Hanukkah, Christmas, and New Year's Day.

What makes it really interesting is that, during all of this, we also have elections every couple of years. Yes, we're going to elect mayors, senators, members of the house, and a president. But not only that, we also get to vote on numerous laws, propositions, council people, school boards, and on and on and on.

Media love this time of year. Many television and radio stations, with a good number of newspapers and magazines, make the bulk of their advertising revenue during the Thanksgiving, Christmas, and New Year holidays. But when you add in elections, particularly presidential elections, well, it's jackpot time at Caesars.

Please understand, I'm not complaining about any of this. I love advertising; we all must make a living. I just got to thinking that it might be better if it was spread out a bit more during the year. Keep Christmas, New Years and Hanukkah where they are; religious traditions are hard to change. Thanksgiving, however, can certainly be moved. Who wouldn't mind having Thanksgiving during, say, March? March could use a good holiday, and Thanksgiving would be perfect.

Halloween could also be moved. In fact, it would probably be safer to have all those little trick-or-treaters out during the twilight of a summer month (and warmer, too) than during the dark of winter.

The big one to move would be elections. What would be a good month to hold elections? Yes, I know that the days we use are in the Constitution, so it would take a bit of doing to change. But it could be done by an amendment. So, let's get after it and change the day for elections to one in, say, August. Or May. May would be good, and so would June.

What the elections need are a nice, warm day and evening. It might even get more people to come out and vote. But most of all, the advertisers would love it.

Raking in the dough

Sure, there are some summer ads of various kinds, but nothing approaching election advertising. Just imagine, by moving elections, it would free up more ad space for Halloween, Thanksgiving, New Years, Hanukkah, and Christmas. More dough than ever could be made then. Plus, think of all the available ad space in the summer months that could be used for candidates and various and sundry propositions. The benefits to the nation, not to mention businesses, would rise into the billions (yes, it does sound somewhat like a political ad and, just like most of them, I don't have any proof either). So, let's do it before it's too late. Too late for what, I don't know, but it sounded good.

I know, let's start a grass-roots campaign on a shoestring. We'll appeal to the working person and reject the special interests. Our only concern will be children, the elderly, education, and safety. And saving money. And lowering taxes. Then, when we get in, we'll start working on our ideas to move the holidays. Change won't happen quickly, but with a couple of terms, we should be halfway there.

The Good, the Bad, and the Ugly

In 1966, a western film directed by Sergio Leone, *The Good, the Bad, and the Ugly*, was released. I've always loved that title, and it so aptly states what this is about: a list of things that are good, bad, or downright butt-ugly.

The Good

Elementary and pre-schools: I am constantly amazed at what goes on in these schools. There is such a range of students' ages, abilities, medical problems, learning and physical disabilities, needs, desires, and wants. The fact that they receive an education that starts them on the road to life demonstrates the work of the elementary faculty is something that must be noted and praised.

Middle schools and high schools: Teaching hormones in sneakers is worthy of all the cash one can throw.

Colleges and universities: Think medicine, science, electronics, technology, economics, business, and most everything else that makes this world better.

Museums and art galleries: the places where history and other ways of seeing exist and can be seen and shared.

Human beings: we love each other, care for each other, play with each other, befriend each other, enable each other.

The Bad

Politics: this should be in the good column, and sometimes is, but most of the time, it's a miserable thing. Oh, not politics itself, but the people involved in politics.

Food: Yes, I know, it should be in the good column, but it also belongs in the bad column. Why? Remember calories?

Human beings: we hate each other, ignore each other, hurt each other, injure each other, steal from each other, kill each other.

Cranky people: every neighborhood has at least one cranky person (and sometimes has quite a few, depending on the neighborhood).

Guns, bullets, and the NRA: It's a different world now—the shootings in schools prove it—and gun laws need to reflect that change (and so should the NRA, as good and well-meaning as most of the individuals in the organization are).

Sharks, rattlesnakes, and cockroaches: because they're sharks, rattlesnakes, and cockroaches (how much of a reason do you need?).

Other bad things: death, dying, destruction, war, pestilence, famine, murder, blind dates (threw you with that one, here, didn't I? But admit it, blind dates are, for the most part, a bad thing), ex-husbands and –wives (although this can also go in the good column, if you're really happy and lucky to be rid of them), and pimples.

The Ugly

Landfills: Yes, they're better than having all the trash blowing around on the street, but just imagine how many landfills there are in this country, how big they're getting, how much bigger they're going to get. Staggering, isn't it?

Hate, racism, ageism, bias against individuals with disabilities, and any other way people use to push people apart and create misery based on simple human makeup.

Evil and all the many ways it's exhibited every day—from spousal abuse to the Nazi party.

New examples of all this keep appearing every day and old ones can (occasionally) disappear, and the world goes on.

Watch out for the Soccer Parent

Soccer Alert, Soccer Alert, Soccer Alert! The dreaded soccer season. Oh, not dreaded because of the kids or the sport. Oh, no, no, it's dreaded because of…soccer parents.

So, how have your weekends been, lately? I have spent the last couple of weekends with sports fanatics. Oh, I'm not talking about the usual beer-guzzling, yelling and screaming at the TV type of sports fanatics. No, no, the kind of sports fanatics I'm speaking of here are—get ready—soccer parents. Yes, soccer moms and dads and grandparents and brothers and sisters are some of the spookiest people on earth.

Now, in a way, of course, I too am a soccer parent. My kids play soccer, I buy the candy they're supposed to sell to help raise funds for the league, and I take them to games and root for every play. I do those things and do them happily and with a bit of pride. But pride is one thing; being an insane fanatic is another.

The true fanatic comes out during games. Oh, sure, the parent may holler words of encouragement at their child from time to time during a practice, but it's only during a scored game that the lunatic comes out.

Wait—did I say lunatic? No, no, no. I meant concerned, caring, loving parent who wants nothing more than to see their son or daughter succeed in whatever it is that they want.

Yeah, right. Sorry, but these folks are absolute, certified, one hundred percent get-out-the-straight-jacket parents who can't quit screaming at their kid for an entire game.

Go Johnny, Go

One team that our son was on a year or two ago had a terrific group of kids on it. But one of the kids had to have had the most obnoxious parents I've ever seen. These people brought their kid and then went jogging around the field so they could get in their exercise while the kid played. Now, that's not a bad idea, except from the entire perimeter of the soccer field, you could hear these people screaming, "Go Johnny, go! Go Johnny, go!! Go Johnny, go! Go Johnny, go!! Go Johnny, go! Go Johnny, go!! Go Johnny, go! Go Johnny, go!! Go Johnny, go! Go Johnny,

326

go!! Go Johnny, go! Go Johnny, go!!"

Are you starting to get an idea of how maddening that sounded after an hour? But to be fair, they didn't scream it for the entire hour. After every few "go Johnny, go" they would scream instructions—tell the child which plays to make, which way to run, how to be more aggressive, less aggressive, how to kick, how to block, how to run, how to score. Then it was back to "go Johnny, go." And all this is going on, remember, while the coach is trying to, well, coach.

Some of the parents wanted to get a fund started to send the parents on a one-way trip to the nearest iceberg, but the coach wouldn't let us (even though I'm pretty sure that the idea started with him). And the really sad thing is, the kid was terrifically nice. Sure, he's probably going to grow up with severe psychological problems, but as a kid, he was really wonderful.

It's all about the kids

One thing that so many parents seem to have trouble remembering is that it's all about the kids. It's not about the parents, not about how good a job they do raising their child, not about the kind of people they are. Nope, it's just about the kids. Young kids learn all sorts of lessons from team sports—they learn sportsmanship, good teamwork, the importance of listening and leading, and the value of exercise, among others. However, some parents need to remember that *everything* can be a lesson. Kids learn both good and bad things from their parents. Do you want to teach that screaming is the best way to get something? That pushing and pushing and pushing someone who is already trying their absolute best is the best way to show you love them? What are you showing your kids? What lessons are you teaching your kids?

Yes, I realize that the parents who can't quit screaming at their kid will tell you that what they're doing is for the good of the child. They want him or her to grow up healthy, with a respect for teammates and with a can-do attitude toward life. Yeah, yeah, yeah. I've heard it all before, and it's just so much BS. If that were true, the parents wouldn't get mad at the child for faltering, wouldn't get mad at the coach for letting another teammate play, wouldn't get red-faced and hoarse from screaming directions from the sideline. Nope, those parents are control freaks who have placed far too much of their own worth on the achievements of their children. And that's sad for the parents and, particularly, for the kids.

At one of last season's games, one of the parents was so loud and obnoxious that he got thrown out of the stands.

What are you teaching your own kids? All of us want our children to grow and become healthy, happy, successful members of a productive, free society. How are you doing your part? By screaming or supporting? By pushing too hard or just enough? By being a soccer parent or a parent who is there for their child while that child plays, and enjoys, soccer? Remember, your child learns from everything you do…everything.

Note: Names have been changed to protect me from being sued by the guilty.

Watching Clocks

There is an interesting thing about aging: the older you get, the faster time flies. The phenomenon is called "time dilation," and it's not a particularly good thing. Personally, I hate it…okay, I also hate getting older, but there you go. When you combine the two—aging and time dilation—well, you're just out of luck.

When I was in college, I took a class on aging. We discussed all the various aspects of getting older, including everything that happens from the instant of birth to the moment of death. The class was interesting at the time, but this was probably due to the fact that I was much younger. For that matter, everyone in the class was young; hell, we were a bunch of college kids who knew everything, would never grow old, and would rather be out on a date than sitting in that classroom talking about aging. We didn't have a clue.

Now, however, since I went through that door marked "Horrors Ahead – No Turning Back," I recall the lessons from that class with wry amusement…or horror—take your pick.

Pain is not a good thing

I am thinking about this subject today because of a recent trip to a physician. Last week, I was working around the house, cutting and sawing on a kitchen floor (no, I don't know why I was doing it on the kitchen floor, probably because it was closer to the refrigerator), and a few days later, I moved some boxes of books out of my office. Normally, this would not be any big deal. But the morning after I finished all this work, I awoke to shooting pains in my elbow whenever I moved my arm. (The old joke here is, a man goes to his doctor and tells him, "Doctor, my arm hurts whenever I move it like this." The doctor replies, "Well, quit moving it like that.") I figured the pain would stop in a day or two, took a couple of Tylenol, and pretty much ignored it.

Well, the pain didn't stop. So, I made an appointment with Roy, the physician who has been keeping this body in more or less working order for the past couple of decades. Roy and I, it seems, are simply growing old together. He knows where I hurt because he hurts there as well.

Roy examined my arm and gave me the bad news. He told me I had something with a name that I can't begin to pronounce. I asked him what it meant, and he said, "You've got tennis elbow."

"Tennis elbow? I haven't played tennis in years."

"It's just the slang term for lateral epicondylitis. You can get tennis elbow from all sorts of things, especially from doing things with your arms you don't normally do."

"So, what can you do about it?" I asked.

He gave me a few options, but mostly it came to waiting it out and perhaps taking some laser treatments. My elbow problem was transient (it means temporary, but you know how doctors are with language).

A few years ago

The main thing is, a few years ago, I never would have had this problem. A few years ago, I could have built a house, shoveled a mountain, arm-wrestled a pro quarterback (yes, I would have lost), and still not had any pain (at least, not in the elbow). But that's the key, "a few years ago."

I hate saying "a few years ago"; it makes me seem even older (remember a grandparent saying, "Why, just a few short years ago, your grandmother and I..."). Yep, I hate saying it, and yet I find myself saying that exact thing more and more. Part of it, of course, is because things happened a few years ago that I remember (when you're young, there just aren't enough years going back to remember).

One of the terms people tend to use with aging is "age is catching up with me." This is nonsense. Age doesn't catch up with anyone. Age couldn't care less. Age is simply a process that goes on. The problem is not with age playing catch-up but with our bodies losing the battles with:

1. Gravity
2. Sunlight
3. Free radicals
4. Chlorine
5. Red meat
6. Pollution
7. Sugar
8. Saccharine

9. Tobacco

10. Caffeine

11. Dust mites

12. Plastics

13. Liquor

14. Too much exercise

15. Too little exercise

16. Not enough chocolate (okay, this is a personal belief, but hey, it's my book)

17. Electromagnetic radiation

18. Falling meteors

19. Synthetics

20. Artificial ingredients

21. Bad drivers

22. Environmental problems and/or disasters

23. Not enough oxygen

24. Too much oxygen

25. Stress, stress, stress

And on and on and on. There are so many things that contribute to aging that just when you find one answer (don't smoke), a new question rears its ugly head.

Personally, I don't have a clue regarding what to do about it all except complain. And since I do that so extraordinarily well, I'll just keep it up. If nothing else, complaining about it is worthwhile just because of how much it annoys people.

One last thought: Nothing, and I mean *nothing*, makes you feel older than sitting in a hospice room and with a parent as he or she spends their final few days on earth. And nothing makes you feel more whole…

When Devastation Happens, Friends Appear

After the horrific Hurricane Katrina hit the Gulf Coast, and people were homeless, jobless, and suffering, it wasn't just our own services that helped. More than fifty countries have offered to help with the devastation on the Gulf Coast.

I often hear people say, in discussing American Foreign Aid, "When does anyone come to our rescue?" Well, this helps answer that absurd question. Many people came to the help of the US, and they did before Katrina and have since.

The list below will amaze you to see who came to the aid of people in trouble—even countries often thought of as very poor or not so friendly. Indeed, Mexico not only sent supplies, they sent members of the Mexican Army and vehicles to help search. In fact, according to Wikipedia, "In September 2005, units of the Mexican Armed Forces responded to the emergency situations after Hurricane Katrina with aid and assistance, appearing as a flagged, uniformed force in the United States for the first time since World War II in the 1940s and the first operational deployment of Mexican troops to the U.S. in 159 years."

The Mexican contingent was based out of Kelly Air Force Base in San Antonio, Texas for the duration of the deployment. The Mexican military conducted aid and cleanup missions in Harrison County, Mississippi, in conjunction with Dutch navy sailors, U.S. Marines, and the U.S. Navy. When humanity suffers, there will be others to help ease that suffering. Just like a squabbling family that nonetheless helps each other when the need arises.

Countries that helped or offered help after Hurricane Katrina

Armenia
Australia
Austria
Azerbaijan

Bahamas
Belgium
Britain
Canada
China
Colombia
Cuba
Dominica
Dominican Republic
Ecuador
El Salvador
France
Germany
Greece
Georgia
Guatemala
Guyana
Honduras
Hungary
Iceland
India
Indonesia
Israel
Italy
Jamaica
Japan
Jordan
Lithuania
Luxembourg
Mexico
The Netherlands
New Zealand
Norway
Paraguay
The Philippines
Portugal
Russia
Saudi Arabia

Singapore
Slovak Republic
Slovenia
Spain
Sweden
Switzerland
South Korea
Sri Lanka
Taiwan
Thailand
Turkey
Venezuela
The United Arab Emirates
NATO and the United Nations

It kind of makes you think, doesn't it? Despite everything, the USA is surrounded by friends. And yes, like all friends, sometimes we don't get along. Sometimes we've even fought—just like personal friends will do. But it's important to remember that, when horror happens, we help each other. The US has responded to situations around the world and will continue to do so. It's nice to know that help will also come to us when we need it…it's just what families do.

Whoever Called Them "The Golden Years" Must Have Meant Fool's Gold

You've heard it all your life, that simple expression, "The Golden Years." This is the time of life generally seen to be sixty years of age and beyond. But my mother-in-law calls all of the years after sixty "The Mildew Years."

She has a pretty convincing argument, when you stop to think about it. Picture all of the things that change or start to go downhill after you turn sixty:

* You and your doctor's receptionist are on a first name basis.

* You have more medical specialists than you can keep track of, if you bothered to even try, which you don't, because if you did, you would still get them confused with all of the ones your spouse has.

* There are far too many aches and pains to do all the things for which you worked hard and scraped and saved money to do.

* Your favorite entertainer has been dead for at least twenty years.

* Your eyes seem to get worse by the minute, which wouldn't be that big of a deal except you need those eyes to read the small print on all the medicine bottles. So, you get new glasses with thick lenses and then add reading glasses because there's no way you're ever going to wear bifocals. Now, if you could just remember where you last put them. My father solved the problem by placing glasses in every room of the house, because even he got tired of accusing my mother of hiding them from him (not that she wouldn't do it).

* Speaking of medicine bottles, every time you go to see one of your doctors (not *the* doctor but *one of* your doctors), he or she has to write a prescription for a brand-new medicine. Your medicine cabinet is starting to look like the pharmacy at UCLA Medical Center.

* Even taking a new medicine would be okay, except that it simply is another reminder (like you needed another reminder) that your health isn't what it used to be.

* Your health will never be what it used to be.

* You are never going to feel better than how you feel now (now, there's as good a reason as any for anti-depressants).

* You've started spending more time at hospitals than you ever thought you would. About a year ago, the time you've spent there surpassed time you've spent on the golf course, which is okay because you can't see the hole, the flag, or even the green anyway.

* The hospital receptionist knows you by sight and asks how your grandchildren are.

* Not a day goes by that you don't worry about money. Will your savings/retirement/investments run out?

* If your money does run out, what will you do? You can't go around the neighborhood mowing lawns or delivering newspapers from a bike. And as far as your old career goes, well, there were a whole lot of young sharks working their way up to the position you had, and they sure aren't letting you have it back now.

* You take an inventory every day of all the things that either have quit working entirely or are getting heavily rusted. The eyes see a little less clearly, the legs are a little more wobbly, the knees either squeak or have been replaced, the hearing is fine as long as you don't forget your hearing aids, things you used to pick up with a finger now require both hands, and even your sense of taste isn't what it used to be.

* Your energy level is much, much less. You never want to miss your nap, and nap time is exactly that, nap time. Those "afternoon delights" (wink, wink) are now a hard board in the bed for your aching back instead of your spouse's hard body.

* Your spouse's hard body must have disappeared to the same place yours did.

* Even with all of this, you're still somewhat optimistic and enjoy the simpler things in life, things like a morning drive along the coast. And you would have taken one yesterday, if only you could have remembered what you did with the car keys. And speaking of car keys, you and your significant other have a standing bet as to which one of you the DMV will first disqualify to drive.

* Your house starts to look messier than it ever did, but you can't see the dust anyway, so why bother?

* You would get together with your friends more, but trying to

schedule it all based around everyone's doctors' appointments, who can drive, who needs to be picked up, which restaurant to go to that will fit everyone's special diet...well, it all just becomes too much.

* You and your friends say how much you miss the good old days, knowing full well those days weren't all that hot.

In looking at it all, I suppose that the years after sixty are, indeed, somewhat closer to mildew than gold. Does that mean you can't have an enjoyable, meaningful, relevant life? Of course not. It just means that The Mildew Years, like anything else with mildew, need more care.

I have so very much to look forward to. And yes, you are hearing a bit of sarcasm there...

I-10

never meanders
It blasts
    through the
    swamps hanging with Spanish moss
    the occasional forests
    and mile after endless mile of deserts
It blasts
    through towns like
        Las Cruces
        Indio
        Tucson
        Lordsburg
        Deming
        El Paso
    And the water places, the humid places
        Baton Rouge
        Pensacola
        Lafayette
        Gulfport
        Biloxi
From
Santa Monica on the west   &
                Jacksonville on the east
There is life between the two &
                yet
I-10 is a staggeringly lonely place

In Conclusion

I realize that it may seem hard to believe, but the pieces in this book took decades to write. Not that I sat down at a keyboard for decades but rather, over that length of time, I wrote newspaper columns, articles, stories and such, and from that, I picked the ones that I liked the best.

Words are like atoms of smoke drifting on air currents. Each atom is insignificant but together change the very air we breathe. I hope the words in this collection have given you a moment or two of entertainment or insight or annoyance (I'll take what I can get).

This I know, from everything I've written: It is better to be amazed than be amazing. To be amazed is to be engaged with life, to be connected to people, their places, and their things. It's easy to be amazing; to be amazed is to live.

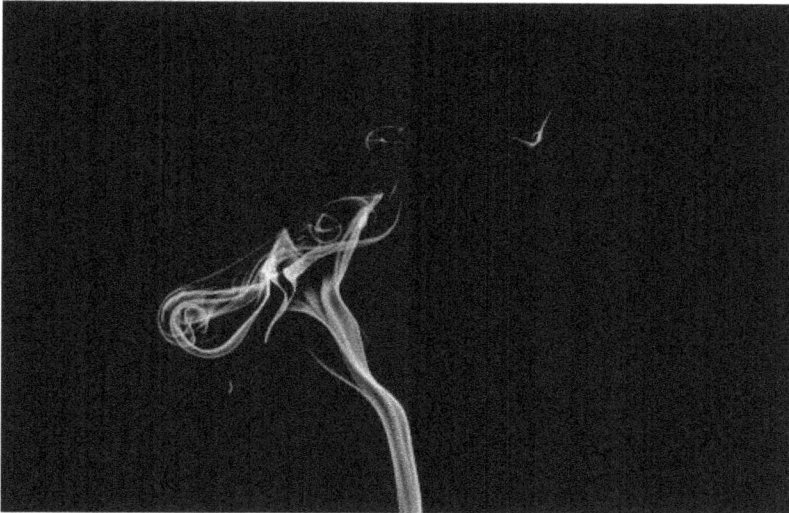

Thanks

I'm grateful to many people for this book and so much more. My family tolerates me, friends still return my calls and texts (and usually don't make snarky comments on my tweets), and my colleagues are some of the best on the planet. I don't know how I ended up luckily enough to be born into a family of hardworking people who supported my nasty habit of writing. Go figure. A special warm appreciation goes to Michelle, Ryan, Paige, Jo, Hank, Pauline, Jim, Jan, Shirley, and so many others. Y'all make life a whole lot better.

About the Author

Miles Beauchamp is a native Californian and is Associate Editor and columnist at the Asian Journal, an English-language, pan-Asian newspaper. In addition to writing his often-irreverent column, he writes and conducts research in social media for enterprise and the professions, mass media social communications, and the portrayal of individuals with disabilities in American Literature. He blogs at: It's Just (all of) Us at milespb.com. Follow him on Twitter @milespb1, and find his other works on Amazon.

www.ingramcontent.com/pod-product-compliance
Lightning Source LLC
LaVergne TN
LVHW041210080426
835508LV00011B/895